SCIENCE VS. RELIGION

SCIENCE VS. RELIGION

What Scientists Really Think

ELAINE HOWARD ECKLUND

OXFORD
UNIVERSITY PRESS
2010

OXFORD
UNIVERSITY PRESS

Oxford University Press, Inc., publishes works that further
Oxford University's objective of excellence
in research, scholarship, and education.

Oxford   New York
Auckland   Cape Town   Dar es Salaam   Hong Kong   Karachi
Kuala Lumpur   Madrid   Melbourne   Mexico City   Nairobi
New Delhi   Shanghai   Taipei   Toronto

With offices in
Argentina   Austria   Brazil   Chile   Czech Republic   France   Greece
Guatemala   Hungary   Italy   Japan   Poland   Portugal   Singapore
South Korea   Switzerland   Thailand   Turkey   Ukraine   Vietnam

Published by Oxford University Press, Inc.
198 Madison Avenue, New York, NY 10016

www.oup.com

Oxford is a registered trademark of Oxford University Press

Library of Congress Cataloging-in-Publication Data
Ecklund, Elaine Howard.
Science vs. religion : what scientists really think / Elaine Howard Ecklund.
p. cm.
Includes bibliographical references and index.
ISBN 978-0-19-539298-2
1. Religion and science. I. Title. II. Title: Science versus religion.
BL240.3.E25 2010
215—dc22   2009034731

3 5 7 9 8 6 4 2

Printed in the United States of America
on acid-free paper

to Karl

CONTENTS

PREFACE

As a college sophomore at Cornell University, I witnessed a debate between William Provine, a Cornell professor of evolutionary biology, and Philip Johnson, a U.C. Berkeley professor of law. They were there to debate the merits of the theory of evolution and the theory of intelligent design, and the two men clearly disagreed vehemently with one another. In attendance were committed evangelical Christian students (who agreed strongly with Johnson) and committed atheist students (who agreed strongly with Provine). And there were many students, like myself, who were not really sure what they thought about these issues and had simply come to listen. A wide-eyed collegian, not raised in an intellectual environment and having never heard such ideas expressed so persuasively before, I was struck by how civil the men were to each other and to the students gathered. They stayed there for three hours, debating and answering questions. Even after the formal lecture ended, each man continued in informal discussions with interested students. I came away thinking that discussion about controversial topics surrounding science *can* happen. I felt enlivened and eventually embraced a career in social science myself.

Fast forward to nearly 15 years later. I was sitting on the opposite side of the room now, as a faculty member, watching a prescreening of *Flock of Dodos*, a film that investigates the differences between scientists and religious people who are on opposite sides of the debates about teaching intelligent design in secondary school classrooms. The premise of the film is that while most scientists find the intelligent design movement unequivocally wrong, it appears that those who support intelligent design have a greater spirit of dialogue than the scientists who act instead like a "flock of dodos." (The dodo was a bird native to the island of Mauritius that evolutionary theorists think became extinct because it was not able to fly and hence could not escape from European explorers and the animals they brought with them.) Filmmaker Randy Olson, a trained biologist, implicitly argues throughout the film that scientists too will die out if they do not learn how to change with the times, to act more respect-fully to those who disagree with them, and how to present science in a more favorable, understandable light. As the film ended, discussion began. And I watched incredulously as some of the scientists in the room confirmed Olson's accusations. They erupted with totalizing criticisms of religion and religious people, calling them "stupid fundamentalists," oblivious that there were religious academics seated in the room. Sadly, when dialogue breaks down, those scientists with the loudest voices seem to drown out those with a different, sometimes more open perspective.

That's why I have written this book. At its core, it's about the scientists whose voices have been thus far overlooked in the science-and-religion debates and who might have powerful contributions to add to the cause of translating science to a broader public audience, especially a religious audience.

This book was helped through its gestation by a community of scholars, friends, and family, who tirelessly read and helped edit the manuscript. The conversations and practical help received from this community only made the work stronger. Any remaining weaknesses are mine alone.

Those scientists who made this research possible by welcoming me into their labs and offices and sharing openly with me about their views deserve my sincere thanks. I have endeavored to represent their views as accurately as possible. I am thankful also to Oxford University Press for supporting this work, particularly to my editor, Cynthia Read, marketing manager Brian Hughes, and copyeditor Mark LaFlaur.

This research was supported by several grants. Support for data collection came primarily from the John Templeton Foundation. In addition, I received funding from the University at Buffalo, State University of New York, Rice University's sociology department, and the Center on Race, Religion, and Urban Life (CORRUL) at Rice University. The primary data collection was completed during a postdoctoral fellowship at Rice. I am appreciative for the questions (both formal and informal) I received about the research after lectures at Princeton University, New York University, University of Virginia, Baylor University, Northwestern University, University at Buffalo, SUNY, the Faraday Institute for Science and Religion at Cambridge University, and Rice University. Several individuals provided useful feedback on portions of the manuscript through lengthy discussions at various phases of the research. Special thanks go to Nancy Tatom Ammerman, Robert Bell, Philip Clayton, Penny Edgell, Michael Emerson, Robert C. Fay, George Gallup Jr., Ian Hutchinson, Stephen Klineberg, Elizabeth Long, William Martin, John Polkinghorne, David Richardson, Robert M. Stein, Jennifer Wiseman, and Robert Wuthnow for serving on a study advisory board. I had ongoing conversations with Wendy

Cadge, Roger Finke, Bridget Gorman, Conrad Hackett, Kristen Schultz Lee, Anne Lincoln, Gerardo Marti, Jerry Park, and Martha Stipanuk about fundamental issues related to research design.

My thanks to Stephen Adams, Phillip Conner, Catalina Crespo, Timothy Dy, Elizabeth Gage, Leigh Anne Jackson, Devra Jaffe-Berkowitz, Tariq Kahn, Rita Kasa, Patrick Kelly, Angela Ling, Windsen Pan, Mor Regev, Christopher Scheitle, Nicholas Short, Brad Smith, Phil Todd Veliz, and Chloe Walker for help with data analysis. Thanks to Melanie Daglian for editing help and to Meagan Alley for assistance with manuscript preparation.

Betsy Stokes came along just at the right time and provided help with editing the manuscript.

Several mentors, friends, family members, and colleagues read (sometimes multiple) drafts of this work. These include Jenifer Bratter, Marian Ecklund, Stanley Ecklund, Ian Hutchinson, Karl Johnson, D. Michael Lindsay, Kirstin Matthews, Robert Matthews, Gwynn Thomas, Robert Wuthnow, and Pablo Yepes. I benefited, in particular, from discussions on spirituality and science with Elizabeth Long. I received feedback on the manuscript from John H. Evans, Ronald L. Numbers, John Schmalzbauer, and John Wilson, who were invited guests to a seminar on public sociology sponsored by the Center on Race, Religion, and Urban Life and the sociology department at Rice University.

The constant support of family was the reminder that life outside the academy only serves to strengthen scholarly endeavors. Thank you to my parents, Betty Howard and the late Robert Howard, to Bonnie Howell, Fern Vaughn, and Stan and Marian Ecklund. I have received no end of encouragement towards academic excellence from each of you. I thank my siblings Carolyn Howell August, Kathryn Howell, Ella May Vaughn, Anthony, Aaron, Elissa, Amy, Andrew, and Adam Vaughn, Kier and Hung Ecklund, and Karen and Kreig Ecklund.

My daughter, Anika Elizabeth Howard Ecklund, was born in the midst of the publication process. Witnessing the next generation makes even small efforts toward a spirit of intellectual and sincere dialogue between contested ideas seem all the more pressing.

My deepest gratitude goes to my husband, Karl, a physicist. As one who cares deeply about translating difficult ideas within and outside of the academy, your support of this work—both personal and intellectual—has surpassed anything I could have hoped for.

PART I

Crossing the Picket Lines: The Personal Faith of Scientists

CHAPTER 1

The Real Religious Lives of Scientists

It is a centuries-old debate: Is there truly an inescapable conflict between science and religion? Many today—mostly scientists and policy makers—argue that there is, and the existence of this "irreconcilable" difference is coddled as fact. But how then does one explain a scientist such as Margaret, a chemist who teaches a Sunday school class? What about scientists like Evelyn, who embraces a spirituality that she feels is more compatible with science than traditional religion. Or the physicist Arik who, well before science took root in his mind, decided at a young age that he did not believe in God?[1] These are real people, not stereotypes. We can't simply assume that they live in conflict with their religion or that they avoid religion because it conflicts with their science. We need to *ask* them why they walk the paths they do.

A LONG HISTORY OF THE CONFLICT PARADIGM

Galileo, a father of modern science, insisted that the earth revolved around the sun—not the other way around, as then commonly believed. According to the Church, this contradicted Holy Scripture. The scientific findings did not conflict with religion, Galileo argued; unfortunately, the people in charge didn't agree.[2]

The idea that religion and science are necessarily in conflict has been institutionalized by our nation's elite universities. When Cornell was established in 1865, Andrew Dickson White—one of the university's founders—announced that it would be different from the other colleges of the time; it would be a safe place for science, protected from the authorities and constraints of theology.[3] The idea that science was oppressed by religion—and would over time even replace religion—was nicely encapsulated in the title of White's landmark volume, *A History of the Warfare of Science with Theology in Christendom.*[4]

In the early twentieth century, scholars who championed this conflict paradigm sought support for it in studies of how scientists themselves approached matters of faith. In the early decades of the twentieth century psychologist James Henry Leuba argued that religion was a creation of the human imagination rather than a rational response to a divinely ordered cosmos. Leuba reasoned that scientists—as those who know the most about the natural world—would be the first to apprehend this truth and consequently the least likely to believe in God or attend church. Surveying the National Academy of Sciences, the most elite scientific body in the United States, Leuba indeed found that these scientists were generally much less religious than were other Americans. He reasoned that it was only a matter of time until science would overtake religion. Leuba thought that for religion to remain "a vitalizing and controlling power in society, [it would] have to organize [itself] about ultimate conceptions that are not in contradiction with the insight of the time."[5] Over the past hundred years, scholars have continued to find that scientists are generally less religious than other Americans, pointing to this as proof that religion and science remain in conflict.[6]

The God gene. Embryonic stem cell research. Teaching evolution in public schools. The religion-science conflict narrative is upon us again, returning with a vengeance in the early twenty-first century. The debate, propelled by current controversies, depicts higher education in particular as the enemy of religion and the friend of science. And there is some evidence that the more educated individuals become, the less likely they are to be religious. Highly religious individuals, especially those Christians who believe that the Bible must be taken literally, tend to have a more adversarial relationship with science, particularly evolutionary theory. Increased knowledge of science does seem to suppress some traditional religious forms, just as Galileo's discovery forced a rereading of the Old Testament's claim that the earth "cannot be moved."[7] But many Americans see scientists as not only lacking faith, but as actively *opposed* to religion. This perception further sustains the conflict paradigm.[8]

MAKING NEW HISTORY

Aggressive attacks on religion such as Richard Dawkins's *The God Delusion* do not accurately represent the complex ways in which scientists—even those who are not religious—actually engage religion and spirituality. The general public misunderstands what scientists really think about the relationship between science and religion; many accept the extreme hostility of a few as representative of all scientists' views about faith. As for the scientists themselves, they are not generally prone to religious discussion, and have very little idea about what their colleagues really believe.

It is important that we uncover the complex truth about what scientists practice and believe as well as how they encounter and engage (or disengage from) religion in their lives, rather than cede the floor to the hotheads on both sides of this contentious issue.

The religious views of scientists who work at the nation's top universities are especially important to understand, because these are the scientists who shape the views of future leaders of our society. Half of the heads of corporations and nearly as many governmental leaders graduated from one of 12 highly selective universities, places like Princeton, Harvard, and the University of Chicago. Future politicians, business leaders, and public opinion makers are currently sitting in the science classrooms on America's top campuses. These very leaders will make decisions about future science policy—such as how much funding science should receive and what types of research should be funded.[9]

Until now, no one has explored how religion and spirituality enter the lives of scientists at the nation's best universities. Neither a polemic nor a manifesto, this book offers a balanced assessment of information gathered scientifically from scientists themselves. These pages present the diverse views of elite scientists from seven natural and social science disciplines at the nation's top research universities. To tell their stories, I draw on data collected during four years of intensive research I conducted between 2005 and 2008 as part of the Religion among Academic Scientists (RAAS) study, including a survey of nearly 1,700 scientists, one-on-one conversations with 275 of them, and notes from lectures and public events where top scientists talked about matters of faith. In their interviews and survey responses, these scientists revealed what they think about religion, spirituality, the role of religion in teaching, and the current debates about religion and science. At the center of these data are the thought-provoking and at times touching stories from their lives.

THE REAL STORY AND ITS MAIN CHARACTERS

After four years of research, at least one thing became clear: Much of what we believe about the faith lives of elite scientists is wrong. The "insurmountable hostility" between science and religion is a caricature, a thought-cliché, perhaps useful as a satire on groupthink, but hardly representative of reality. Scientists face a plethora of religious challenges, both public and personal, and employ just as many diverse responses to these challenges. Some, pressed by the needs of (and their concern for) their students, engage the topic of religion in the classroom. This is what I call *environmental push*, when events outside the university challenge scientists to reexamine the barriers between science and religion. Some scientists were raised apart from a religious tradition, have had bad experiences with religion, or simply know very little about different religious traditions or the variety of ways that religion and science might relate. They have not necessarily rejected religion *because* they are scientists. Others who do practice a religious tradition anticipate—whether rightly or not—hostility from their colleagues and so practice a *closeted faith*. Nearly all, from the atheist to the devout, think about how to interact with the increasing number of religious students who are flowing into their classrooms. Some scientists eventually become *boundary pioneers*; because of their institutional legitimacy as elite scientists *and* their deep commitment to religious ideals they are able to cross the picket lines of science and religion, introducing a measure of kinship to the controversy. And others are what I call *spiritual atheists*, who practice a new kind of individual spirituality—one that has no need for God or a god—that flows from and leads into science.

This isn't chiefly a book about social forces or conflict resolution. It's about voices. Throughout my research and during countless probing discussions, certain voices have stuck out. Some individuals seem to perfectly capture what entire groups are thinking, so I decided to structure the narrative around the lives of a few scientists who embody many of the major findings and themes revealed by the larger study. Other interviews and the survey results provide a supporting cast for these protagonists.[10]

The stories of scientists like Arik, Margaret, and Evelyn emerged over and over during the systematic analyses of the one-on-one conversations I had with individual scientists. As we journey from the personal to the public religious lives of scientists, we will meet the nearly 50 percent of elite scientists like Margaret who are religious in a traditional sense and the over 20 percent more like Evelyn who, though eschewing religion, still see themselves as spiritual to some extent, with spiritual sensibilities that often derive from and are borne out in the work they do as scientists. For the proportion of scientists who are, like Arik, indeed committed secularists, we will draw out the complexity in their reasons for rejecting, leaving, or ignoring religion.[11]

Max Weber, a founder of sociology, described people he called "carriers," who were "types representative of the various classes who were the primary . . . propagators" of major world religions. In particular, these carriers perpetuated ideologies of "the kind of ethical or salvation doctrine, which most readily conformed to their social position."[12] Scientists have been perceived as carriers of the secularist impulse, a group responsible for building the modern research university and undermining religious authority by their success in deciphering the mysteries of the natural order without recourse to supernatural aid or guidance. But I argue here that elite scientists who are *boundary pioneers* and *spiritual atheists* might actually be carriers of a new religious impulse, one characterized by a deep commitment to the scientific enterprise and the achievement of elite status among their scientific peers. This new religious impulse doesn't just cope with science. It crosses boundaries. Stories of reconciliation between religion and science that make logical sense to scientists, structural supports for religion (like centers and programs), and new science-friendly models of religion all contribute to the strength of this new impulse.

Science and religion *can* transition from warring factions to twin states with a contested border. And under certain conditions, there might even be "free trade" between them.[13] Other sociologists of religion, upon whose work I build, have described both the secularization of the academy as well as how the institutional infrastructure of the academy has changed to allow more of a place for religion.[14] Now that religion is again a vital force in the academy—as a result, some say, of a countermovement complete with resources, infrastructures, and active student involvement—the most secular of scientists are finding it hard to handle the resurgence in traditional forms of religion. Some, never having encountered such discussions before, simply don't understand the vocabulary.

A traditional sociology-of-religion approach that focuses on religious organizations and institutions does not allow for the complex pursuit of spirituality in everyday life, particularly the new kinds of science-linked spirituality I find among scientists. These spiritual atheists are creating something new, outside of religious organizations and conventional religious understandings.[15]

A MESSAGE TO SCIENTISTS

Scientists routinely criticize the American public for their lack of appreciation for science compared to the esteem with which science is held in other developed nations. (Schoolchildren in the United States have a poorer education in science than do those in most other industrialized nations.)[16] But to better engage the broader public with science, scientists must be more introspective about their own relationship to religion and how they talk to the broader public about the connections between religion and science. Regardless of what the scientists personally believe about matters of faith, there is a surrounding social environment—including public debates about intelligent design, embryonic stem cell research, human cloning, public funding for science, and much more—that simply can't be avoided.

Scientists tend to view the impact of religion on science education entirely through a frame of conflict, often blaming Americans' poor understanding of science on religion, arguing in particular that fundamentalist forms of Christianity inhibit science learning. There is some evidence to support these accusations. About 40 percent of Americans believe that creationist accounts of earth origins should be taught in public schools instead of evolution, which is a fundamental concept of modern science. And 65 percent think that some form of the Old Testament creation story should be taught side by side with evolution. In comparison, nearly all of the scientists I surveyed think that evolution is the best explanation we have for the development of life on earth. As debates about teaching intelligent design in public school classrooms intensify, outspoken scientists have lashed out, perhaps angered by what they see as an outright attack on evolution.[17]

But "much more needs to be done by scientists . . . to overcome public indifference or outright hostility to science," according to noted political scientist Sanford Lakoff.[18] It is clear that scientists at elite universities do shoulder the responsibility of translating science to the broader American public. But this public includes a great many religious people. Beyond their own personal attitudes toward religion, scientists in my research revealed that they know little about how their own colleagues came to their views on religion, much less about what drives a typical American worshipper. Secular scientists need better information—including a more informed grounding in the basics of the world's major faith traditions—to think through how to engage the believing public and religious scientists about matters of faith. Without this knowledge to serve as a bridge, boundaries can't be crossed, the benefits of common dialogue are wasted, and potential allies for science remain untapped within a religious public.

Americans have placed science on a precarious throne. In one sense, they know that they benefit immensely from it. They immunize their children, enjoy the benefits of technology, and clamor for new discoveries and breakthroughs. Yet at times they mistrust the very scientists from whom they expect miracle cures, especially when it comes to issues such as embryonic stem cell research, environmental degradation, and the origins and development of life. Debates around these issues sometimes leave much of the American public with the impression that scientists do not think enough about the potential ethical implications of their work. And this impression can have very negative consequences for science. Even with a more science-friendly administration in

Washington, public funding for science might continue to be cut by unsympathetic members of Congress. Scientists must provide a better rationale for the types of research that they do and how their research helps the general public.

American public schools have suffered from the religion-science conflicts. Young Americans are not learning what they should about science because their parents' quarrels and impasses are holding them back from studying topics like evolution or from pursuing science careers (out of fear that such pursuits are incompatible with their religious beliefs). Scientists need to do a better job of communicating the importance of science to religious people. And to the extent that religion could be a resource to motivate people to study science (in order, for instance, to better care for God's creation), this resource should not be left untapped. If the public thinks that to be a successful scientist, you have to be either antireligious or clueless about religion, this can only be to the detriment of scientific progress and public funding.

Since the dawn of the scientific revolution there have been religious challenges to science, and there will be more in the future. Scientists have usually taken a defensive posture in the face of these threats, but they need to go on the offensive. They can begin by examining themselves. This book puts scientists in a virtual conversation with one another—looking inside their own lives and the lives of their peers to better understand their own collective forms of religion and spirituality and where these differ from and overlap with those of other Americans. The time to accomplish this self-investigation is now, not later, at a school board hearing on evolution in front of TV news cameras on the lookout for a catchy sound bite. The scientists I talked with were sometimes afraid of this study, suspicious that, as one psychologist put it, "the findings could be interpreted or misinterpreted as just confirming the public stereotype of academia as nonspiritual, nonreligious . . . the liberal enemies." Fortunately, what scientists really think about religion is far more complex and far more interesting.

A MESSAGE TO RELIGIOUS NONSCIENTISTS

Whether or not scientists are religious, or philosophers see an inherent conflict between religion and science, or psychologists discover something in the chemistry of the brain that makes certain individuals predisposed to be religious, faith is indisputably a central thread in the fabric of American life.

Americans also *care* about science. About 90 percent of Americans express interest in new scientific discoveries and new inventions and technologies.[19]

Often, simply saying "scientific studies show" is enough to gain a public hearing for a new product or idea. But the general public is often either deluged with misinformation or woefully underinformed. Most have little idea what scientists actually do or the true value of their efforts. Scientists are routinely criticized by other Americans for taking too much public money for research that seems of little practical benefit to the public good. More than 50 percent of Americans agree that "we depend too much on science and not enough on faith" and that "scientific research these days doesn't pay enough attention to the moral values of society." Nearly 25 percent of the American public think that scientists are hostile to religion.[20]

The message of this book for Americans of faith is that even the most secular of scientists often struggle with the implications of their work for religion, especially in that many of them look to religious communities for the moral education of their children or for guidance in ethical matters. Moreover, there are scientists who share your faith and who work to maintain their traditions in the midst of the demands of their scientific career.

WHY STUDY BOTH NATURAL AND SOCIAL SCIENTISTS?

When I speak of scientists, I mean both natural scientists (for this study, physicists, chemists, and biologists) and social scientists (here, sociologists, economists, political scientists, and psychologists).[21] Those who work in the natural sciences are most likely to become involved with the public controversies over evolution/creation and embryonic stem cell research. Social scientists are often characterized by the general public as "village atheists" and as the most politically liberal of academics and for that reason potentially biased in their research.

The relationship between natural and social scientists is sometimes uncomfortable, but they are usually of one mind in the defense of science. Although my study was designed to illuminate the differences between natural and social scientists, it uncovered a lot of similarities. Both see themselves as engaged in a search for the truth of scientific fact. And there was very little difference between natural and social scientists in their religious propensities. In fact, it was surprising how closely (with some notable exceptions) the social scientists' conceptions of science and the generation of scientific "facts" meshed with the views of the natural scientists.[22] Where there are true differences I point them out. Social scientists were included in this study in part to facilitate interdisciplinary dialogue.

They are now looking more closely than ever at the place of religion in society, and they have useful commentary for natural scientists on issues of public science, particularly those public science issues connected with religion.[23]

BOOK OVERVIEW AND DISTINCTIONS

As only good social science can, this work will, I hope, add depth and personality to a debate that has remained largely academic and abstract. Other studies have been predicated on narrow definitions of religion. A weakness of such research is the assumption that scientists will define religion in the same ways as do other groups of people. I both analyzed my respondents according to conventional definitions of religion *and* allowed them to tell me the different ways in which religion and science might operate in their lives outside of a conventional understanding (allowing the generation of a category like "spiritual atheist"). Consequently, I do not use a singular definition of religion throughout the book but allow the respondents to define religion in their own terms.

The following chapters will proceed in two broad sections along the lines of the *personal* and the *public*. The first section of the book, "Crossing the Picket Lines: The Personal Faith of Scientists" (chapters 1–4), provides an intimate look at how scientists respond to and incorporate religion and spirituality in their lives. Chapter 2 examines the lives of scientists who do not have any religious beliefs, with particular focus on their reasons for not being religious. Chapter 3 moves on to explain how scientists maintain faith in the midst of demanding careers, while Chapter 4 tells the stories of scientists who are charting new forms of spirituality.

In the second section of the book, "Society and Broader Publics" (chapters 5–8), I explore how scientists handle their interactions with nonscientists about matters of religion, both inside and outside the academy. We begin in Chapter 5 with their first line of engagement with the American public—the students in their classrooms. In chapters 6 and 7, I invite the reader onto the campuses of some of today's top universities, where scientists struggle with how to talk about religion in the context of their lives as scientists. We also investigate the subtle suppression of discussions about religion that occurs within their departments. These chapters examine how scientists who are not religious approach the current issues related to their particular disciplines— whether it be the origins of the earth for natural scientists or questions of social or economic policy for social scientists. This section ends with Chapter 8's

discussion of how scientists might better engage with the broader public outside the university. The chapter investigates whether scientists who are part of
a faith tradition have a special role in the religion-and-science debates—I argue
that they do—and how they could be in dialogue with nonscientists in the
American public on the important subject of faith and reason. Culling from
the 275 interviews, I present some of what scientists think are our best hopes
for moving our public discussions about religion and science from divisive
arguments to productive dialogue. In the conclusion (Chapter 9) I present
some of the myths that scientists believe about religious people along with
misconceptions held about scientists by religious people in the general public.
I hope that dispelling these myths will help us learn to respect and honor one
another at a time when science *and* religion are fundamental parts of the fabric
of our pluralistic nation. Such greater understanding could help bring a divided
nation a little closer together, for the sake of both science and religion.

CHAPTER 2

The Voice of Science

Physics is Arik's[1] lifework. He knew at age 13 that he wanted to be a physicist; even then, he found himself drawn to scientists and their stories, particularly the life of Einstein. Arik's tone was easygoing and friendly, but when the discussion turned to religion, he became passionate. Arik truly believes that religion should not exist. He was raised Jewish and has abandoned Judaism in any formal sense over what he views as its meaningless rituals and anti-intellectualism. He describes religion as a form of "intellectual terrorism." The only time Arik turned to Judaism was when his children were young; he joined a liberal temple for a little while to give them cultural education about their heritage. After the September 11 terrorist attacks, however, Arik left Judaism for good, even more convinced that religion in any form has the potential to lead to violence. He did not want to associate with any group based on "supernaturalism." Arik has not raised his children religiously since he left the temple, and he remarked proudly that his "children have been thoroughly and successfully indoctrinated to believe as [he does] that belief in God is a form of mental weakness."

To Arik, religion opposes science; it's a tool to wield power over those who are not intelligent enough to know better. As we talked, Arik often applied the metaphor of a virus to describe religion or faith. As a child, he was "infected" by religion, but now he is "immune." He believes that this view is shared by other scientists who are all "just astonished at this sort of viral nature of faith-based thinking [which] only exists because parents infect their children and then there's a new generation and they go on to infect more."

In contrast, science holds almost a magical quality for Arik. He and his colleagues view science as a "dear product of human minds and marvel frequently at how astonishing it is that this collection of atoms and molecules that constitute the human body has managed to figure out such a vast level of understanding of the natural world." He is "furious" that others do not understand the importance of basic science. For example, Arik does not see why Mother Teresa got more attention than antibiotics, MRI machines, or doctors. He acknowledged that other scientists believe in God but said right away that these individuals are something of a frustration to him because they give legitimacy to the extreme wing of religious fundamentalism. As if to sum up his irritation, he said, "too many people believe in the power of prayer over the power of science."

Whenever I asked a question that struck Anthony,[2] a chemist, as thought-provoking—such as how science has influenced what he thinks about religion—he would take off his tortoiseshell glasses, placing a sidepiece in his mouth, and rub the front of his head. He would then lean toward me with his elbows on his knees, as if he wanted to talk like we were old friends. I had a sense that Anthony is a professor students find engaging.

During his high school years, Anthony "wanted nothing more than to be an auto mechanic." Because his mother did not graduate from high school, she wanted something more for him: she wanted Anthony to have a college education. And as he described it, college "opened my eyes to what learning is." With a big smile on his face, Anthony remembered that one of his favorite classes was chemistry, because "you understand what makes things explode!"

Anthony described himself as a "lapsed Catholic," who as a child never enjoyed attending Mass. At one point, his father had told him that if he got a job, he wouldn't have to go to church anymore, so he immediately went out and got a job. He described his religious upbringing as both positive and negative: positive in the sense that it gave him a "grounding in ethics" but negative because all the religious rules he had to follow "left [him] with a permanent guilt complex." Today, he is an agnostic.

Anthony generally does not talk about religion with his colleagues, though they have on occasion talked about religious challenges to the theory of evolution. He thinks most of the other scientists he works with are atheists, probably because, given the facts of science, they do not see a need for God. For Anthony, the main conflict between science and religion is that religion says that God is necessary in order to "get the whole thing rolling" (by which he means the beginning of the earth). The more Anthony understands about chemistry, however, the less he sees room for God; for example, evolution can take place without God. And on top of what science has shown him, Anthony's own experiences with suffering have led him to believe that even if God does exist, He certainly is not all that active in the world.

During our hour-long conversation, we moved past the questions I had prepared, meandering into other areas that Anthony thought we should discuss. He told me how he would like to respond to people who have a belief in God. If they would listen, he would say to them, "If you knew more about biology and the sequence of proteins from all different parts of the tree of life," then you would realize that "God did not just invent beavers! Beavers arose from a common ancestor of something else. And you would realize that you do not need to believe in God to understand how life came about."

Arik and Anthony and others like them are part of a tradition of scientists who think that eventually science will make faith irrelevant. And their words would appear, on the face of things, to confirm the image of the godless scientist. Some scientists said in conversations with me that it is only a matter of time before science completely replaces religion, which was simply trying to answer the wrong questions in the wrong ways. As science continues to make further advances in the pursuit of knowledge, they reasoned, it's going to be harder and harder for religion to have a place in society. It is clear that these scientists have a very particular notion of what constitutes science: Science is fact. Those who adhere to this unwavering conflict position hold religion under the lamp of what they see as empirical reality. In this light, religion is vacant.

But our goal is to dig deeper, pursuing dialogue between scientists and the general public that goes beyond thin views of science *or* thin views of religion. We need to ask how even atheist and agnostic scientists such as Arik and Anthony view the connection between religion and science, and why.

Statistics make starkly obvious the differences in religious commitment between scientists and the general public; while nearly 28 percent of the American population is part of an evangelical Protestant tradition, about 2 percent of natural and social scientists at elite universities identify themselves this way. The only traditional religious identity category where scientists comprise a much

TABLE 2.1. Religious Affiliation of Elite Scientists Compared to all Americans[3]

Religious Affiliation	Percent of Elite Scientists	Percent of U.S. Population
Evangelical Protestant	2	28
Mainline Protestant	14	13
Black Protestant	0.2	8
Catholic	9	27
Jewish	16	2
Other	7	6
None	53	16
Total Percent	100	100

larger proportion of believers than in the general population is Jewish. While a little less than 2 percent of Americans identify as Jewish, about 16 percent of academic scientists do—with many of these considering themselves ethnically, rather than religiously, Jewish. For our current discussion, the most important gap is between the two nonreligious groups. Fifty-three percent of scientists have no religious tradition, compared to only 16 percent of Americans.

In *The God Delusion*, Oxford University evolutionary biologist Richard Dawkins argues that science proves wrong "the God hypothesis." Dawkins's brand of science-based atheism is a hard sell, however, among the broader public. (Many of the scientists I talked with also thought that Dawkins is doing little to further the cause of science among the public.) Still, about 64 percent of scientists at elite research universities either are certain that they do not believe in God, the classic atheist position, or they do not know whether or not there is a God, the classic agnostic view. Natural and social scientists are similar in their thinking here. In a radical show of difference, only about 6 percent of the general public consider themselves either atheist or agnostic. Looked at the other way around, only 9 percent of scientists say they have no doubt that God exists, compared to well over 60 percent of the general public.[4] The discrepancy is no secret. But what brought about this current state?[5]

Like the atheists and agnostics (in nineteenth- and early twentieth-century British society) chronicled by historian Susan Budd, present-day scientists have myriad reasons for rejecting faith.[6] Scientists are not a monolithic faith group.

TABLE 2.2. Scientists' Belief in God Compared to the General Public

Which one of the following statements comes closest to expressing what you believe about God?	Percent of Scientists	Percent of U.S. Population
"I do not believe in God."	34	2
"I do not know if there is a God, and there is no way to find out."	30	4
"I believe in a higher power, but it is not God."	8	10
"I believe in God sometimes."	5	4
"I have some doubts, but I believe in God."	14	17
"I have no doubts about God's existence."	9	63
Total	100	100

For some, not believing has everything to do with learning more about science. For others, science itself had little influence on their decision to not believe. In fact, for the majority of scientists I interviewed, it is not the engagement with science itself that leads them away from religion. Rather, their reasons for unbelief mirror the circumstances in which other Americans find themselves: they were not raised in a religious home; they have had bad experiences with religion; they disapprove of God or see God as too changeable.[7] For others, religion is simply irrelevant to their life's passion of science.

REASON ONE: BECAUSE SCIENCE
TRUMPS RELIGION

Sociologist Robert Merton has called the collective set of values that uphold the scientific enterprise the "normative structure of science."[8] This conception of science holds that science is inherently protected from personal bias because scientists work together in groups. They replicate one another's experiments, thus ensuring the objectivity of the collective rather than the subjectivity of the individual. For the Mertonian normative structure to work, a sense of organized skepticism is required, a choice agreed to by all scientists not to believe in a theory until suitable evidence has been presented to support it. Another important aspect of the Mertonian structure is the concept of disinterest (or nonattachment). If a scientist, for instance, has a personal stake in his or her discovery, its veracity is automatically suspect.

When scientists take the norms they perceive as governing science and apply them to all of life, religion is weighed against science, and it does not measure up. Religious views are not based on the kind of information that can be judged impartially, such scientists would argue. There is a personal bias in religion; religious individuals have a stake in findings that support their faith (they lack the disinterest that scientists have). These scientists do not entertain the possibility that some religious followers might be more reasonable than others; they compare all religion to science and find it wanting.

Scientists who have this view think that in all spheres of life, only knowledge that is found through science is reliable. Likewise, for them, only questions answerable through science are worth exploring. Questions concerning the *meaning* of life are not even worth asking. The sentiments of Joel,[9] a political scientist who is a practicing Christian, provide some insight here. As we talked, Joel said in a discouraged tone that "the main battle you find in academia is simply getting people to take [religious questions like] the question of whether there might be a God or not, seriously." Joel seems to be right. I talked with a chemist at a Big Ten university who said that questions about why we are here and the purpose of the universe are simply uninteresting to him. (To his mind, these are the kinds of questions about which religion is generally concerned.) What did matter to him was what could be tested by scientific experiment. If the answer to a question could not be found through science, then why ask it at all?

Similarly, when asked about his answers to the meaning of life, an easygoing neuroscientist[10] who joked a lot as we talked said that he did not think that there was any real purpose to life beyond furthering evolution. He then went on to compare human existence to that of a cockroach: "What's the purpose of a big cockroach? What's the purpose of a cockroach's life? One is to eat and mate and create progeny. . . . I don't see a purpose—in the sense of a noble purpose—other than to survive." This speaker, or his perspective, might be described as Kafkaesque, reminiscent of Franz Kafka's early-twentieth-century novella *The Metamorphosis*, in which Gregor Samsa, a traveling salesman, wakes up one morning to find himself transformed into a giant insect. The entire novel is the story of Gregor being separated from human relationships because of his state. This neuroscientist took his beliefs about science being the only type of knowledge worth pursuing to their logical conclusion. Because science is capable of comprehending the totality of life, humans are separate entities pursuing their own rational outcomes. Higher questions of meaning and purpose are not important. Human life is no more noble than that of a cockroach.

Over and over, from school to school, I discovered sentiments similar to those raised by Arik, Anthony, and other scientists like them. These scientists found questions addressed by religion so utterly insignificant that they did not want to waste time thinking about them. For them, science had superseded religion. It was not restricted to doing experiments in their labs but offered a pervasive worldview, a way of conceptualizing and talking about life.[11]

Championing the Conflict

Rather than regarding religion as merely a waste of time, a small proportion of scientists I interviewed who claimed no religion saw it as a threat to science. These individuals (like all those who reported that religion and science are necessarily in conflict) generally are not part of a traditional religion and do not consider spirituality important. They often have a narrow definition of religion, seeing all religion as (indistinguishable from) fundamentalist Protestantism.

And they often have a narrow definition of science, too, seeing all science in the pure Mertonian form as described above. These scientists do not only come from fields like biology—fields currently embroiled in public debates about religion and science. Scientists across all disciplines have adopted a "conflict paradigm," although this group makes up only a small percentage (15 percent) of the 275 scientists I interviewed. A few scientists, some of whom alluded to Galileo's conflict with the Catholic Church, flatly declared that there is no hope for achieving a common ground of dialogue between scientists and religious believers.

The public conflict is most clearly manifested in debates about teaching intelligent design in public schools.[12] There are also controversies about research on embryonic stem cells and about human genetic engineering.[13] Beyond such public conflicts, 10 percent of scientists also mentioned personal conflicts with religion that led them to reject faith once they learned more about science.

From a very early age, Arik was convinced that science had largely replaced religion. Although he was raised in a Jewish household, for his parents, being Jewish was largely a matter of following rules and cultural practices rather than religious belief. As an adult, he has become even more convinced that religion is deleterious to science. (He wondered aloud if he was extreme in this view compared to the other scientists I talked with.) He told me that the conflict between religion and science is "not a conflict between opposing forces," since what science is up against is nothing but "garbage—the detritus left over from the age of enlightenment and the scientific revolution." He said, "It's the only realization of the battle between good and evil that I know of." For Arik, science embodies everything good, and religion is beyond irrelevant. It's evil.

Although perhaps less contentious than Arik, a sociologist[14] who taught at a large research university in the Midwest said that religion is "a response that people generate to [deal with] general basic fears about life and death and where we come from." He quickly added that the more he learns about science, the less religious he becomes. When I asked him whether he thinks there is a conflict between religion and science, he said without hesitation that there is. The conflict arises because science is, at its core, about observing. By contrast, religion involves believing in things that you cannot observe. As he thought about it further, he reasoned that scientists who have faith must be experiencing "some kind of schizophrenia between two parts of their lives and fulfilling different functions [rather] than [having] an integrated way of looking at things." For this sociologist, science and religion seemed so very much in conflict that it was hard for him to imagine how one could even *be a* scientist and a religious person at the same time, apart from some measure of mental distress.

REASON TWO: BECAUSE RELIGION HAS LET THEM DOWN

One could argue that maybe nonreligious scientists just haven't given religion a chance. But for at least some scientists at elite U.S. universities, religion had its chance and it left them wanting—or even scarred. Of the nearly 1,700 natural and social scientists surveyed, about 39 percent were raised in a Protestant home. Less than half of these still identify as Protestants. About 23 percent were raised Catholic, and fewer than half of these are still Catholic.[15] A former Catholic, a chemist,[16] explained that being a scientist and thinking like a scientist were a big part of his early doubts about religion. He remembers going through a difficult period in high school around the time he was confirmed in the Catholic Church. He started to have doubts about his faith, and the church offered no answers to his deepest questions. These doubts eventually blossomed, resulting in what he called his "anticonversion." In our conversation, he connected his anticonversion to thinking like a scientist and approaching the world from the perspective that science alone can answer its questions.

Social scientists raised in a religious home who then decided to leave their faith often found reading works by the founders of their respective disciplines to be a critical turning point. The works helped them see the aspects of religion that are *socially constructed*, created by groups of people to meet their own needs rather than being based on a supernatural reality. A sociologist[17] I talked with had this experience as a college freshman through reading the work of Emile Durkheim, one of the founders of sociology and a seminal thinker in understanding the social construction of religion.[18] Finally, she felt released from her ties to her parents' faith. In her words, "It was just like, 'Okay, I can finally let this crap go.'" Even before college, grade school science class was another place where it became clear to her that science was more reasonable than religion: "In school . . . we learned about Galileo, and we learned about how crazy backwards people don't believe in evolution, but evolution is what really happened. . . . I pretty much learned that religion was sort of superstitious and science had . . . facts." In her sense of things, learning more about the bases of social science theory further solidified her view that religion is less about seeking answers to genuine questions and more about communities of people meeting their own social needs.

Most scientists want to live their lives sincerely. And for some, a belief in God seems impossible given what they know of science. What some call their assent to science and others more broadly call a commitment to reason makes it so that, in good conscience, they just cannot believe. For one chemist[19] in her late thirties, a belief in God and what is written in some parts of the Bible do not make sense. She has tried to ask believers her questions about the Bible but has not yet found anyone who can answer them to her satisfaction. Although she would like to believe in God, because believing might give her a sense of relief from her difficult life as an assistant professor, this young chemist finds that she cannot, "because it doesn't make sense to [her]." Belief in God cannot come at the cost of what she sees as her professional commitment to science and to reason.

Bad Experiences with Religion

I spoke with Evelyn[20] for nearly an hour and a half about her views on religion, spirituality, and science. She had gone into science because of what she described as her "fantabulous" grades and because, as she explained, she was a "total geek." While taking her pre-med requirements in college for medical school, she discovered that she really liked her chemistry classes and decided to pursue chemistry instead. For Evelyn, much of religion has strayed from the noble purpose of loving and caring for others and often "ends up being a mechanism by which people's thoughts and lives are controlled or meant to be controlled." She said, "[if] I were a religious person, the thing that I would want out of religion is that sense of community and that sense of common purpose." In the rare times when religion does work, Evelyn thinks, believers do seem to achieve that sense of common purpose.

It is clear, however, that as a child Evelyn did not have these sorts of positive experiences with religion. She felt more like an outsider. She grew up in what she describes as a "Christian fundamentalist family." As with many scientists, Evelyn was naturally inquisitive as a child. When she asked questions about faith, however, she was rebuffed by her religious leaders and told to just believe. She recalls once asking in a Sunday school class how she could believe despite all the bad things that are happening in the world. She had been told simply, "You just make a decision to believe." She remembers learning of a passage in the Bible that condones "beating your wife with a stick that's not thicker than your thumb." (In fact, nothing at all like this appears anywhere in the Bible.)[21] She also told me the heartbreaking story of how, as a child, she was abused by family members who were religious. Evelyn wondered—given the abuse she experienced at home—how her family could still go to church and pretend that what was being said there mattered in how they lived their lives. Yet sometimes even now she yearns for a sense of what it would mean to have faith. "What is it that keeps people believing?" she muses. "There's a part of me that really longs for that sense of comfort that people must get from knowing that there's a purpose to everything."

The Problem of Pain

For Evelyn and a plurality of other scientists, it is not the long, arduous struggle with science itself that leads them away from God. Rather it is life's big questions, such as the problems of evil and pain—problems that plague many believers as well.[22] A chemist[23] explained that he has no problem with the ceremony and community of religion. But when it comes to belief in God, he asks, "If God is all-powerful, all-knowing, and good, then how do you explain the quantity of evil in the world?" He has "read various discussions of that problem, from people [who are] pro-religion and anti-, but [he] could never see any credible response from the theological side to that problem." I talked with a chemist[24] around the time that hurricane Katrina, the most deadly hurricane in recent U.S. history, hit New Orleans. He told me he finds it difficult to talk with those who believe in God about events like this devastating hurricane:

> I have a conversation with a believer, and I ask him to describe God. Ah! Forget it. What evidence do you have for the existence of God? None! None whatever! I just say New Orleans as case in point. I asked a believer, "If you believe in God, why did God permit New Orleans?" And the answer came back, "Oh, there were sinners in New Orleans." . . . There are sinners everywhere. There are more sinners in Chicago than there are in New Orleans, and we don't have hurricanes. I mean, come on! Eventually they give up. They just walk away.

For these scientists, it is not the hard, cold facts of science that lead them away but their struggles in response to questions such as "How can a good God allow bad things to happen?" that make belief difficult.

Bad Religion in Society

Greg Graffin studied evolutionary theory at Cornell University, but he is best known as the lead vocalist of the punk rock band Bad Religion. One of the band's most popular songs, "American Jesus," describes in detail the problems that the band feels fundamentalist Christianity brings to the United States:

> We've got the American Jesus
> He helped build the President's estate . . .
> He's the farmer's barren fields
> The force the army wields[25]

These lyrics show that intellect, emotion, and politics are often closely intertwined when it comes to discussions about religion and science.

Often scientists I interviewed cited the ills they have seen perpetuated at the hand of religious leaders as the primary reason for their lack of belief. These scientists would tell me about evils done in the name of faith, broader societal problems they saw resulting particularly from fundamentalist and evangelical religions, and, in Evelyn's case, their own negative personal experiences with the traditions of their past. Evelyn remembers being taken to church with her family on one occasion; the preacher talked with her after the sermon and told her that she would probably have more friends if she would lose some weight.

A physicist[26] I spoke with was raised in a Protestant tradition and, like Evelyn, did not have good experiences with religion as a child. He was part of a tradition "where you go to church every Sunday, you go out and proselytize and try to save souls, . . . you accept Christ as your personal Lord and Savior." The people in his family's church were often afraid of any challenges to their faith and provided no forum for asking difficult questions. Worse, their personal ethics seemed inconsistent with living life as Christ lived it. Although he once gave faith a chance, in his words, "I don't really have any association myself that there's anything positive about religion, and I certainly think that there are a lot of negatives." This physicist says that rather than follow a religion he lives simply by the golden rule and tries to treat others as he would like to be treated himself.

His sense that he does not need the particular doctrines of a religion to live as an ethical person is typical of the way many Americans see Christianity, according to sociologist Nancy Ammerman. Ammerman finds that individuals who practice what she calls "golden rule Christianity," unlike the physicist above who was raised a Protestant, might actually go to church but attend less often than others. What they take from their religious tradition is a sense that one should pay more attention to "right living rather than right believing"—caring humanely for others rather than holding to a particular doctrine.[27] Those scientists who eschewed the organized religion of their childhood often remained committed to the codes of ethics learned from their traditions.

Leaving *or* Retaining Religion Brings Criticism

The decision to not believe in God or to raise one's children without religion is not without public consequence. Indeed one study finds that Americans dislike atheists more than almost any other group of people, including various ethnic and religious groups, and shows that "increasing acceptance of religious diversity does not extend to the nonreligious."[28] Pollsters find that among a range of types of potential candidates, Americans say they are the least likely to vote for an atheist for President. This tension sometimes came out keenly in my one-on-one discussions with scientists. A biologist[29] I talked with said that dealing with the topic of religion in her broader life has been especially difficult because "people in our society are so religious, and that makes me feel like there's something wrong with me." Most acutely she struggled with how to raise her children. Because she and her husband did not share the same religious beliefs, they brought their children up without religion. Although her children are now adults, religion is still, as she put it, a "thorn in my side." She said, "I try to console myself by saying that most people don't get to see what I do in my work, into the inner workings of things the way I do in my work." The beauty she sees and the meaning she gets through her work as a scientist lead her to feel somewhat at peace without having a religion, even though much of the world outside her scientific haven is religious.

Scientists who do practice religion can face intense pressure to give it up as they are sometimes harshly judged by their secular peers. They might be viewed as not fully engaging the scientific part of their brains, simply putting their reason on hold to find comfort in religion. A chemist[30] who has been in the field for years remarked that if you are a scientist, you "cannot believe in things that are supernatural, because that's a total cop-out. That's really antiscience. The whole purpose of doing science is to figure out how nature works. And as soon as you . . . say, 'Ah-ha, I'm going to push the supernatural button,' then you're just abdicating yourself as a scientist." For some, like this one, believing in God actually puts research at incredible risk. That is why, for the sake of the profession, they think other scientists should give up religion. Believing is the opposite of exploring; it means to leave questions unanswered that are simply too difficult to ask.

REASON THREE: BECAUSE RELIGION IS FOREIGN OR UNIMPORTANT

Frederick William Faber was born June 28, 1814, in West Yorkshire, England. His hymn "Faith of Our Fathers" has the following chorus: "Faith of our fathers, holy faith! We will be true to thee till death."[31] A popular song in both the Catholic and Protestant traditions, "Faith of Our Fathers" was sung at the funeral of President Franklin D. Roosevelt. The song's theme confirms that the primary way religious traditions survive is by being passed through families.

And just as traditions and practices individuals acquire in childhood influence their belief or nonbelief as adults, what scientists learned (or did not learn) about religion as children also influenced their direction. About 13 percent of scientists were raised in homes with no religious tradition. Much more important, for the remaining nearly 87 percent of scientists whose families were part of a religious tradition, membership was sometimes only significant as a label rather than a matter of regular practice. Consequently, these scientists did not learn much about their tradition, nor were they taught to see religion as an integral part of everyday life. Scientists who said that religion was not important in their families when they were growing up are currently less likely to believe in God or attend religious services. When we consider that a larger proportion of top scientists compared to other Americans in other occupations came from backgrounds where faith traditions were weakly or seldom practiced, some of the differences between elite scientists and other Americans make more sense.[32]

Eight percent of the general population were raised with no religion, compared to 13 percent of elite scientists. And while 54 percent of the general population were raised Protestant, only 39 percent of scientists at elite universities were raised in this tradition—a significant difference in statistical terms. Much more important, those scientists raised in a religious tradition were often in homes where religion was only a tangential part of life, while nearly 40 percent of Americans attend religious services at least once a week. Consider two sociologists who are similar in other respects. If one was raised in a Protestant home where religion was very important and the other was raised without a religious tradition, the sociologist raised without a tradition is statistically four times more likely to be an atheist.[33]

These figures came to life as I talked with scientists. I asked a political scientist[34] in his early forties how religion was approached in his family while growing up:

> It basically wasn't there. I knew that my mother was . . . Episcopalian, but she never went to church when I was growing up. And my dad never gave any evidence [of having] religious beliefs at all. He's a scientist, and . . . I don't think he went to church when he was a kid. . . . So I never really had any exposure to religion.

The experiences of this political scientist were typical of some of the other scientists who did not have faith. They were raised as atheists or without religion.

Possibly their parents had gone through a struggle of leaving the faith of their own families. Such scientists are part of a group that is rare in the rest of the American population: the second-generation atheist or nonreligious person. Going on to describe his scant experiences with religion, this political scientist said that he had only attended two religious events: a wedding, and a church service that he was obligated to go to when he was a Boy Scout. For Boy Scouts, "being an atheist was not an option, so [he] had to choose a church, and [he] was a Catholic for a day."

WORKING TOWARD DIALOGUE

Scientists at elite research universities are indeed less religious than many other Americans, at least when we measure their levels of traditional religious commitment. Some do drop their religious identities upon learning more about what the religion involves. Others experience an anticonversion (or aversion) after difficult or painful encounters with religion as children. The assumption that becoming a scientist necessarily leads to loss of religious commitment is not supported when we take into account the fact that scientists seem to self-select from certain kinds of religious background—most importantly, from backgrounds where religion was practiced only weakly. (Religious socialization and heritage are strong influences on present religiosity, even among elite scientists.) And others, whose only exposure to religion is the fundamentalist Protestantism they see represented in the news media, are disgusted by the idea of affiliating with any religion at all.

The work of sociologist Basil Bernstein brings some insight to how we might begin to assess the implications of scientists' religious backgrounds. His work primarily analyzes social class differences by examining what he calls language codes. Bernstein's research focuses on the factors in working-class families that affect how their children learn to talk—not just their first words, but their particular way of talking. Bernstein thinks these ways of talking help to determine whether a child will grow up to be a janitor or to work on Wall Street. Middle- and upper-class children benefit from being taught elaborate codes that are complex and accessible; lots of people can understand them. In comparison, the restricted codes used by many working-class children—for example, using phrases like "I ain't" repeatedly—have lots of shorthand and shared meanings, making it more difficult for these children to interact with a variety of people outside their social class. This inability to relate to those outside their class means that working-class children do not possess the language necessary to expand their networks and so move up the social class ladder. The implication is that it is not enough simply to put working-class children in the midst of upper-class social settings. Rather, working-class children must be taught to effectively communicate with the people in settings outside their usual milieu.

Wholly unlike the working-class children Bernstein studied, the scientists I talked with are among the most educated people in our society. Therefore I expected them to have very complex and unrestricted speech codes. But although scientists have extraordinarily elaborate codes in some areas of their intellectual lives, when it comes to talking about matters of faith, they often have a *restricted code* based on shorthand stereotypes. In other words, they are not articulate. Thus they might lump all religion into fundamentalism, or discredit religious claims based on premature assumptions. And because most elite scientists have limited interactions with religious people who share their views about science, the stereotypes persist.

A scientist's restricted code poses a challenge to dialogue with the general public. And a scientist who becomes less religious from learning more about science (10 percent of those I interviewed think—against evidence to the contrary—that increases in education always lead to a decrease in religious commitments). To work toward dialogue, nonbelieving scientists would need to understand that while over 50 percent of scientists do not have a religious tradition, nearly 50 percent do. There are believers in their midst. But the scientists who renounced or never embraced faith might also have a difficult time understanding the perspective of their religious colleagues. If there is a way to foster dialogue, scientists without faith might view scientists with faith as *allies* in better translating science to the general public.

CHAPTER 3

The Voice of Faith

When I talked with scientists at our nation's elite universities about their religious colleagues, no one was mentioned more often than Francis Collins, director of the National Institutes of Health. At the time of these interviews, Collins was at the helm of the Human Genome Project, the largest effort ever to map the intricacies of DNA, the road map of life. Collins is also an outspoken evangelical Christian and recent author of *The Language of God*. In a book that is part autobiography and part science, he writes about his upbringing by flower-child parents who met at Yale and raised him on a farm in the Shenandoah Valley of rural Virginia.

Although I did not interview him as part of this study, Collins represents a group of scientists for whom religion is important now but was not an important part of childhood. These individuals came to faith—and particularly to an understanding of how their religious traditions connected with their lives as scientists—over the course of a struggle. Another group of religious scientists were raised in a religious home. These too experienced a struggle, trying to maintain faith in the midst of traditions that often suppressed questioning. For religious scientists, the struggle between faith and science generally occurred in adolescence or young adulthood rather than after receiving their training in science.

Surprisingly, given public stereotypes of scientists as atheists and religion-haters, these scientists came through such struggles to a place where they do not see any conflict between religion and science.[1] As we'll discover, scientists who have achieved such reconciliation generally understand their faith traditions differently than do the nonscientists who share their faith. If we look closely, however, it's possible to see some areas of overlap between these scientists and religious members of the general public. Also contrary to stereotypes put forth by some nonreligious scientists, believers did not consider their traditions and beliefs influential on how they conducted their research. None of the religious scientists I talked with supported the theory of intelligent design.

(Ninety-four percent of religious scientists think that evolution is the best explanation for the development of life on earth).

There was some agreement among these scientists that their faith commitments ought to influence the kinds of *relationships* they had with others; 53 percent of scientists who identify with a religious tradition see religion and spirituality influencing their interactions with students and colleagues. In the midst of the competition involved in trailblazing scientific discoveries, these scientists retained a faith-based emphasis on personal relationships.

Some thought their faith should influence the kinds of projects they chose. For a physicist, this might mean refusing to participate in studies that support nuclear proliferation because of a Christian conviction to care about the welfare of humanity.[2] Their faith commitments might also influence their decision to work on translating science to a broader audience or to do work that has a humanitarian application.

THE COMPLEXITIES OF KEEPING THE FAITH

On the one hand, it's clear that the majority of religious scientists were raised in homes with a faith tradition. According to my survey, about 50 percent of those from a Protestant tradition retained religious beliefs and practices of some type.[3] And unsurprisingly those who said that religion was important in their family when growing up were less likely to say that they currently see no truth in religion, do not believe in God, or do not attend religious services.

On the other hand, just because scientists were raised with faith and eventually retained faith does not mean that they went through their lives without experiencing a personal struggle between religion and science. The majority of religious scientists I talked with experienced as adolescents a *sincere* struggle in which they tried to figure out how being a person of faith connected with or could be reconciled with a burgeoning interest in science. These struggles often brought scientists to a deeper understanding of how science and religion connected for them personally. As those who have developed a thinking faith, they are potentially poised to be public commentators to an American public that often views faith and reason at odds, or even mutually exclusive.

For Tobin, an economist I interviewed, such a struggle as an adolescent led to a stronger and more outwardly focused adult faith than what he had as a child.[4] Economists are often stereotyped as hard-nosed, hyperrational number crunchers, but Tobin had a warm, almost tender, way of speaking. Only in his late thirties, Tobin has achieved outstanding professional success. He is a full professor, chair of his department, and has already served as the major adviser for nearly thirty PhD students. Tobin talked openly with me about his experiences as a Catholic, in particular the tension he experiences between faith and science.

Tobin was raised in a Roman Catholic family, with a faith that he described as "not very deep." He found that simply being raised Catholic was not enough for him to remain a person of faith through his late teens and early twenties. The shift away occurred at one particular Mass, when Tobin had the sense that he was no longer able, in good conscience, to be a Catholic. He described this turning point as a "quick shift" that "had been building." While Tobin walked away from the Church for a time, a "deep faith" experience ultimately led him back. His return to the Church was more gradual than his turning away had been; what Tobin now sees as "a true faith" crept up on him quietly. It involved a lot of reading to figure things out—reading without "any particular intent to become religious but more to engage seriously with people who are religious." Looking back, Tobin said he wanted to figure out how far he could "get through reason," and how much beyond reason he "would have to go to be religious."

After a period of agnosticism, during which he did not know whether or not he believed in God, Tobin said that ironically it was the "depth" of Catholicism that led him back to the Church. The traditions of the Church helped him make sense of what it would mean to believe in God, in Jesus Christ, and to find a way that was "indeed consistent with reason." The process was not easy. He spent hours reading Church scholars and through this process became aware that "the Catholic Church was much more than what people perceive it [to be]." Tobin concluded that Catholicism was especially good at reconciling faith and reason. And the ability to reconcile reason with faith was the linchpin that helped Tobin remain both a Catholic and a scientist. He mused, "I do not think that two gifts from God should contradict one another." When I asked Tobin to name the specific Catholic doctrines that are most important to him, he talked about belief in God and belief in Jesus Christ. He described these "core beliefs" as very different from the "bells and whistles" of Catholicism and went on to say with a touch of humor in his voice that "if I picture myself as I die and I find out what things are really like, I'd be stunned if there wasn't a God, but I wouldn't be stunned if a particular teaching on the Virgin Mary wasn't exactly the way the Church had said it was." In contrast to those who find faith irrelevant, scientists like Tobin say they walk a more complicated path, revealing that the scientific enterprise need not crumble under the weight of faith.

A DIFFERENT FAITH FOR SCIENTISTS

It might seem that Tobin would have a lot in common with other Catholics who, although they are not scientists, share his faith. And it might seem, since Tobin is a committed Catholic, he would even be in a position to help fellow parishioners see that faith and science do not have to contradict each other. But even for scientists with a meaningful faith tradition, gaining common ground with others in their tradition is not always easy. Yes, the majority of Americans have a faith tradition. Most are Protestants. And many Americans view public issues such as science policy through a faith-informed lens. But before we can fully understand the potential for scientists with faith to have a role in public discussion about religion and science, we must understand how the faith of scientists compares to the faith of other Americans. Such understandings will establish whether and where there are common points of religiousness or belief between scientists and members of the general public that could lead to further dialogue. So here we explore how faith is lived out for the significant minority of scientists who are traditionally religious, those who belong to one of the major world traditions.

Who Is Religious?

When studying religious and nonreligious people, we can also look at the other aspects of their lives. In this way, we can determine what "types" of people within a certain group (such as scientists) are more likely than others in that group to identify themselves as religious. Gender, for instance, plays a role. Although a variety of reasons have been given for the gender differences in religious belief and commitment among Americans, there is almost universal agreement that women tend to be more religious than men and more involved in the activities of their congregation.[5] When looking at differences in religiousness between men and women *scientists*, however, women are not any more or less likely than men to be religious—even when measuring religion in a variety of different ways, including both beliefs and practices.[6]

Similarly, when social scientists survey the general population, they find that older individuals are much more likely to express higher levels of religious belief and practice than younger individuals.[7] My survey of scientists, however, turned this relationship on its head. It was the *younger* scientist who was more likely to believe in God and to attend religious services. And when I compared my survey of scientists to another study conducted over thirty-five years earlier, the likelihood of younger scientists having faith had increased. If this holds throughout the career life-course for this cohort of elite scientists, it could indicate an overall shift in attitude toward religion among those in the academy.[8]

Other insights from sociology are helpful here. Those who study religion label an individual "religious" based on three types of criteria. One of those is the major religious body with which she identifies. Does she consider herself Jewish, Unitarian, or fundamentalist? Another facet of studying religious people is examining *what* an individual believes: Does he believe that God exists? Does he believe that his religion is the only true religion? Scholars also describe degrees of faith through examining the practices religious people use to display and maintain their faith. Does an individual attend a house of worship or spend time meditating at home instead? And how are these practices connected to her beliefs and identities?

Perhaps unsurprisingly, scientists in general are much less likely than are members of the general population to identify as part of a traditional religion. As the figure below shows, over 50 percent of the scientists I surveyed had no religious affiliation.[9] Compare this to only about 16 percent of those in the general population who have no religious affiliation.

But to pay attention only to those who do not avow a faith would be to ignore the nearly 50 percent of elite scientists who do identify with a religious tradition. Of these, the highest proportion are Jewish (about 16 percent), but many of these identify as Jewish as an ethnicity, not in terms of an active religious faith. About 14 percent of the elite scientists—and 13 percent of Americans—identify with one of the major mainline Protestant traditions (such as Methodist or Episcopalian). And 9 percent of elite scientists see themselves as Catholic, as do 27 percent of general Americans. In the future, might we look for more Catholic spokespersons for science?

The differences in how U.S. religions are represented among university scientists are most stark when comparing Jews and evangelicals. Roughly eight

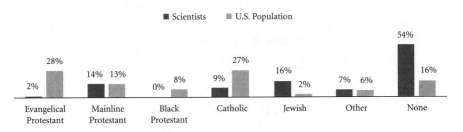

FIGURE 3.1. Religious Traditions: Elite Scientists Compared to the U.S. Population. Sources: Religion Among Academic Scientists Survey 2005, General Social Survey 2006.

times more elite scientists are Jewish than general Americans are.[10] And looking at things the other way around, 14 times more Americans are part of an evangelical tradition (about 28 percent) than elite scientists (about 2 percent) are. When considering the proportion of scientists who are part of traditions that are not Judeo-Christian—such as Buddhism, Hinduism, and Islam—the differences between scientists and other Americans are still noteworthy. There are twice as many Buddhist scientists as Buddhists in the general population.[11] And there are over three times more Hindus among scientists than in the public.[12] For Muslims, the proportion is about the same. These scientists are normally first-generation immigrants or not U.S. citizens. (Recent immigration is largely responsible for the increase in the U.S. presence of non-Christian religions.)[13] Indeed over 30 percent of natural scientists at the top 21 U.S. research universities are either first-generation immigrants or noncitizen U.S. residents.

The greatest commonalities in religious identity between scientists and other Americans are the similarities in proportion of those who identify as mainline Protestant and as Catholic. This is a big surprise in some ways, since more recently it is evangelicals who have been engaged in writing books trying to reconcile Christianity with science.[14] We might be hearing more, however, from Catholic scientists in the future. Noting changes in the religious composition of scientists over time will help us tease out what types of people might be the future religious spokespersons for science. So I compared my 2005 survey of elite scientists to the 1969 Carnegie Commission survey mentioned above of those in the same science disciplines. The proportion of Catholic scientists in some fields has grown dramatically, while the proportion of Protestant scientists has consistently decreased in most disciplines.

It is obvious that there is a much smaller proportion of evangelicals among scientists at top research universities when compared to the proportion of evangelicals in the general population. Yet when I interviewed scientists, I also found a considerable reluctance in using the term evangelical as a self-descriptor, especially when we compare its use in the general population. Even when scientists fit the traditional description of an evangelical, they didn't want to embrace the term for themselves. More important for them than labels were beliefs and practices.

What Do They Believe?

Core beliefs are another important way that scholars determine how important religion is to an individual's life. I can say, for example, that I am a Protestant or a Catholic, but what really matters, scholars would argue, is what I

TABLE 3.1. Opinions of Religious Truth: Elite Scientists Compared to the U.S. Population

Religious Truth Position	Percent of Scientists	Percent of U.S. Population
There is very little truth in any religion	26	4
There are basic truths in many religions	71	84
There is the most truth in only one religion	3	12
Total Percent	100	100

Sources: Religion Among Academic Scientists Survey 2005, General Social Survey 1998.

believe. And scientists' religious beliefs are different from those of the general population.

On the whole, scientists tend to view themselves as religiously liberal. For example, when asked to compare themselves to other Americans along a continuum of religion from liberal to conservative, a 7-point scale on which 1 represents extremely liberal religious beliefs and 7 represents extremely conservative, most of the scientists I interviewed saw themselves as measuring around 2. This means that when they are religious, scientists tend to see themselves as religious liberals. It also means that they view other Americans as having much more conservative beliefs than they themselves do.[15] And this is important to understand as they converse with the general public.

When we hold this liberalism alongside the fact that scientists at elite U.S. research universities are the least likely to be evangelicals (at least to label themselves so) *and* that evangelicalism is heavily represented in the general population, we see that scientists who care about translating science to a general public might need a lot of help to do so effectively.

The table above reveals that 71 percent of scientists think there are basic truths in many religions—the pluralist position—compared to 84 percent of the general public who have the same view. In contrast, only 3 percent of scientists who work at elite universities see one religion as holding the most truth—the exclusivist position—and that is the position most likely to be held by evangelicals[16] (the majority of the religious population).

About 36 percent of scientists have some form of a belief in God. When this same question about belief in God is asked of members of the general public, about 94 percent claim belief.[17] (Indeed it is virtually impossible to find a group of Americans who do *not* believe in God.) About 28 percent of scientists who are part of a religious tradition do not know whether or not they believe in God (the agnostic position). But agnosticism may mean something different to scientists than it does to members of the general public. By definition, their life-work of science requires insurmountable evidence, so for a scientist to say that he is not absolutely convinced that God exists may still be consistent with his religious tradition. A scientist is rarely absolutely convinced about anything!

In comparison, 15 percent of scientists say that they have a religious identity yet do *not* believe in God at all. Many of these are Jewish. In fact, among scientists who are Jewish, nearly 75 percent indicated an atheist position.

What Do They Practice?

Sociologist Peter Berger explains that human beings are constantly faced with the choice of how to interact with their world. An individual's social reality, he argues, is produced by her interaction with social structures.[18] One prominent social structure is religion. Religion is always at risk of no longer being plausible to the individual, because she lives in a social world that often appears ordinary, mundane, and devoid of the supernatural in the day-to-day experience. Hence, Berger thinks that religion requires a way of upholding its unique symbols and doctrines, what he calls a *plausibility structure*. This structure manifests as an actual social community (such as a church congregation) that is less likely to question than uphold the norms and doctrines of the religion.[19] In this way, the believer, in the midst of a world that may contradict her beliefs, can rely on her community of like-minded others to reinforce the content of those beliefs. So then, how religion is practiced within the community—even more than how a person identifies himself or what he believes—may be the key way of keeping the believer's faith intact. While he can pray in his own home without anyone else knowing, attending a worship service means an outward identification that shows others he is religious. Indeed, a central way that scholars determine how committed an individual is to his faith is by looking at how outward his faith is, whether he is an active part of a religious community.

According to sociologist Robert Merton (discussed in Chapter 2), scientists have similar communities that uphold their ideals. Merton thinks that one reason why science is so successful is that the community of scientists all adhere to the same norms—common guidelines for appropriate behavior—of what constitutes good science.[20] However, there would be a stark difference between the communities of the religious and of Merton's communities of the scientific.

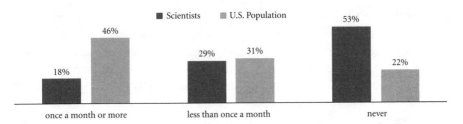

once a month or more   less than once a month   never

FIGURE 3.2. Religious Attendance: Elite Scientists Compared to the U.S. Population.
Sources: Religion Among Academic Scientists Survey 2005, General Social Survey 2006.

While the religious group would be based on acceptance of certain beliefs, a Mertonian scientific community would be based on the opposite: a relentless questioning of what is believed to be true.

Merton's model, though, is only one way of viewing science. And in practice, there are clearly many things that scientists no longer question. Few dispute the theory of evolution or the law of gravity, for example. And, as we'll see, there are many scientists who live well in both communities.

When we look at the numbers for attendance at religious services—a key part of religion's plausibility structure, or social community that reinforces its norms—there are stark differences between scientists and members of the general public. About 18 percent of scientists attend religious services at least once a month or more, compared to about 46 percent of those in the general population. Yet these numbers tell us very little about how the nearly 1 in 5 scientists who attend a house of worship at least monthly *experience* their particular religious communities. Religious scientists live in a precarious state, because the work of science is constantly reminding them of the mundane natural world. As we've seen, however, religious scientists at elite schools have been exposed to and practice the best plausibility structures for science and are still committed to the plausibility structure of religion. If we are able to understand how they live comfortably with this tension, their experience might be the perfect model for how science and religion can coexist as plausibility structures within the same person. It is to this interpretive task that we now turn.

How Do They Live?

The famous mid-twentieth-century Protestant theologian Reinhold Niebuhr (1892–1971) was perhaps best known for taking his faith beyond the doors of the church sanctuary. He consistently related and held in balance the importance of two key Christian doctrines: equality and respect for all humanity, and an awareness of human pride and sinfulness. This understanding led to his advocacy for the voiceless within the broader public sphere. He championed Christian intervention against human rights violations and has been widely influential among a broad range of modern-day thinkers, from journalist David Brooks to the late Pulitzer Prize–winning historian Arthur M. Schlesinger Jr.[21]

Like Niebuhr, many of the religious scientists I talked with placed great value on their coworkers and students as people created in the image of God in the midst of a competitive scientific profession that often seems to chew up and spit out individuals with little regard for human dignity. This desire to care for others even in this competitive environment often means that these scientists live according to values and with worldviews that are quite different from those of their nonreligious peers. These scientists' worldviews and practices made them different from their colleagues in how they thought of themselves. Their religious identities contributed to and shaped their identities as scientists.

Scientists specifically drew on aspects of their religious selves to make sense of the competitive environment of academic science. In doing so, they engaged in what sociologist Michèle Lamont has called a *boundary ideology*, using a moral barrier to create distance between themselves and their colleagues who did not share their philosophy of providing help to others.[22] I spoke with a biologist[23] in his mid forties, on the faculty of a large state university in the Midwest, who was raised in a Presbyterian church where his mother was the choir director for fifty years. Religion has a powerful impact on the way that he treats his colleagues and students. Indeed, he says, religion "always influences" how he thinks about mentoring those who work in his lab. This biologist described his beliefs as classically Christian, holding that "Jesus Christ was born and died and rose again, and there's some afterlife." While he "hires good people," he knows that it is sometimes better for those he works with—better for their overall professional success—to allow them to "move on" to other jobs where they can get more experience. This biologist contrasted himself with some of his nonbelieving colleagues who "don't like to see success in other people, because they think it makes them look bad." His sensibilities as a Christian have also helped this biologist put his own intelligence in perspective. He explained, "I hang out with people who are a lot smarter than I am, and that's okay. I have tried to live my life helping people as much as I can. That includes my students. Their success is my success. And I think my upbringing obviously influences that." In an intensely competitive environment, coming to terms with his own abilities—or, as he would put it, being content with the person God made him to be—was generated from his understanding of the Christian faith and freed him to develop genuine relationships, including with potential competitors.

A political scientist,[24] one of the leading scholars in her field, told me that her moral commitments as a Christian influence how she treats others. She explained, "As a Christian . . . I believe that people are equal and that everybody has the potential for good that makes them intrinsically valued, a very Christian belief." Other political scientists were even more explicit about how their commitments influenced their views of humanity. One[25] argued that you can reason your way into acting ethically toward others. This is a core part of how he understands Catholic doctrine—in particular, "the doctrine of natural law," which implies to him that "ethical norms are not arbitrary judgments of God revealed from on high . . . but rather [part of] the integral directedness of the human good." He believes that God has given us the capabilities to "infer principles of right conduct including something like the golden rule." He explained that the golden rule is actually "directly from the mouth of Jesus and the Gospel, [where Jesus said] 'Do unto others as you would have them do unto you.' . . . So my belief in the golden rule [as] the right way to behave is significantly bolstered by my belief that [it] is a clear teaching of Christ." Other scientists also said that their ideas about how to practice science ethically—including how to treat others in their labs and classrooms—came directly from religious principles. It should be noted that there are obviously many nonreligious scientists who also care deeply for the needs of their students and others. The point here is that the characteristic of "caring for one's students" is how scientists with faith perceived themselves as different from their colleagues.

Scientists who considered themselves part of a traditional religion generally did not want to keep their faith entirely compartmentalized from their scientific lives. They often invited their faith traditions to implicitly influence how they thought about the implications of their science. But they never saw religion as influencing how they applied their scientific methods (that is, how they *did* their science). Rather they emphasized their uniqueness in considering the broader relevance for humanity of the particular science in which they were engaged.

A biologist[26] who described himself as part of the "liberal, progressive tradition of Christianity" and who attended a Congregational Church said that he had a "strong, strong belief in God." As we talked about how his faith influences the work that he does as a scientist, he said it had a very direct impact on his "choice of research problems." His faith motivated him to find out how "we as humans . . . function, how things work, as a way of revealing what is broader and more general and wonderful about life." This desire to find out more about the wonderful nature of life has a direct relationship to his interest in understanding human disease. He was clear to point out that being a person of faith in no way compels him to accept creationism, which he called a "conservative approach." Rather, his faith has an influence by making him interested in doing work that "has a positive impact on people around [him]." He told me that it is "very clear that sort of sense comes out of [my] religious background and upbringing."

Like many of his believing peers, Tobin, the economist introduced at the beginning of this chapter, also said that his faith entered his work by directing the kinds of research topics he chooses and the ways he thinks about their influence on the broader public (though not the methods for his science). At the beginning of a project, his faith framework helps him decide what issues to consider. For example, Tobin attributed his interest in doing work that "benefits underprivileged children" to his Catholic faith. After the research topic has been chosen, he said, being an economist takes over, and it is a little like being a surgeon. Once you start cutting, it does not matter whether you are religious or nonreligious. The only important thing to the person lying on the table is that you are good at your job. But once Tobin has the data from his studies, being a person of faith starts to make a real difference again, this time on "the policy recommendations [he makes] based on the data." His perspective as a Catholic compels him to look beyond what he sees as the "narrow calculations" of other economists and to think more broadly about how the results of his studies could be used to truly improve the welfare of children.

A FAITH AT ODDS WITH THE FAITH COMMUNITY: "DOES THIS GRILLED CHEESE SANDWICH REALLY LOOK LIKE JESUS?"

Like many people, religious scientists sometimes create boundaries between themselves and those in their labs and departments who are not people of faith. The boundaries can manifest in various ways and might indicate differences in beliefs, priorities, or what is considered acceptable behavior. They also create boundaries between themselves and the nonscientists who are part of their own faith traditions. A chief line of demarcation for these boundaries is scientists' questioning of (and at times even full-blown cynicism about) what goes on in their houses of worship. The biologist[27] just mentioned who grew up in a church where his mother was the choir director said that his current church is a fairly liberal Presbyterian parish attended by several other biology professors. A group of biologists in the church "got together and gave lectures . . . in church on evolution and how religion and biology come together." But even though he is part of a religious environment that is generally supportive of his work as a scientist, he often finds himself at odds with what his church believes. It is difficult to know if scientists are really that different from other inquisitive people who naturally question assumptions, but this biologist is like the other scientists with faith I talked to: he thinks he probably questions the core tenets of Christianity because constant questioning is simply part of who he is as a scientist. Being a scientist is a central piece of his identity, shaping his world-view and causing him to be more critical—not so much that he gives up on religion altogether, but enough to give him pause when pastors and leaders claim something as "truth." For example, he talked about sitting in his church service and "wondering from a scientific point of view how this process got started and how Christianity could go from nothing to taking over the world as it has."

Similarly, a psychologist[28] who said he is a Christian (although not part of a particular denomination), finds that having the kind of "critical-thinking skills" that you develop as an academic makes you become "more of a doubting Thomas."[29] He went on to say that sometimes when he sits in a church, it is hard for him not to implicitly define and test in his head what a pastor or leader is discussing from the pulpit. He finds it especially difficult when pastors start "using pop psychology, which they often do because they think they're psychologists." He also finds it troubling when they try to manipulate people through their preaching styles, using "the power of persuasion, of images, and of repetition." His training leaves him always assessing the "intent behind their practices" when he attends worship services. In this way, our psychologist thinks he is probably quite a bit more critical "than the average Joe or Jane" churchgoer.

Another biologist,[30] who described himself as a practicing Catholic, said that being a scientist has influenced his faith by causing him to question certain aspects of his tradition. He explained that he thinks some of his fellow Roman Catholics might accept many things at face value. For example, "stigmata, or some of these sorts of phenomena that are observed and interpreted by some as evidence of a religious force acting." As a scientist he simply doesn't take these testimonials for granted. He jokingly said that being a scientist makes him want to raise objections such as, "Well does this grilled cheese sandwich really look like Jesus, or is it somebody's imagination?" (This memorable quote refers to instances in which religious people find religious imagery in natural phenomena.) Still, some of what he believes as a Roman Catholic he accepts "as a matter of faith," as he put it, even though he knows he cannot "prove these things." He sees himself as somewhat unique, though in this description, he could resemble countless other questioning Catholics, both within and outside science.

THE OCCASIONAL PUBLIC FAITH

There is controversy among religious scientists about how outspoken they should be about their faith. Some think that being open about faith practices and beliefs is paramount to what it means to be a practitioner of their tradition. Yet few scientists I talked with at elite universities are as outspoken about their faith as Jack is. Jack is a biologist[31] in his late forties who researches the neural processes of the brain. When I asked him how he defines religion, he immediately referred to the Latin root of the word, as "that which keeps us together." (The etymology of "religion" is uncertain, but the word may derive from the Latin *religare*, to bind.) Jack thinks that being raised a Catholic made him the person that he is. This experience with religion followed a typical path for the religious scientists I examined. He was raised a Catholic but became frustrated with some of the teachings of the church and went through a period he described as "very worldly." When Jack married and began to have children, he returned to church, this time finding himself in a nondenominational Christian tradition. He explained that many of his beliefs are consistent with evangelicalism, although he stressed that he is "not a fundamentalist" and that his church would "not really be called evangelical." When I asked Jack to explain the particular kinds of beliefs he held, he said, "I ask myself, how should we live, and what should be the guiding principles? I think Jesus Christ provided those. I can't come up with any better way to live than the way Jesus taught us. And that pretty much sums up my religious view." This and other assertions he made about his faith as we talked would align him doctrinally with many conservative Protestants. However, like many of the elite leaders sociologist D. Michael Lindsay interviewed for his work, *Faith in the Halls of Power*, Jack was quite unwilling to label himself as evangelical.[32]

Jack is fairly open about his faith, although he thinks that most other biologists would prefer not to talk about religion. Referring to those in his specific department, he added, "I think faculty members are very uncomfortable with the subject. Most of my colleagues are unreligious or areligious or atheist or even hostile to religion." Jack went on to say with a touch of humor in his voice that enough people know he is religious that "some of my friends on the faculty actually try to persuade me against religion. This is sort of a fun kind of activity for them . . . to try to put religion down and then to get me to renounce it," although he admitted that this kind of teasing is not common. He finds that conversations about religion are hard to get started, and often his fellow scientists are just "uncomfortable talking about it." Jack added later in our discussion that "probably more of them are religious than admit it."

Tobin, our economist,[33] is now well known on his campus for being a person of faith. But this outward focus came only after another struggle—different from the one he had had earlier in his life. He talked about being a Catholic with a few students along the way and was asked by them to give a couple of lectures on what it means to be a person of faith and an economist. As other economists became more aware of his faith, Tobin found their responses surprising. He explained, "I thought that people might not be respectful [of my faith]." Instead, he experienced just the opposite reaction. His colleagues were intrigued by how he reconciles being Catholic with the fine-tuned scientific work he does as an economist. He does find colleagues who would prefer not to talk about matters of faith. But those who do want to talk do so from the vantage point of trying to "figure out how it is that a person that they respect and think is smart and does good work could also have that side which they don't have."

THE MORE COMMON, CLOSETED FAITH

Few scientists are as open about their faith commitments as Tobin and Jack. The majority of religious scientists are rarely public with their colleagues about their views. As Jack correctly surmised, religious scientists generally tried to keep their faith to themselves because of the perception that other faculty in their departments think poorly of religious people and religious ideas. Whether or not this perception is true, it perpetuates a *closeted faith* and a strong culture of suppression surrounding discussions of religion within departments. Although Jack thought there were no other Christians in his department, I found through my research that there were some. They were practicing a closeted faith, but they were interested in the same kinds of issues surrounding faith in the academy as Jack was.

Social scientists talk about the differences between "strong cultures" and "weak cultures." Strong cultures within organizations are characterized by a "system of values widely extended and intensely shared."[34] Within a weak culture, shared values are fewer, and the ties they create among group members are less potent. If the desired outcome of an organization, for instance, is economic in nature—to make more money—then groups with strong cultures are going to be more successful. Intense ties foster cooperation and therefore high economic performance.

But what about when organizational goals are not economic in nature? What if the desired outcome is expanded understanding? Or the spread of knowledge? Is a strong culture that suppresses discussion of religion the *best* one for an academic science department?

One characteristic of this strong culture is that it is generally considered better not to discuss religion than to discuss it. When religion unavoidably comes up, such as when discussing news events, the conversation ends abruptly. Or everyone—religious and nonreligious alike—tacitly agrees that religion is generally negative and has a negative relationship to science, or at least that the subject is delicate and is best avoided. The hallmark of a strong culture is that there is widespread public agreement about certain issues—in this case, the issue of suppressing religion—even in the context of individual dissent.[35] Most relevant here, strong departmental cultures related to religion made religious scientists feel as if they could not talk openly about being religious because they might face negative sanctions from their colleagues. When religious individuals participated in and upheld the strong culture surrounding religion in their particular departments, they perpetuated a closeted faith.

Janice[36] is an example of a scientist who feels trapped in a closeted faith. A physicist, she landed a job early in her career at a prestigious university on the East Coast. And of all the physicists at the elite research universities where I interviewed scientists, only 9 percent are women. So Janice feels marginalized in the world of physics as a woman, as a young person, and—most germane to our discussion here—as a religious person. When I asked Janice to describe her particular religious beliefs, her long silence became uncomfortable. She later explained just how difficult it is for her to talk about religious topics in the academic setting. Janice knows of a few others in her department or broader university who are religious but said that they talk about their faith only occasionally and then only "off line," as she put it—her shorthand way of explaining that these conversations simply do not occur in the work environment.

Janice said that the recent controversies over intelligent design have made her even more reticent, reluctant to discuss religion with science colleagues. She explained, "I think academia is not always a very accepting environment. And intelligent design has made it a lot worse. Intelligent design has made it really hard to be a religious academic, because they have polarized the public opinion such that you're either religious or you're a scientist!" Janice went on to say that to let others know that you are religious might undermine how colleagues view your academic work. When I asked her if she personally has experienced this sort of discrimination, she quickly added that she has not, because most other physicists do not know about her faith.

Regardless of whether or not scientists do or would experience religious discrimination, to paraphrase sociologist W. I. Thomas's famous maxim, "If men define situations as real, they are real in their consequences."[37] Janice perceives that the climate surrounding religion is so hostile that if she were to talk about her faith, she would bear the brunt of negative sentiments that would affect her ability to succeed as a scholar. There is evidence for Janice's perception. For example, she recounts the experience of talking with colleagues about teaching and her colleagues' dismay that students come to their university with much less background in math than should be expected. A colleague quipped to Janice, "It's stupid intelligent design. It's stupid Christianity." The fact that Janice's colleague immediately assumed that all Christians reject evolution makes her uneasy about being open with her faith.

Janice is not only frustrated with her colleagues but also with those outside the academy:

> It is really unfortunate that science has been undermined so much, and it's so frustrating to me. . . . I see this world in perfect order that we're trying to figure out, that we mere humans are trying to understand, and it's so beautiful. Everything is so self-consistent, everything is so beautifully described by this mathematical language. . . . That's to the glory of God more than some imperfect world that needs constant intervention to run properly. So it's very frustrating to me that such a large fraction of our country seems to denigrate science, and think that they have to, in order to be properly religious.

Janice would like to see more done to translate science to the broader public but feels stuck within her closeted faith. Because of what she sees as threats to her career, she's in no position to serve the religious American public as a spokesperson for the science that she so dearly values. When religious scientists feel suppressed, science loses its most fluent translators to the broader American society.

THE BOUNDARY PIONEER

Although many of the religious scientists I talked with thought that their secular colleagues were negative toward religion, this perception was not always borne out in my actual discussions with nonreligious scientists. There was a group of scientists—even among those who were not religious—who pointed amiably to fellow scientists who had successfully reconciled religion and science. These models they referenced are what I call *boundary pioneers*. And, surprisingly, these exemplars sometimes adhered to traditional forms of religion, showing that under certain conditions, secular scientists perceive religious scientists in a very positive light. Scientists often described evangelicalism and fundamentalism—labels used interchangeably—in particularly negative terms.[38] But secular scientists generally described those they perceived to successfully combine religion and science in very *positive* terms, despite the high levels of religiosity (even evangelicalism) of these boundary pioneers.

When I asked a sociologist,[39] who described himself as culturally Jewish but not personally religious, how he sees the connections between religion and science, he explained that he has great respect for some religious scientists:

> There are some people with very deep religious beliefs who simply don't let those things conflict. One of the lovely examples that I heard about just recently is this guy, Francis Collins, whom I actually heard talking about some new developments in gene mapping this morning on NPR. He is the director of the gene-mapping outfit at NIH, and he's a very serious born-again Christian and obviously a firm believer . . . and obviously manages to live very well with that.

But Collins is not so much a boundary pioneer because of his ability to reconcile his own faith with the work that he does as a scientist; I met many scientists who have found a similar peace. Collins is a boundary pioneer because of his willingness to *talk openly about* such reconciliation. He also probably gains a hearing because he is very skilled at how he talks about such reconciliations and because he is a scientist at the top of his field.

Scientists who are not religious also participate in the efforts of boundary pioneers. A chemist[40] with no religious identity talked about the intersection religion has with her discipline. Concerned for the science education of her religious students, she tells them, "There are creative ways to integrate these different parts of your life." She often refers students to a web site developed by a scientist who does radiometric dating of fossils that are billions of years old and is "a self-professed, practicing, very religious Christian, taking on a lot of the myths that are out there—that are on a lot of fundamentalist Christian web sites—about radiometric dating being wrong." This chemist, then, is pointing to a boundary pioneer to show future scientists that full commitment to science can be held alongside full commitment to Christianity (of a certain kind). Rather than leading students away from faith, she provides them with examples of how different religious scientists have reconciled their faith with their life-work because she "want[s] students to be able to integrate those things."

Because their identities as scientists are respected by their colleagues, boundary pioneers have legitimacy within the world of science. So as religious scientists are more outspoken within their departments about their faith, prejudice against religious groups as a whole ought to decrease. It was very telling that both religious and nonreligious scientists talked about how much they disliked evangelicals, yet I could not find a scientist who had anything negative to say about Francis Collins, who speaks openly about reconciling his work as a scientist with his faith commitments as an evangelical Christian. Collins's respected scientific identity ushers in acceptance of his religious identity. Even his public endorsement of religion is received well by scientists because of his legitimacy within science. In contrast, his colleagues probably would not have *nearly* as much respect for a Christian pastor who spoke at their university about how science and religion might be compatible. That Collins's faith did not become so public until after his scientific career was in the stratosphere and he had written his *New York Times* best seller (*The Language of God*) raises questions about the potential for success of a junior scientist or a less elite scientist engaging in the same sorts of efforts.

CONCLUSION

The scientists with a faith tradition whom I interviewed often displayed what Harvard-trained psychiatrist Robert Jay Lifton has called a protean self: an identity that is many-sided and fluid. And, as we've seen, the multiple identities gained from practicing both religion and science—two things the public often regards as opposed—sometimes does cause angst. Religious scientists often feel embattled, both in their scientific and religious communities. At work, they might experience subtle discrimination. At church, if they were to express all facets of their identities as scientists, they might face misunderstanding and rejection, especially within religious communities that sometimes question (or outright reject) the theory of evolution. However, if they can survive the struggles, such protean identities provide religious scientists with enormous potential to translate the value and benefits of science to religious nonscientists as well as to nonreligious scientists.

Yet this potential is rarely realized. Scientists with faith often struggle over how public they should be with their colleagues about their faith. Many of the religious scientists I talked with have the perception that their secular colleagues are universally negative toward religion. Little can dispel their notion. To be sure, some nonbelieving colleagues do discriminate against religious people, making it difficult for religious individuals to talk about faith participation openly in their departments or voicing suspicions about faculty candidates who have religious beliefs. And a large majority of the scientists I talked with, both those with faith and those without, were especially negative about American evangelicalism.

What religious scientists fail to realize, however, is that a significant proportion of their colleagues, although not religious themselves, are open to talking and thinking about matters of faith. Some are even looking for scientists with faith traditions to help them connect better with a religiously believing American public. These "open but nonbelieving" scholars are looking in particular for models like Francis Collins—even though he is an outspoken evangelical—to serve as boundary pioneers leading the way in crossing the picket lines of the science and religion debates. But because religious scientists rarely talk candidly about their faith in the science environment, they are not aware of these open but nonbelieving scientists. The actions, then, of both groups end up perpetuating closeted faith, further hardening an embedded custom that religion should not be discussed in universities and science environments.

The Boundary Pioneers of the Future

The sizable group of elite scientists who are committed to their faith traditions are potentially crucial commentators about science to the American public. That the scientists in this population are from prestigious universities makes them all the better positioned to contribute to significant dialogue about what distinguishes scientific and religious claims. But who, exactly, are our future religious spokespersons for science likely to be? And how can this positive dialogue come about? Elite universities are extremely hierarchical, with the academy generally giving preference in voice to senior scientists—those with the largest labs and the most publications and the richest research grants. But my research finds that it is the younger scientists who are more religiously minded. So when it comes to translating science to a broader believing public, it might be younger scholars who lead the way—suggesting that the effort might also take a while to be realized.

Religious scientists of all professional stages, however, might need to lead their own denominations and congregations toward a publicly accessible science that takes seriously the concerns of a religiously motivated American public. There is significant common ground, for instance, to be gained between scientists and other Americans who are part of *mainline* Protestant denominations. Sociologists Robert Wuthnow and John Evans (editors) point out in *The Quiet Hand of God* that mainline Christians—Methodists, Episcopalians, and mainline Presbyterians—have often taken a public backseat to their more outspoken cousins, American evangelicals.[41] Also, while the public has looked to the Protestant traditions for outspoken religious scientists, it is *Catholic* scientists who are currently increasing in number and who might lead the way in contributing insights to the public dialogue. And religious scientists should take heed that sometimes, their secular colleagues look favorably on already accomplished scientists who successfully reconcile faith and science, regarding them as boundary pioneers, even when they are part of religious groups described by these same scientists in fairly negative terms.

Special Opportunities for Religious Scientists

Sociologist Gordon Allport, in his classic work on prejudice, has talked about the importance of groups having contact with one another in an effort to decrease prejudice among them.[42] Allport's ideas are relevant: Individuals will be most likely to accept certain identities of others who are not like them if these others *also* have identities that are similar to them. That some secular scientists show respect for their boundary-crossing peers demonstrates that there is room for scientists who are religious to reduce prejudices against their particular faith traditions. The problem is that most of their nonbelieving colleagues are not aware of the faith commitments of these religious scientists (as when Janice's colleague derided "stupid Christianity," above). For Allport's ideas to be invoked in the realm of religion among scientists within the academy, there would have to be more personal discussion between religious and nonreligious scientists about issues of faith.

Another way scientists might take a more active role is through mentoring science students with faith through their involvement with religious organizations, both within and outside of their campuses. I am not recommending the imparting of particular moral stances on issues such as abortion or political party affiliation. Rather, scientists could help students develop frameworks that would allow them to consider issues of science and religion from the viewpoint of their faith traditions. I am also not suggesting using religion as a filter through which one accepts or rejects scientific assertions. (Remember that both religious and nonreligious scientists at top universities generally see themselves as holding to the same methodological framework for science.)[43] Rather, by using their own lives as models, religious scientists would show students that faith and science can be successfully and sanely integrated. Such efforts would allow religious students to reconcile science and religion so that they do not feel forced to reject either one. (It's tragic to lose a gifted scientist.) This kind of mentoring work should not be left only to university chaplains and religious leaders. It's also the work of any scientist within a faith community who values the scientific future of our nation.

CHAPTER 4

Spiritual Entrepreneurs

Evelyn,[1] the chemist we met in Chapter 2, said that when "[religion] doesn't work, it ends up being a mechanism by which people's thoughts and lives are controlled or meant to be controlled." Evelyn feels differently about *spirituality*. "Spirituality is a much more individual, personal thing," she remarked with a voice of firm conviction. After saying this, she paused reflectively and then continued, "When I think of a spiritual person, the word 'judgment' doesn't even pop into my mind." Although she does not consider herself religious in a conventional sense, her spiritual views influence her actions in a number of ways. For instance, she would not contribute to research that might lead to the destruction of the environment, and she tries to bike rather than drive in order to help the environment. This is part of her general philosophy of "mindfulness." She has taught her son to be a vegetarian, which also seems to stem from her spiritual beliefs. And for her, running is a spiritual and meditative "Zen experience."

Like Evelyn and the over 20 percent of scientists who see themselves as spiritual but not religious in a traditional sense, more and more Americans are exploring a unique spirituality that may still borrow from traditional religions. Some scholars even think that to be "spiritual-but-not-religious" may indeed be quintessentially American. According to a recent national survey, over 70 percent of American adults consider themselves spiritual to some extent.[2] But spirituality by itself evokes a sense of cynicism among the highly religious in some circles; it is considered to be a term used by those who want to partake of some broader framework to find meaning in life but avoid any responsibility to religious communities or fellow sojourners. Scholars and practitioners alike have difficulty defining the term. Religion scholars think that Americans tend to link spirituality to interaction with *some* form of a higher being. And most Americans actually do see spirituality as including facets of traditional religion. In his book *After Heaven: Spirituality in America Since the 1950s*, Princeton University sociologist Robert Wuthnow asked his interview subjects to give their own definitions of spirituality. Their answers ranged from near-death experiences, unseen spirit guides, and belief in angels to meditation and prayer fellowships. Wuthnow concluded that while some Americans hearken to the spiritual practices of early traditions, others partake of endless spiritual seeking that starts to look entirely foreign to traditional religion. American spirituality is often fragmented, as individuals develop their own personal belief systems from bits and pieces of traditions. The individual attending Mass on Sunday, for example, might follow a form of Buddhist meditation during the week. This base in religion means that most Americans use the vocabulary of traditional religion to also describe spirituality. "The spiritual, for the ordinary person, is most often and most easily described in language that has religious connotations," says Wuthnow.[3]

There is disagreement about the cultural implications that new forms (or a return to old forms) of spirituality have for American religious life. Some hold that "new" forms of spirituality stand in sharp but benign contrast to traditional religion. These scholars argue that spirituality might be a "cultural resource" that helps people retain meaning in life and a connection with the transcendent when they are uncomfortable with traditional religious communities.[4] Proponents of spirituality argue that spiritual practices—those that might be part of no particular religious tradition or that have homes in many traditions, such as meditation—can lead to a peaceful outlook that deemphasizes the importance of the self. This awareness, which results from meditation, for example, could decrease war, poverty, and a host of other social ills.[5]

Others posit that the new spirituality could be a negative result of and/or a cause of secularization (decline in religious authority) in American society. Berkeley sociologist Robert N. Bellah and his colleagues think that Americans are becoming more individualistic and less committed to strong local communities. In this vein, researchers argue that while traditional religious involvement promotes concern for the common good, those who are spiritual but not religious are more concerned with self-fulfillment. Increasing emphasis on spirituality rather than religion can lead, then, to an inward focus that neglects the needs of others. Picture the person in a solitary room meditating to achieve enlightenment versus the person volunteering with a religious community at a soup kitchen.[6]

THE SPIRITUALLY THIN

Scientists who consider themselves spiritual generally view their sentiments and practices as less robust than that of other spiritual Americans. Nearly 29 percent of Americans say they are very spiritual. But only 9 percent of scientists give this answer. About 32 percent of scientists consider themselves slightly spiritual, compared to 21 percent of the general population.[7]

My research supports these statistics. Nearly 60 percent of scientists I interviewed displayed a spirituality that scholars might call "thin."[8] If we think about spirituality as a continuum of relevance, there would be many scientists on one end, whose spirituality seems to be lacking in content, or an accompanying sense of responsibility. Thin spirituality is epitomized by a young nurse, Sheila, who was interviewed by sociologist Robert Bellah. In his chapter on religion in *Habits of the Heart*, Bellah talks about Sheila and her fully individualized form of spirituality; Sheila "has received a good deal of therapy and describes her faith as 'Sheilaism.'" He goes on to say, "This suggests the logical possibility of more than 235 million American religions, one for each of us":

> "I believe in God," Sheila says. "I am not a religious fanatic. I can't remember the last time I went to church. My faith has carried me a long way. It's Sheilaism. Just my own little voice." Sheila's faith has some tenets beyond belief in God, though not many. In defining what she calls "my own Sheilaism," she said: "It's just try to love yourself and be gentle with yourself. You know, I guess, take care of each other. I think God would want us to take care of each other.

Sheila's spirituality is so disconnected from the tradition of a community that she can develop her own faith and even name it after herself.

Although Sheila might be an extreme example of thin spirituality, a portion of the scientists I talked with did express elements of this less reflective, diluted form of religious practice. Indeed, some of the scientists have spiritual practices so thin that they are almost nonexistent, only described as "spiritual post hoc," after the interviewer introduced the concept of spirituality. And some of their spiritual experiences could be better described as good feelings rather than epiphanies. Consider one memorable response from a sociologist[9] at a university in the midwestern United States. He is in his mid thirties and was raised without any religious tradition. He describes himself as an agnostic who is loosely part of a Unitarian group. When I asked this sociologist how he would define spirituality, he explained that it had to do with "relationships with the rest of the world, both people but also nature and other animals of the planet. It has to do with my place in the world and being aware of that and acting accordingly." Although it seemed from his definition that he had an idea of what it might mean to be spiritual, when I pressed him to describe a spiritual practice that he had engaged in, he talked about attending baseball games. At first I thought that my respondent—as one sociologist might chide another— was subtly telling me not to take my study too seriously. But as I listened, he paused for more than a few seconds and then went on in a totally unassuming way to describe his spiritual experience at baseball games, times when he is "really aware of being connected with everyone here and with nature and with my place in it and with time." It was an experience that the less introspective might simply have called "contentment."

Similarly, when asked about the role spirituality plays in his life, a chemist,[10] who described himself as nominally Jewish, responded that spirituality is simply "getting up every day and putting [his] pants on." Spirituality, then, is nothing special. As with this sociologist and chemist, many of the scientists I talked with do not often think about what it might mean to be spiritual or whether spirituality is connected in any meaningful way to the work they do as scientists. After talking to many scientists who expressed similar views, it became clear that to some extent, their definition of religion and spirituality only arose during the actual interview. It was as though putting them in a context where they were asked about spirituality forced them to develop a definition for something that would have never concerned them otherwise.

SPIRITUAL ENTREPRENEURS

At the other end of the continuum are those scientists who do have a deep sense of spirituality. These are the *spiritual entrepreneurs*—scientists looking for new ways to hold science and faith together yet still free of the constraints of traditional religion. These entrepreneurs have a spiritual impulse that is "thicker" or more substantial, marked by a search for truth compatible with the scientific method, belief in a meaning that is greater than the individual, a coherence that unifies the various spheres of life, and, for some, engagement with the ethical dimensions of community living. Like other entrepreneurs, they are inventive in their practices, discovering and applying new forms of spirituality as needs arise. They embrace what works and discard what they find outdated or irrelevant.

Over 40 percent of the scientists I interviewed who see themselves as spiritual but not religious could be described as spiritual entrepreneurs. They specifically labeled themselves as spiritual without my prompting. They articulated a specific set of spiritual beliefs. They engaged in practices that they saw as a further outworking of their spirituality, and they had had experiences that they specifically described as spiritual.[11]

Most of these spiritual entrepreneurs eschew traditional forms of religion altogether (although some admit that they borrow from the religious traditions of their past). Rather than trying to reconcile science with a particular religious tradition, as religious thinkers have done for ages, this group of scientists says that spirituality is a better fit with modern science than is any traditional religion.[12] In fact, this group could be part of a small movement arguing that science and spirituality are deeply connected. (For example, in 2005, the Dalai Lama was the keynote speaker at the 35th Annual Meeting of the Society for Neuroscience, where he spoke mainly on embracing meditation within science and tried actively to disconnect this practice from any particular Buddhist belief.)[13] This group, the spiritual entrepreneurs, sees religion and spirituality in distinctly different terms, with many viewing the two as nonoverlapping categories.

Contrary to some secularist accounts of religious change in American society, natural and social scientists at elite research universities have more of a spiritual impulse than I would have expected. While different from that of the general population—which is often characterized by angels and demons—scientists' spirituality has implications for the others-focused practices that researchers often find lacking in the lives of spiritual Americans in the general population.

Spirituality as Different From Organized Religion

Evelyn thinks that religion often becomes a way to control people's thoughts and lives. Spirituality, by contrast, fosters individual freedom. It is this sense of individuality—being able to pick and choose as they make spiritual sense of their world—that appeals to people like Robert Bellah's Sheila and the countless number of Americans who define their spirituality in their own terms. The difference between scientists and most of the nonscientists who see themselves as spiritual is that members of the general population often compile bits from various forms of religion (a spiritual salad bar) to put together an individualized inner life that works for them. The effort of the spiritual scientist is more about pursuing reality and discovering the truthful aspects of spirituality that will be most in line with science. Most often scientists see this individual pursuit of truth, which allows science to stand in the face of criticism, as completely incongruent with religion. For Evelyn, religion connotes a sort of "groupthink." Spiritual entrepreneurs, on the other hand, conform to nothing but their discovered truth, or search for meaning. And these individual pursuits of truth can often lead to an outward focus rather than shallow preoccupation with oneself.

Scientists who are spiritual entrepreneurs do not consider religious communities likely sources of truth. Nearly 40 percent of the spiritually minded scientists I talked with one-on-one had not attended religious services in the past year. And of those surveyed, 31 percent who agreed or agreed strongly with the statement "I am a spiritual person" had not attended religious services in the past year. In comparison, among those in the general population, only 14 percent of those who see themselves in the same way spiritually had not attended religious services in the past year. This comparison shows that elite scientists might have a very different kind of spirituality than those in the general population, one much less connected to traditional religious institutions.

Interestingly, scientists who are spiritual entrepreneurs often have the same kind of criticism of religion as highly religious people in the general population have of spirituality: it's just too undefined, too open to interpretation. Religion, its creeds, and its holy books can mean anything. Spirituality, in contrast, because it's open to being shaped by personal inquiry, has more potential to align with scientific thinking and reasoning.[14]

Scientists in one sense are partakers of extreme Enlightenment thinking, which emphasizes that reason is in contrast to faith. This philosophy is thought to make a place in the world for science and the distancing of many major research universities from their religious roots. Historian George Marsden argues that modern elite universities were originally founded on Protestant beliefs but that today, the "free exercise of religion does not extend to the dominant intellectual centers of our culture."[15] Other scholars, however, see a renewal of religion on campuses, especially among undergraduates.[16] As I discovered, and as is surely becoming clear to the reader, spiritual-but-not-religious elite scientists are a breed apart. Let us understand first the concept of postmodernism, an idea that means on its most basic level that many truths, even contradicting ones, are equally valid. It's also extremely relativistic: no truth really exists at all apart from another. Postmodernism, in one form or another, has touched nearly all academic pursuits in recent years. Science, however, as a pursuit of unique truth, tries to resist postmodernism. Most scientists remain "modern" in the sense that they endorse wholeheartedly the idea of science as objective and truth as existent. For them, the truth is out there, even if it's as yet undiscovered.[17]

Yet the metaphysical seeking of these scientists is more postmodern, in a way, than modern. Spiritual entrepreneurs are both traditionalists as regards their relationship to truth and revolutionaries in their manner of religious understanding and practice. They share with the spiritual-but-not-religious person on the street the same desire to cast off the shackles of religion. But they cling with devotion to the existence of objective and knowable truth.

Spirituality as More Congruent with Science

So for those scientists who consider spirituality important in their lives, their deepest sense of self still comes from their work in science, and their spirituality flows from the same characteristics they value in their identities as scientists. This is a spirituality characterized by *coherence*. The scientists do not want spirituality to be intellectually compartmentalized from the rest of their lives; they seek a core sense of truth through spirituality in much the same way that they seek it through their research. They perceive spirituality as valid in so far as it suffuses their everyday lives and is instantiated in their practices as teachers, as citizens of the university, and especially as scientists.

Scientists see religion and spirituality as qualitatively different constructs. "Religion is institutionalized dogma" was a common response when I asked how religion and spirituality are different. Translation: Religion is most about the rule of powerful persons who propagate information that is not true. "Religion is organized against individual inquiry" was another frequent response, meaning that people cannot think on their own in the midst of religious communities, which have a primary aim to stifle individual adherents who might be trying to ascertain the truth on their own. Their traditionally religious colleagues would certainly have disagreed with this characterization. Often cited as examples of what was meant by power going awry were "Waco," "Jim Jones," "the religious right," or the sex abuse scandals of the Catholic Church. Conversely, individual spiritual inquiry protects people from groupthink, say the spiritual entrepreneurs. Spirituality—as separate from religion—is good for people. It allows and even encourages them to think on their own.

There is a distinct group of scientists who think that the kind of faith necessary to sustain religious commitment means necessarily buying into an absolute absence of evidence. For example, when asked how he distinguishes between religion and science, a biologist[18] who described himself as ethnically Jewish explained simply that "science goes by facts that are empirically verifiable." He stressed that there is no prejudice in science: "You would find a large number of people of any cultural, racial, or gender background that will agree on those facts." He went on to say that religion, in contrast to science, "works by faith." Religion even tries to stand "in the face of evidence many times." Science is what you can "see and test," while religion "is predicated on personal revelation . . . that is not testable . . . or has been tested and shown to fail, but you still believe it anyway."[19] This same biologist does not think of spirituality in the way that he thinks of religion. Instead he said that for some people, spirituality could "mean sort of religious feelings," but for him (solidifying his place as a spiritual entrepreneur), spirituality was broadened to "include the sort of feelings of going outside yourself."

Like this biologist, spiritual entrepreneurs seem to come up with an intuitive definition of spirituality. It is most often and at its core about meaning-making without faith. This idea of spirituality meshes beautifully with their identities as scientists. An individual can pursue a spiritual journey much as a researcher pursues scientific knowledge. They also see spirituality as an individual journey, a quest for meaning that can never be final, just as is the case for scientific explanations of reality. For this group, meaning is important. They discuss aesthetics and meaning when discussing science, just as they do when talking about their spirituality.

THE SPIRITUAL ATHEIST

This distinctive rhetoric contrasting spirituality with religion was most evident when listening to the group of scientists whom I would call *spiritual atheists*, a category that is nearly exclusive to scientists. As sociologist James Alan Neff explains,[20] in the general population, spirituality is almost inherently linked with some conception of God—although not always a religiously orthodox one. Many scientists who clearly see themselves as spiritual, though, have no connection to a particular belief in God or, in some cases, even in the transcendent. For the general public, it is an act of trust and courage to believe in God, since there is no way of proving or disproving God. In comparison, these spiritual atheist scientists see the very act of deciding *not* to believe in God in the face of an American public preoccupied with theism as an act of strength. Their spirituality makes room for this disbelief and so is, again, more congruent with science than religion is. The table below shows the intriguing prevalence of atheism in the midst of spirituality among scientists at elite universities.

Of the scientists who do not see themselves as spiritual, 59 percent state that they are atheists. As populations go, this is a lot of atheists. But their relation to also being nonspiritual would seem to make sense, given our assumptions about the atheist scientist. Note, though, that about 22 percent of scientists

TABLE 4.1. Belief in God, Listed by Level of Spirituality[21]

	Not at all Spiritual	*Spiritual*
Atheist	59%	22%
Agnostic	34%	27%
Believer	8%	51%

who are spiritual also state that they are atheists. Is this spiritual atheism truly unique to scientists? It would appear so, though there are so few atheists (2 percent) and agnostics (4 percent) in the general population that comparable statistics cannot even be generated.

The idea that the existence of God cannot be definitively proven through physical evidence has radical implications for these scientists, who generally trust nothing outside their five senses. But this does not mean that they give up on spirituality altogether. Its pursuit is often seen as independent of the supernatural. These scientists seem to have an inherent sense that their spirituality is qualitatively different from that practiced among the general population. A biologist[22] explained the differences between her understanding of spirituality and the view held more broadly among Americans: "People who have spirituality believe in God, and they think of it that way. Personally I believe in nature, and I get my spirituality . . . from being in nature. But I don't really believe there's a God, so I don't consider it's necessary for what I do or how I behave." For these scientists, spirituality is about the wonder of the natural world, how it all fits together, how it is bigger than oneself—for example. Some scientists perceive that leaving God out frees them to admire the complexity of the natural world and praise it. Spirituality without God helps some keep in tension the mystery they often encounter in their work with the framework of the scientific method.

For social thinkers Max Weber and Émile Durkheim, belief in God as an external authority that guides action and, particularly for Weber, provides a way of understanding meaning outside of oneself is essential to religion's role in a society. To reject God entirely goes hand in hand with eventual "disenchantment," to use Weber's term, or secularization, as we label it today.[23] When I surveyed scientists, nearly 65 percent gave answers consistent with an atheist or agnostic perspective. But many of these were still spiritual to some extent, because the supernatural was irrelevant to their pursuit of spirituality.

Many spiritual atheists were attracted to eastern religions, particularly Buddhism. There were more self-identified Buddhists among elite scientists (about 2 percent) than among the general population (less than 1 percent).[24] Spiritual atheist scientists are not, however, practicing a particular form of Buddhism, such as Theravada or even the less tradition-laden Mahayana, and most do not even call themselves Buddhists. Instead scientists borrow concepts that they perceive to be part of Buddhism and appropriate them through the lens of their lives as scientists.

I wrote in my notes after I interviewed a named-chair professor of psychology[25] that he was a "down-to-earth sort of person" who gave long, considered answers to my questions, especially those concerning spirituality. This psychologist explained that his own "spirituality might be closer to almost an eastern kind of tradition than a western tradition," even though he was raised a Catholic. He added that spirituality involves a "person's own motivation and feeling about their relationship with things beyond them." One does not have to believe in God to be spiritual, and one can certainly be spiritual without being religious.

Irving,[26] a social scientist who was one of the few African Americans I interviewed as part of this study, described himself as "a completely secular individual" and a Darwinist. He added, however, that he is "as curious as the next person as to where we come from and what it all means and where we're going when this whole thing is over." He made a strong distinction between himself and his "religious compatriots" in that he did not invoke notions of the "divine" or "supernatural" to answer this curiosity. For this social scientist, religion (such as Christianity and Judaism) is inherently "supernatural," whereas Buddhism is just a "life philosophy." Spirituality is "almost orthogonal" to, going a different direction than, religion. Naturally then, one can be spiritual without believing in the supernatural or being religious. Like other spiritual entrepreneurs, he connects his spirituality to the kind of science that he does. For him, being a spiritual person is to "wonder about the complexity and the majesty of existence." He is influenced by Buddhism, which he describes as a "system of ethics" and a "philosophy imbued with a lot of spirituality." He believes that his science is a "spiritual act." He explains, "It's a way of being a student of the forces which are shaping the world, and for me, that's almost being a priest of life or a priest of existence." He views hiking through the woods as a spiritual practice because it is a "kind of act of worship" that enables him to "connect with this great wheel of existence." As an entrepreneur would, this scientist takes pieces of religion and melds them with science to create his own sense of spirituality, one that has an influence on his own life philosophy.

SPIRITUALITY AS FLOWING FROM AND INTO SCIENCE

For some scientists, being spiritual is a way to recognize the multiple forces that can influence the scientific process. In this way, spirituality can influence which research questions scientists ask. This is somewhat similar to the dynamics of the artists Robert Wuthnow studied, who saw themselves not just as creators but as spiritual receptacles during the creative process.[27] One psychologist,[28] who chairs his department, said that while organized religion cannot be a legitimate part of science, "acknowledging what spirituality is, what personal values are, should be a part of all science, because that's how we get to the questions we ask." He described himself as a "nonbeliever" with respect to God and said that his religious/spiritual beliefs are very "informal" and relate to things such as the "subtle connectedness between people [and] valuing quieter moments and reflection." For this scientist, research questions do not always naturally proceed from one to another. He, therefore, rejects what he calls "scientism," which proposes that all science is completely objective. For instance, he explains that in "the hypothesis-generation phase, there may be multiple personal, spiritual, familial, cultural roots . . . which we have to openly acknowledge." Notice too that this psychologist has a very different view of science than do many of his colleagues; he accepts that scientific questions are sometimes informed or influenced by sources outside science itself. He does believe, however, that one should at least strive to be objective in the hypothesis-testing phase. Being spiritual in some sense distinguishes him from colleagues who see science as the supreme form of knowledge, impervious to influence by forces outside the scientific method.

Deriving spirituality from nature is another way spiritual entrepreneurs see their unique form of coherent spirituality flowing from what they know of science. In one sense, this way of seeing spirituality connects them to members of the general public who also see spirituality as related to a sense of awe or transcendence in relation to the natural world. For example, according to one survey of American spirituality, a common aspect of daily spiritual values is, "I am touched by the beauty of creation."[29] The relationship of spirituality with nature for those in the general population, however, is often correlated with at least a vague sense of the transcendent and more often with a particular notion of God, often the sense of God as Creator. For the spiritual atheists, it was connected to a deeper sense of appreciating the natural world.

An assistant professor of political science[30] in his late thirties linked his view of spirituality to nature but at the same time also tried to distance himself from a belief in God:

> I have spiritual commitments. . . . It's kind of a view like [the philosopher] Spinoza, without God, in the sense that I like being outdoors and I think there's some sort of meaning and beauty and value to everything around me and what I do. And so there's a way in which I feel very spiritual.

Others, when asked how their spiritual beliefs or practices connected to a belief in God, more adamantly distanced themselves from belief in a personal God. A biologist[31] said, "I guess religion implies that one believes in some kind of God. . . . I always assume that people who have spirituality believe in God and they think of it that way." Like Irving, the self-described Darwinist social scientist, this biologist feels that spirituality is also about a belief in nature. In his words, "I get my spirituality, if you want to say that, from being in nature, but I don't really believe there's a God." He believes that this view makes him different from most other Americans, and he's right.

Some scientists feel that science actually frees them to admire the complexity of the natural world and praise it. Their spirituality helps these atheists appreciate the mystery they often encounter in their work. As we all know, the work of scientists—especially natural scientists—requires highly technical knowledge about the natural world, as well as skill in its manipulation. Some scientists see themselves as genuinely unlocking nature's secrets through their research. And for this group of spiritual scientists, their sense of access to the deepest aspects of nature also enlivens a sense of spirituality. A biologist[32] said that spirituality could come from being connected to nature, as when seeing the mountains of the Himalayas: "I've done it! You get sort of a feeling of awe before nature. And that's not really a religious feeling, more of a spiritual feeling, so I find that it's a feeling of transcending your own being and feeling part of a great force and greater energy." Many of these scientists intimately connect their spirituality to their understanding of the natural world but are clear to distinguish this from a connection with God.

Some scholars would say that this sense of the spiritual but not religious is similar to some of the ideas of the New Age movement, some of which borrow from Ralph Waldo Emerson and other transcendentalists. Yet I rarely heard the interview subjects mention Emerson or any of the other Transcendentalists—and scientists emphasized that they were not, as one scientist clearly put it, "some flipping New Ager."[33] Still, in their connecting of spirituality to nature, these scientists are similar to Emerson and the New England Transcendentalists hailed by religion scholar Leigh Schmidt as partially responsible for connecting spirituality to a deep appreciation of nature and the environment.[34]

According to another biologist,[35] spirituality helps students understand how large the natural world really is. Raised as a conservative Jew, this biologist described himself as an atheist and said that his spirituality helps him to transmit to his students the sense of wonder found in the natural world: "I'm always trying to remind my students that what they're trying to understand is how everything fits together. . . . That's included for me [in my definition of spirituality], but it's not included in everybody's definition." Some scientists made the triangulated link between spirituality, science, and nature very explicit, such as the physicist[36] who talked about his time in an observatory. The hours that he spends alone in his work as an astronomer give him the time to "think of my place in the world and the universe and its vastness." He contrasted this deep sense of spiritual connectedness to the world with what he feels when he is just, say, "sitting here in my office." This comment (and the many others like it) reveals that, for some scientists, it's not science that is replacing religion. It's spirituality that is replacing religion.

Another biologist,[37] who told me that he is a committed atheist, quickly related his spirituality to his experiences with nature:

> That feeling you get standing by the seashore looking out over the endless expanse of water. Or standing in the rain forest listening to the insects and the birds and their huge diversity and incomprehensibility. Or the feeling you get considering the age of all things in existence and how long it could go on. Sort of awe at the totality of things. If that's what spirituality is, then I get it. But I have the feeling I am missing the point when I say things like that, because my Christian friends don't talk that way. They seem to mean something else.

Notice that in this interview excerpt, he contrasts his own sense of spirituality with how he thinks more *religious* individuals might view spirituality. This scientist is not only discussing the boundaries between the knowledge categories of religion and science, but also between himself and spiritual seekers who are not scientists, whom he perceives to have a very different sense of spirituality than he does.[38]

A Way Out of Conflict

For some elite scientists, embracing spirituality rather than religion is a way of avoiding the conflict between religion and science. The scientists who were the most spiritual seemed the least interested in policing the boundaries between science and religion or even the boundaries of discourse between the two. For example, the ethnically Jewish chemist[39] introduced earlier in this chapter (for whom spirituality is simply "getting up every day and putting [his] pants on") also linked his sense of spirituality to his science. In particular, he sees religion and spirituality as having very different relationships to science. When I asked him if there is any conflict between religion and science, he paused for nearly 10 seconds, a seemingly interminable time in a conversation. Just as I was ready to repeat the question, he went on—with what I interpreted as a sense of frustration—to address the whole debate. He said rather adamantly that "there is surely not any irreconcilable conflict between *spirituality* and science." As other scientists did, he referred to Einstein's supposed sense of spirituality, telling me that he would "adopt the views of Einstein on this, who always claimed to be an extremely spiritual person, but he had no use for religion. He was always in awe and wonder at the universe." Spirituality, then, specifically links this chemist with science and is even generated from his science. He finds his ideas about spirituality, although not religion, to be perfectly reconciled with his work. And for him, Einstein serves as a legitimating trope (a concept that one links or identifies with to appear more valid or truthful). Surely, then, Einstein could serve as the last word on the matter.

AN ENGAGED SPIRITUALITY

Sociologist Michele Dillon and her coauthors say that spirituality often spurs impulses that make a person more concerned with his own spiritual enlightenment and path to peace than with the welfare of others. In contrast, for scientists who are spiritual entrepreneurs, about one-third specifically link their spirituality with helping others. Some go so far as to consider their engaged spirituality worthy of a boundary between themselves and scientists who are strict secularists and who, these respondents think, often do not reflect carefully on the implications of their science.

At the point where spiritual practices are "thick" (see the section "Spiritual Entrepreneurs" near the beginning of this chapter) for this population of scientists, such practices also reinforce the notion of belief and/or the quest for coherence and truth. The quest then spurs more action, and the circle of coherence continues. This spirituality emanates naturally from the work that they do and manifests in a sense of care for the people around them. For example, on the survey I gave to 1,646 scientists, I asked if they had participated in any volunteer activities in the past six months. Nearly 84 percent of those who saw themselves as spiritual to some extent had engaged in some form of volunteering. In comparison, about 71 percent of those who are "not at all spiritual" had volunteered, a modest but significant difference.

I found that a higher proportion of those scientists who engage in any spiritual practices do some form of volunteering than do those who do not practice

TABLE 4.2. Spiritual Practices and Volunteering

	Meditation		Yoga		Reading Sacred Text	
	Yes	No	Yes	No	Yes	No
Any Volunteer Activity	89%	72%	83%	76%	93%	72%

spirituality. For example, 89 percent of those who engage in private meditation are involved in at least one volunteer activity, compared to 72 percent of those who do not meditate. And 83 percent of those who do yoga and 93 percent of those who read any of the sacred texts are involved in at least one volunteer activity, compared to 76 and 72 percent, respectively, of those who do not engage in any form of yoga or reading of a sacred text.[40]

More complicated statistical analyses reveal that engaging in at least one of the spiritual practices makes it more likely that a scientist will also engage in a volunteer activity.[41] Even when we take religious attendance out of the picture, engaging in a spiritual practice (such as meditating) still makes scientists more likely to volunteer. That means that, independent of some of the indicators of traditional religion, engaging in spiritual practices retains a significant and positive influence on the likelihood of volunteering.[42] Even for *religious* scientists (those involved in one of the major world traditions), engaging in a spiritual activity still makes a scientist more likely to volunteer.

These conversations with biologists, physicists, economists, and other scientists help to expand our understanding of what they actually mean by particular spiritual practices and how they link these spiritual practices and identities with other kinds of acts. Most significant, being spiritual and/or engaging in some form of spiritual practice often generates a different approach to research and teaching. For example, a political scientist[43] whose interest in the discipline derived partly through growing up in a politically involved family used her sense of engaged spirituality to distinguish herself from her colleagues. "I spend a lot of time in my course preparations. I could spend a lot less time and invest more time in my own writing and publications," she explained. She has a deep sense of caring for the less fortunate, particularly the financially disadvantaged undergraduates who are numerous at the research university where she teaches: "My part of making the world better is helping those [students] succeed. I feel a certain kind of spiritual obligation to help in the best way that I can, which in that sense is teaching them, trying to figure out how to reach them so that they understand," she said with a sense of conviction in her voice. "[I do this] in ways that I know some of my other colleagues don't." For this political scientist, spirituality provides a lens, a worldview, for the way that she teaches. Spirituality also provides a demarcation, specifically an ideological boundary to define her as different from her colleagues.[44] While her colleagues might focus on their own research at the expense of student interactions, her sense of spirituality provides nonnegotiable reasons for making sure that she helps struggling students succeed.

For others, the very research that they choose to do has a spiritual component, with some even attributing the choice of a particular topic to spiritual reasons. A sociologist[45] (who told me that the only religious academic she knows of is a guy who has eight kids whom he homeschools to bring them up "in the religious way") said she doesn't "practice religion, but [is] a spiritual person." Her specific choice of research topics is partly linked to her sense of spirituality. She studies "poverty and inequality because [she] thinks it is a good use of [her] time and [her] skills." She went on to say, "I would feel like studying something that wasn't going to help society would be a hard thing for me to do. So for me, it's more of a philosophy, a spiritual thing and not a religiously guided thing." This sociologist (who was raised as a Catholic but now considers herself an atheist) chooses to focus on inequality because of the potential her studies will have to help people, and this is linked very directly to her sense of spirituality.

For still others, spirituality is linked to a motivation to care for the environment. When I asked an ethnically Jewish economist[46]—who was drawn to his discipline partly because of his love of mathematics—about God, he told me that a belief in God was not necessary to his spirituality. He also explained that his sense of spirituality influences his commitment to the environment:

> I'm going to sound like some flipping New Ager here. . . . I have a very strong commitment toward the outdoors and the environment, and I think that can kind of be a spiritual commitment. I've made provisions to give a substantial amount of money in my will to the Nature Conservancy, for example.

This excerpt is particularly instructive, because it is reflective of the group of scientists who view spirituality as intimately linked with their practices. This scientist's choice to leave money to an environmental organization is connected to his sense of the spiritual. Also, we see in my conversation with this economist, as with others above, that he views general spirituality as "New Age," which he implies is spurious. He contrasts it with his own state by demonstrating how his spirituality generates true action (and in his case, financial commitment) for the sake of the environment.

IMPLICATIONS FOR FUTURE RESEARCH

The narratives (and the statistics) these scientists provide reveal that engaging in some form of spirituality often helps them to think outside of themselves. Their spirituality is sometimes connected to a form of religion (being Jewish, for example), but more often, it's not. Such narratives reveal that the implications of spirituality are not simple for this population: they cannot be described in clear-cut categories. But for a significant minority, when spirituality is a part of their lives, it spawns acts of generosity.

Where some traditional forms of religion might be in conflict with science for this population, their spirituality isn't. It can actually provide a framework that stresses altruistic acts, even replacing religion in its significance. These scientists' accounts challenge conventional understandings of spirituality, particularly the range of ways in which spirituality might influence its practitioners' lives.

Scientists who are spiritual in the "thick" (or substantial) sense could provide a clear alternative to existing notions of spirituality found among the general population. In the broadest way, then, these findings have implications for modernity and secularism. Although scientists—particularly those at elite universities—are not numerically significant relative to the general population, they are nevertheless culturally influential by virtue of their positions. They might even be at the core of what could be an important spiritual revolution.

What these scientists are doing fits nicely with Max Weber's understanding of what intellectuals do with religion. As Weber explains, intellectuals are more concerned with making meaning from life's problems rather than being rescued from life's problems.[47] Although Weber talks mainly about issues related to a sense of salvation, these scientists seem concerned with a more general search for meaning rather than a specific concern for eternal deliverance. (Weber thinks an emphasis on meaning is typical of intellectuals more than of other groups.) Of particular interest, there is a significant minority of scientists who have a spirituality that is fully engaged. It infuses their work lives through their relationships as teachers and advisers as well as being expressed in the very act of science itself.

One possibility is that scientists share this kind of orientation with other groups of professionals. An engaged spirituality might simply flow from doing work that is an all-encompassing source of identity (for doctors and lawyers, for example). Because of this aspect of professionalism, scientists might be moved to integrate their spirituality with an already coherent sense of self that is organized around their work. For them spirituality cannot be a compartmentalized thing because nothing in their lives is compartmentalized—work overlaps with self to such a large degree. The most natural way to incorporate spirituality into their lives is not only for it to flow from their work but also to be expressed through their work.

Alternatively, or in addition, it might be that an engaged spirituality flows from science itself as a unique worldview, one that compels these scientists to explore a different kind of spirituality than that found among professionals as a whole. This brings us back to scientists' idea of spirituality as coherent. Their pursuit of truth and their desire to understand what others see as the mysteries of the universe lead scientists into awe and the awareness that there might be something beyond the reach of reason. That awe can lead them to spiritual practices that feed back into the work they do as scientists—both research and teaching.

The pursuit of rationality among these spiritual entrepreneurs would not be motivated only by self-interest (how to make more money or achieve personal success) but also by a desire to understand the vastness and complexity of the natural order. If this implication is realized empirically—and we would need a comparison group of professionals with similar levels of education and identification with their professions to examine this definitively—then what has been discovered is a form of spirituality particular to those who most acquiesce to the scientific way of thinking. It might not spread widely among other populations, except through the authority that scientists have as elite carriers of a particular worldview.

Although sometimes not marked by traditional theism, spiritual experience within this population connects them to something outside of themselves through awe at the intricate complexity and vastness of the universe of which they are a part and through concern for other human beings. That their spirituality sometimes has moral and ethical authority over their actions challenges some notions of secularism. Of central significance, their spirituality is not compartmentalized but is integrated into core aspects of their lives and identities as teachers and scholars—in other words, as scientists. This is a different phenomenon than previously investigated by traditional studies on religious practice, or by theories that posit the nature of contemporary spirituality as hyperindividualized or narcissistic. Rather, the stories of scientists who are spiritual entrepreneurs can challenge us to a reformulation of existing theories about religious change.

PART II

Society and Broader Publics

CHAPTER 5

Suppression or Engagement

How Scientists Handle Religion in the Classroom

As I walked into his white, sterile office, Raymond[1] did not get up right away to greet me but kept typing. He was dressed casually in khaki shorts and sneakers—looking more as if he were ready to play golf than teach a physics class. Raymond had become interested in science at a young age and fondly recalls looking through a telescope to witness his first lunar eclipse. He was raised in the Missouri Synod Lutheran church, which "is not just any Lutheran church," he said, alluding to the denomination's extremely conservative reputation. He now views the process of being confirmed in the Lutheran church as "indoctrination." He vividly recalls the minister making him "stand up in front of the church and say things [Raymond] knew weren't true," such as that the age of the earth is only a few thousand years. He now thinks the minister forced him to lie because Raymond's interest in science made him nervous.

Through part of his college years, Raymond continued to attend church with his family. He remembers the particular moment when he decided that he would no longer go to church. It was at a Christmas Eve service held at the time of the bombing of Hanoi (late December 1972) during the Vietnam War. Raymond thought about how "the United States was bombing the hell out of a country and killing all these people for no good reason on Christmas Eve while [his] family was sitting in church praying." At that moment, Raymond had an "epiphany" and "saw through all the hypocrisy." He later told his parents that he would not be going to church anymore.

Raymond thinks there are many things about the world that are mysterious but finds it ridiculous to think that "there's some person sitting on a chair with a beard who has lightning coming out of his fingers or makes pronouncements about how people should live." At this point in his life, he is not pursuing any particular religion and does not have a sense that he is spiritual. One reason is because he "wants to pursue things that [he] knows he can actually make progress with," and he sees the pursuit of spirituality as "a dead end." He chooses instead to use science to approach the complicated, observable issues of the universe.

Raymond would not know if any of his colleagues are religious, because he simply does not discuss religion at work. He added as an afterthought that he *did* work with one colleague whom he now knows to be religious. Raymond found out when a professor at a school where the colleague applied for a job contacted Raymond with concerns about her web site, which had links to "fundamentalist, antievolution . . . web sites." The professor who interviewed her had called Raymond to find out if she was a "kook."

Raymond thinks that all religion should adapt to new scientific knowledge, citing an interview with the Dalai Lama that he had recently read in *Nature* as a positive example of religion adapting. The Dalai Lama said that if a scientific discovery were found to contradict a current teaching of Buddhism, then the religious teaching would have to be changed to adapt to science. Raymond added with a chuckle, "So that's the way religion should be, but that seems very rare to me." When I asked him to elaborate on this, he responded that many people ignore scientific facts and "choose to be ignorant."

Raymond thinks science is the only reliable method we currently have to decide "what's real and what isn't." And, unlike most religions, he says, science is open to revision: "You [should] never get a scientist . . . in an argument with a religious person, because the religious person knows they're right. And if they ask the scientist, 'Are you absolutely sure you're right?' the scientist will always say no," because scientists are constantly testing their theories and making new hypotheses whereas the religious person is not open to change. Religious people do not change their mind when new knowledge becomes available. "Facts just don't mean anything to them," he added.

Religion does come up periodically in Raymond's physics courses. Many of the students who come from the area surrounding the midwestern research university where he teaches were raised in religious homes and are challenged by the things they learn in his courses: "The students are aware of it, that they're being pulled in different directions from what they were taught when they grew up, especially around here." When I asked what he does when students bring religion up in his physics classes, he responded simply, "I just ignore it. They're in the big time now!"

Joel's[2] office was located in the midst of a large group of trees and brick buildings that all looked very similar—buildings with their names etched in tiny letters many years old. After a long trek up a narrow stone stairway to his office, I arrived to our meeting a bit late and a little out of breath. Joel had his door open and stood immediately to shake my hand. Then he closed the thick, glass-pane door with his name painted on the outside and directed me to a chair.

I was immediately struck by how young Joel is. Other things about the way he dressed and his office environment, however, fit the image of a professor at an elite university: the wire-rimmed glasses that he wore slightly ajar on his nose and the shelves and shelves of books that lined his narrow office. Joel's office was not large, but the lighting and the large tree right outside his window made it seem comfortable. A rug in the middle of the floor made a workspace devoted exclusively to scholarship somehow feel a little bit homey.

As we talked about religion, science, and teaching, Joel shifted often in his seat and mentioned several times that he suspected I had handpicked him to interview because he is personally religious. When I assured him that the scientists I chose to talk with were selected randomly, he seemed a little disappointed, as if he had wanted to be asked to tell his side of the story. Joel's sense is that his department colleagues—and probably most of those in his broader field of political science—are not very religious. As a religious person, he feels marginalized in the social sciences.

Joel was eager to have a conversation about the relationship of religion to his teaching and started talking about his experiences before I even asked about the topic. He tries to teach his students about the specific role that philosophers who were influenced by Christianity—such as Augustine and Thomas Aquinas—and Christianity itself had in forming the backbone of Western political thought. Joel struggles, though, to have thoughtful discussions about these figures, because "Christianity plays . . . a very negative role in [the minds of] a lot of current political philosophers [who] find themselves in opposition to it." There is even occasional disgust for traditional religious ideas among his colleagues and those in the broader discipline: For "a lot of political philosophers, the center of their interest is, 'How did we get this weird religion [that leads to] this kind of perverse'—the word 'perverse' is what they would probably use— 'way of thinking about politics?'"

Joel deliberately brings classical Christian political thinkers into classroom discussions, finding that he can present the writings of Augustine and Aquinas in a scholarly way. More difficult is managing to teach the views of these thinkers without offending his students or his colleagues. Joel again shifted nervously in his chair as he tried to paint a picture for me of how students respond when he talks about religion in his classes:

> When you are teaching your Christian thinkers . . . a lot of students will be turned off or they will have an image in their heads of what Christianity means based on

some of the more vocal proponents of Christianity today. And you are playing the opposite battle, willing to take these ideas seriously *despite* the fact that they are religious.

Joel spends time thinking about how best to equip students with a scholarly language to talk about matters of faith. He has considerable difficulty trying to present the ideas of Christian thinkers in his classroom, but he feels obligated to do so because religious and ethical questions are central to the topics he teaches: "In that context I always have to talk about the ideas of original sin and redemption."

If some scientists and members of the religious public are in a battle, then university classrooms are the front lines, where even the scientists who are most opposed to religious interference are forced to deal with the religious students in their classrooms. In his controversial 2005 state of the university address, Cornell University president Hunter Rawlings expressed the need to address a matter of "great significance to Cornell and to the country as a whole." Rawlings said that "religiously based opposition to evolution . . . raises profound questions about the nature of public discourse and what we teach in universities, and it has a profound effect on public policy."[3] Later, several universities (including some in this study) began refusing to give incoming students credit for high school science courses in which accounts of earth origins emphasizing intelligent design were taught. Evangelical Christians were not quiet and took their concerns to the courts. In 2005 an association of Christian schools challenged the rejection of courses that teach intelligent design by bringing a lawsuit against the University of California system. A ruling later occurred in favor of the University of California.[4] Meanwhile, frustrated college science professors are clinging to what they see as already deficient American standards for science education.

Enter the religious students. Their presence in science classrooms often pushes their professors to engage with religious challenges to science. Some scientists respond to this pressure by tapping into public debates and involving their students in dialogue about the connections between religion and science. Other scientists decide to retreat from the front lines and become more entrenched in their view that religion is a threat to science. The need for academic scientists to engage with religion for the sake of science has never been more pressing.

Providing a religious student with a better understanding of science is vitally important, because undergraduate students at elite universities are the future leaders of our society. And as a whole, they are much more religious than the science professors who teach them. Traditional forms of religion as well as spirituality are prevalent on our nation's top campuses. The results of one national study reveal that students are very interested in spirituality, with well over 70 percent of college students saying that "we are all spiritual beings" and that they "gain strength by trusting in a higher power." A four-university study shows that students are interested in traditional religion and especially interested in nontraditional forms of spirituality.[5] Yet, a majority of science professors—nearly 65 percent—come to their positions without a belief in God or with a belief that is much less certain than that found among the broader public. This is in sharp contrast to the nation in general, where only 6 percent do not believe. How will scientists retain interest in science among students who are more religious than they are? If the scientists are too heavy-handed, they might turn the potential leaders of American society off from an interest in science altogether. The solution is not obvious. We must first get a better look at the work lives of scientists and their relationships with their students. A comprehensive understanding of how scientists are currently interacting with students would allow us to assess where scientists interested in achieving dialogue could go from here.

A political scientist[6] in her mid thirties admitted that because she generally does not spend a lot of time thinking about whether or not God exists, she was surprised by a recent encounter with a religious student: "I wanted him to respond to the readings analytically and intellectually, but he took issue with what one writer said and made a statement in his work, something like, 'What she doesn't understand is that Jesus Christ is in fact the son of God.'" With exasperation in her voice, she told me, "Responding to that as a teacher is hard!"

THE CULTURAL SCRIPTS OF SCIENTISTS

Knowing how science professors interact with those in their classrooms about matters of faith involves understanding their particular *cultural scripts*. We might think of a script as a blueprint or road map that tells us what to do. In this context, cultural scripts are the different ways that the training and socialization scientists receive has taught them how to interpret and talk about the world of religion. Some—frequently those who teach at large state institutions—use language focusing on the separation of church and state to suppress all discussion of religion. We could call this a script of suppression. Others use a script that revolves around being a nonspecialist. They are not professors of religion, so they do not see themselves as adequately skilled to discuss matters of religion. Still another group believes that religion is just irrelevant to science. They see no reason why religion should ever come up in science classrooms. As we saw in Chapter 2, some have had negative experiences with religion. These scientists seemed strongly committed to one script, unwilling to entertain other possibilities. Further, some scientists reside entirely within their scientific plausibility structure (see "What Do They Practice?" in Chapter 3) and are entirely unhelpful when students raise issues about faith.

We can learn something about the content of scientists' scripts for dealing with religion in university classrooms by returning to the ideas of sociologist Basil Bernstein (discussed in Chapter 2 under "Working Toward Dialogue"). Common codes for dealing with religion are often reinforced through shared social relations with other academics who have similar views. In environments where there are a limited number of religious scientists who have developed elaborate ways of connecting religion and science, even religious scientists might contribute to the suppressing of discussions about religion simply because they lack conversation partners.[7] And many scientists who do identify with traditional forms of religion—a large minority of those I surveyed—give in to strong departmental cultures and practice a closeted faith. So although their faith traditions could potentially provide them with helpful alternatives, these scientists use a particular script that suppresses conversations about religion on the grounds that personal religious preference is not an appropriate topic of conversation among colleagues or in the science classroom. Sadly, such constrained scripts are often inadequate for translating science to believing students.

But there is another group of scientists who do want positive engagement with religion in university classrooms. These professors think they simply cannot be effective teachers when they ignore student concerns about religion. They want a script for engagement, yet they sometimes lack one because they know so little about religion. This chapter responds to their dilemma by highlighting the kinds of scripts some scientists (religious or not) have developed to discuss religion in science classrooms.

In today's America, all science teachers must engage religion; it's unavoidable. Some do so by expending effort to suppress discussion of religion or to combat its influence on science. Others give religion a wider berth, allowing their faith traditions or spiritual sensibilities to influence how they teach. Thirty-nine percent of the scientists I surveyed said their religious or spiritual beliefs influence personal interactions with students or colleagues. This represents a sizable group of scientists who see faith as shaping interactions with students. For this group, however, bringing religion into the classroom is almost entirely a personal, private matter of being motivated by the desire to care more for students. Other scientists, by far the smallest minority, work toward actual, dynamic, public discussion.

SCRIPTS OF SUPPRESSION

As I talked with scientists, I found some who were propelled by current religious challenges in public schools to erect a strong barrier between science and religion. The most benign argument was that science and religion are in completely separate realms. To a lesser extent, some argued that religion and the opinions of religious people are so meaningless that they are simply not worth discussing. So even if students bring up religion in the classroom, these scientists believe it is best to simply ignore it. In particular, many of those who taught at public universities could not imagine how religion could be discussed in the classroom in a way that would not violate the separation of church and state. Responses like these reveal the kinds of boundaries that some scientists set up between religion and academic life. And boundaries have powerful implications for how religion and science connect in university classrooms.

"That's Not What I'm Here For"

I asked a chemist[8] who teaches at an Ivy League school how he responds when students bring up issues related to religion during the chemistry courses he teaches. He said emphatically that he "would not engage in a discussion about religion with students inside [his] office or [his] classroom." His reluctance to discuss matters of faith occurs out of principle: It is "not because I'm necessarily afraid of the consequences," he said, "but that's not what I'm here for. I'm not a professor of religion, and I would not discuss religious matters with students in an academic teaching or research setting." This chemist's sentiments echo those of other scientists who think it simply wrong to talk about matters of faith in class when they do not know enough about these matters. They are not experts on religion, and such discussions take time away from the areas on which they are.

Even scientists who think that religion should never enter into teaching science often ironically have a great personal interest in matters of faith and their connection to science. This is not to say, however, that they have much respect for religion. My interview with one biologist[9] caught me off guard: Although he thinks that religion should generally not be discussed in academic settings, he was so eager to talk about the negative connections between religion, spirituality, and science that my interview with him lasted over two and a half hours. At one point, I asked him if religion ever comes up as a topic in his interactions with students. He adamantly replied that even if a student does mention it, he tries hard to suppress such discussions. He specifically explained why he thinks students do not talk about religion very much: Since he "teaches advanced undergraduates and graduate students, by that time . . . the people who want to take [the kind of high-level courses he teaches] are just not religious in the first place." In his words, "they're certainly mature enough not to come up to you and start talking about creation or something." One wonders how this biologist knows how religious his students are, since he squelches their religious talk or forces them to face being considered not "mature."

Like many of the faculty I spoke with, this biologist has had little positive experience with religion. He said he has been an atheist since he was four years old, and he subsequently has little knowledge of the range of ways scientists might talk about the connections between religion and science. He further went on to illustrate with an analogy just how irrelevant religion is to science:

> I mean it's as if you were asking me, "Is alchemy a topic of conversation in the chemistry department?" Well, I'm not in the chemistry department, but I feel absolutely sure it isn't. . . . I think that religion should have been discarded at least 25 hundred years ago. . . . I see the fact that we have it at this school as a horrid anachronism.

It should be kept in mind that there is not a large group of scientists who are so extremely hostile to religion (less than 5 percent of those I interviewed). Yet those who are this hostile are often the most outspoken, making it appear to science students as if more scientists are hostile to religion than really are.

"Religion Has No Place Here"

A chemist[10] who teaches at a large state university in the West explained that he strongly "believes in separation of church and state." For much of the interview, he was laid-back, not conveying the ivory tower aura with which academics are so often associated. As he started to talk about religion entering teaching, however, he lost his easygoing manner and became more animated, waving his hands as he talked:

I think that it has no real place in my interactions with students. For example, I had one fellow who was a very devout Christian, and he was always telling me what to do and how to live, and he was sort of evangelical, and how do I handle that? Well I would just make jokes, because it was just so silly. You have to diffuse that kind of energy. It doesn't really have any place in the working environment.

Since this chemist has no real language for talking about religion with his students, he does what he best knows to do; he avoids the situation by quickly dismissing it with either humor or the rhetoric of separation of church and state.[11]

It is not just anti- or nonreligious scientists who choose to suppress mention of religion in their classrooms. An economist[12] I talked with currently teaches at what he described as an "aggressively secular institution." This nature of his university is especially apparent to him, because he is Catholic. After converting to Catholicism as an adult, he taught for a short time at a religiously affiliated college. While he has been trying not to talk about religion at his current university, at the private, religious school, he "would have been comfortable talking about issues [related to religion, since] . . . all of the students were members of the same faith." Students there would even have a prayer before class. In a public institution, however, he "just never would." He attributes his choice not to discuss religion to "institutional reasons"; in short, there is general discomfort about bringing religion into a pluralistic university environment.

SCRIPTS OF ENGAGEMENT

Other scientists, particularly those whose fields—such as evolutionary biology or sociology of religion—intimately overlap with matters of faith, try diligently to bring religion into the teaching environment. A small group of scientists within this category intentionally bring religion into their classes to model for students thoughtful ways of viewing the connections between science and faith. More often, however, these scientists bring in religion as a way of explaining to students how science either differs from religion or even disproves certain facets of religious understanding. This is similar to the journalists and social scientists that religion scholar John Schmalzbauer discusses in *People of Faith*. They are not trying to proselytize. The engagement is much more subtle as they simply try to connect their personal faith with their disciplines.

For all these scientists who employ scripts of engagement, not to examine the connections between religion and science—especially when students raise such topics—would be to abandon their (sometimes spiritual) commitment to quality teaching. All of the political scientists I asked about it said that students *have* raised matters of faith with them. This might mean, for example, discussing the various ways in which Christian ideas form the basis of Western political thought. Among biologists, three-quarters said religion entered teaching at some point. Biologists might talk about the ways in which public debates about evolution have a religious basis, transitioning to a discussion about the differences between religious and scientific understandings of "truth."[13]

Joel, the political science professor introduced near the beginning of the chapter, is an example of a scientist deeply committed to his religious tradition who intentionally converses about religion in order to help his students more thoughtfully consider the connections between religion and political theory. Another political scientist[14] who teaches at a prestigious university near a large city offered an explanation of why his teaching also demands intersection with religion. Unlike Joel, he does not have much personal experience with matters of faith, but he does spend a lot of time connecting the research he does with how to "improve the quality of real people's lives." By linking his own research on social services to the real-life social service efforts of faith communities, he has discovered that religious organizations are fundamental to the growth of civic life in the inner-city area near his university. As we talked, he reluctantly explained why he feels compelled to share these insights with his students and how he goes about deliberately bringing religion into the classroom.

According to this political scientist, talking about religion is simply a practical and necessary piece of the research that he does. He makes it clear to students at the beginning of the semester exactly how he will talk about religion, telling them that he is not interested in proselytizing and does not even go to church himself. "But, if [you] are interested . . . in public life or [you] are interested in urban politics . . . you must be in relationship with church folk," he explains to them. "This so-called wall between church and state isn't a wall that prevents you from communicating and being in relationship with folks in churches. . . . It doesn't mean you can't talk about faith and religion." For this political scientist, a broad understanding of religion makes one better able to help and serve the larger community. Although he teaches at a large state university, he rejects the idea that separation of church and state means that scientists cannot bring religion into the classroom, even at state schools, and especially when it is relevant to their subject matter. The differences between how scientists interpret the need for separation of church and state reveal just how important it is for them to have open dialogue—not just with the general public but with one another—about how to respond to and engage with religion in university science classrooms.

"Religion Is an Important Public Issue": Positive Environmental Push

Unsurprisingly, scientists as a whole are substantially different from the American public in how they view the teaching of intelligent design as part of science curricula. (For an explanation of how scientists understand the meaning of intelligent design theory, see Chapter 2's note 12.) Nearly all of the scientists I talked with—religious and nonreligious alike—had a negative impression of the intelligent design movement.[15] Yet discussions about intelligent design—and others about science and religion—that occur in the environment outside the university actually serve to push many scientists from the realm of science into the realm of religion. This is one example of a phenomenon I call *environmental push*. Even those who have no interest in personal matters of faith find themselves pushed to talk about religious topics, often in the classroom setting. How scientists respond to the push is a matter, to some extent, of their own agency. Sometimes they push back, refusing to allow religion any place at all in their teaching. But when they respond to these outside forces by making room for religion's voice, they are experiencing *positive environmental push*. One example is when religious scientists become more vocal in their classrooms about productive ways to connect religion and science to one another. Scientists, religious or not, might employ religious resources (such as books or web sites) about ways to integrate scientific and religious understanding while retaining all aspects of the scientific method. For example, one chemist I spoke with routinely points her students to a web site by a religious scientist who talks about how he maintains his faith while conducting research that shows that the earth is billions of years old. Such efforts by scientists are made in order to transmit science more effectively to their largely religious students in a way that maintains the integrity of both science and religion.

Environmental push reveals that science does not operate in a social vacuum. Rather, teaching science is an inherently public social endeavor that requires that scientists react to other worldviews and broader debates in the social environment outside the university.[16] A talkative biologist[17] told me about how the intelligent design movement is pushing her to think more about the intersections between science and religion. An atheist, she is proud of the fact that she is not part of any religious tradition, and when she talks with the students in her biology courses she is consistently surprised at how many of them are very religious. In response, she makes a sincere effort to think of ways to present science so that religious students who take her biology class do not need to compromise their faith commitments. Similarly, a psychologist[18] who is an agnostic said that he views discussions about intelligent design as an important opportunity to help students think more clearly about the connections between religion and science. During the course of our conversation, it became clear that even though he is not part of a faith tradition, he thinks a lot about issues related to science and religion. And he feels the environmental push. He said that public debates about intelligent design are forcing him and his colleagues to think about the place of religion in their teaching and about the boundaries that establish what science is and what it is not.[19] He thinks that students should be presented with arguments for and against intelligent design, including the social environment that leads to its acceptance. For this psychologist, his priority is not a matter of supporting or debunking intelligent design but of helping students develop productive ways of talking about the role of science in society. "Students ought to think about what science contributes and what it cannot contribute to knowledge," he explained.

One economist[20] I interviewed was raised in a home that was more philosophically than religiously Jewish but now considers himself an Orthodox Jew (although he also commented that he is a "bad Orthodox Jew" because he does not follow many of the rituals). He explained that religion is naturally part of the courses he teaches on economic thought. He said, "I would start with the Bible, and I would talk about the whole question of rich and poor, the issues that confronted people who lived in biblical times. The whole question of how does society live together in a way that provides the greatest good for the greatest number." This way of incorporating religion into his work as a social scientist establishes him as different from his peers. If they knew he was teaching this way in his courses, most of his economist colleagues would probably "look at [him] strangely," he thinks, because "the profession is not there." He went on to clarify that there are distinct "value systems in the profession" but that these value systems tend to be "very esoteric, really removed from issues that have anything to do with spirituality"—removed from the stuff of real people's lives.

It is important to recognize that those who think that religion should be more openly discussed in science classrooms are not always the scientists who are themselves the most religious. Their common ground is instead the same sense of what it means to be a good teacher and a good scientist. The scientists who experience positive environmental push have a distinctive approach to crossing the boundary between religion and science, one that does not threaten the continuity of science education. In an effort to fulfill their obligation as educators, these scientists are willing to devote at least some teaching time to engaging their students in broader issues of science and society, including the intersection of science and religion.

"Religion Is a Threat That Must Be Addressed": Negative Environmental Push

Other scientists who talk openly about religion do so in a pejorative way. These scientists are often those who would say that religion and science are irreconcilably in conflict, and their actions reveal a *negative environmental push* arising from public debates about science and religion. (Whether the push is defined as negative or positive, then, depends upon the reactions of the scientists who are being pushed.) Though their responses are more derogatory, these scientists are also addressing the question of what science is and what it is not. They differ in that they intentionally talk about religion in a negative light, believing it vitally important to converse with their students about the irrelevance or danger of religion to the scientific mission.

Anthony,[21] the chemist we met in Chapter 2, thinks that learning more about science led him away from believing in God. While he generally believes that any personal expression of religion ought to stop at the university gate, he does talk about religion in his classroom and thinks that it ought to be discussed if it directly relates to the subject matter at hand, as intelligent design relates to chemistry. Consequently, he actively brings up religion in his class, telling students he does not view the theory of intelligent design as science.

No student has ever mentioned religion in Anthony's class; he suspects that this is because he has "headed it off at the pass" by bringing up the topic first. He makes this effort because "intelligent design is rearing its head." He wants to specifically explain to undergraduate students the difference between science and religion, telling them that science is necessarily "hypothesis driven." Religion, he explains, also has a hypothesis: "that there is a God that does everything." Since this hypothesis is not testable and falsifiable through the scientific method, he expounds in class, intelligent design is not scientific and has no place in the study of chemistry.

In another clear example of environmental push, Anthony has begun reading the Bible every day so that he can "react to all these other people quoting the Bible." His reading has shown him the danger of a literal interpretation of the Bible, what he refers to as "fundamentalism."

In light of the public debates about earth origins, I *expected* those in the natural sciences to express strong opinions about distinguishing science from religion. I was surprised, however, that social scientists—those in disciplines generally called the "soft sciences"—also asserted similarly strong distinctions. A social scientist[22] in her mid thirties who teaches at a West Coast campus talked openly—and quite disparagingly—about those in her field who study religion (for example, sociologists of religion, such as the one who was interviewing her). In addition, before she begins discussions in class where religion might come up, she offers students the following preface: "You don't have to distance yourself from religion and think about it from an outside perspective, but you do if you want to succeed in this class. And so if you don't want to do that, then you need to leave." She seems to think that if religion is too personally important to a student, then he will not be able to examine it in the objective, scientific manner necessary for viable social science. In her experience, some religious students waste energy defending their faith that could be used in grasping social science theories and methods.

Similarly, a biologist[23] said that religion must be brought up in science classrooms precisely because, in the current climate, it is approaching so dangerously close to science. He described his typical interactions with students: "I've had a couple of students who in talking to me after class have essentially brought up or even confessed that they have very fundamentalist ideas. . . . I've talked with them briefly about it, but . . . I felt constrained not to be too critical." He then chastised himself for not being more forthcoming about his own opinions in these discussions. When I pressed this biologist to tell me more, he explained, "I see that this issue is not going away. If anything, it's growing. There is a greater confusion over the meaning of science, the meaning of evidence, the ability to judge things on the basis of training." He later added, "I think the whole society in a way is becoming ideological and [has] increasing amounts of demagoguery. . . . It's more important nowadays for people in my kind of position to take what opportunities arise to help, to help sway the balance a little bit." This biologist joins a small but influential group of those who think that academic scientists have a particular responsibility, some would say a moral responsibility, to actively protect the authority of science from the intrusion of religion.

"My Faith Is Simply Part of Who I Am"

About 39 percent of the nearly 1,700 scientists I surveyed considered their religious or spiritual beliefs influential on their interactions with students and colleagues. Specifically, faith can create an ethos for teaching. In other words, the faith of these scientists is a part of their everyday lives to the extent that they see it shaping the *what, how,* and *why* of their teaching.

A Catholic chemist[24] was especially forthcoming about his religious views after I turned off my tape recorder. A recent immigrant, he thinks that academics (and Americans in general) should talk more openly about religion and integrate it into their lives. He blames the present unwillingness to discuss religion on what he called the "political correctness" of the United States, which he contrasts with the religious discussions people have in his home country. Although he clearly had outspoken views about public discussions of religion, this scientist explained that at work, his faith influences him primarily through the ethos it provides for teaching: "I would say religion itself doesn't come up, rather the values that I get through religion. . . . As a teacher you have, for example, a little bit more regard toward weaker students and try to help them out and also communicate to them the joy of studying science." Here, he explicitly contrasted himself with more secular colleagues who he thinks mainly spend time with the better students.

Similarly, a physicist[25] said that his faith causes him to treat those who work in his lab compassionately, going out of his way to do things for them that do not necessarily benefit his own career. In his words, "I'm at an age where I see mentoring as one of the most important things I can do, . . . trying to get [younger scientists] on paths that will get them to the jobs that they want. And you know there's no particular self-interest here. I mean the majority of [other scientists] I don't think do this." This physicist is also establishing a clear boundary between himself and his colleagues who, in his sense of things, care more about their own personal success than making sure that students are mentored well. Obviously, nonreligious professors might also mentor students well. The point is that religious scientists often mentioned this ethos of teaching as something that they believed separated them from their secular colleagues.

The Jewish economist[26] I mentioned earlier also said that his faith has a great impact on how he cares for students. He remembers his mother lighting candles on Friday evenings, a ritual that left him with "very peaceful imprints." Such experiences gave him a sense of "who [he is] and who [his] people are." And this knowledge that he belongs to a broader faith community influences, for instance, how he thinks about promoting character development among his students, such as those who have failed a class. These students might then meet him in his office to request a higher grade:

> And I say, "Well close the door and let's talk now. Aren't you ashamed to be here? What do you want out of life when your parents are spending money to keep you

here? Are you really interested in this? What are you doing with your life?" Never have I had anyone walk out. But I've had people come up afterwards and shake my hand and tell me, "Thank you so much for this conversation."

So, in addition to religion being used by scientists who are experiencing environmental push as a way to (1) help students understand the differences between science and religion and (2) help protect science from the intrusion of religion, there is a specific utilization of religion/spirituality as a basis for a teaching ethos. And those who apply this faith-based ethos generally view it as differentiated from the habits and motivations of their colleagues without faith.[27] We should notice, however, that scientists who talk about faith influencing the ethos of their teaching rarely mention any specific religious doctrines. Most of the students they interact with probably would not know that these scientists are religious. Rather, religion influences their teaching largely through the values it provides. Their faith comes alive through distinct relationships with their students that involve caring for them and promoting their better character.

CHAPTER 6

No God on the Quad

Efforts Toward a Purely Secular University

Of the 21 elite universities where I surveyed and interviewed scientists, eight began with a religious mission. None of the universities is religiously affiliated today. Historian George Marsden, in his eloquently titled book *The Soul of the American University: From Protestant Establishment to Established Nonbelief*, argues that the modern American university began with a soul that sprang from religious roots and was later trammeled by movements to secularize the academy. Historians Jon Roberts and James Turner support his points by arguing that the sciences were at the center of these secularizing social movements. In time, science was separated from any reliance on religious support, and many scientists took up their own unique value system in which science was considered the superior form of knowledge. The sciences basically stopped needing to engage with religion in any meaningful way. (Religion has certainly not disappeared from these institutions as a whole. Four of the ones I studied currently have a divinity school. And 19 house a center, department, or program devoted to the academic study of religion.)[1]

At the same time, the vision of the university itself has changed. Once, a primary mission of the university was moral instruction and character building. In such an environment, efforts to integrate faith and learning were paramount.[2] Universities like Harvard and Duke, with religious roots, have gradually shifted away from their faith origins in favor of an Enlightenment vision of autonomous human reason. For centuries, Harvard's coat of arms had portrayed three open books—two face up and one face down. The face-down one represented the portion of truth that could not be discovered by man but must be revealed from God. In a display of secularization, however, Harvard later flipped the third book, in what some considered an effort to flaunt humanity's potential to obtain all knowledge through reason. And as Harvard's example shows, pursuing this type of reason implicitly means for many of these universities a rejection of religious ways of knowing and an exaltation of scientific ways of knowing.[3] Former Harvard University president Derek Bok argues that another dominant change is the commercialization of elite universities, where more tangible goals such as winning grants, developing patents, and running large research labs replace less tangible goals like the development of students' character.[4]

The rising place of science in American universities paralleled the rising cultural prominence of science more broadly. Over time, Americans began to see science less as a cultural threat and more as a savior, with the ability to ensure the place and prominence of the United States on the world stage.[5] As historian David Hollinger argues, religious ideas were rightly subjected to the same kind of rigorous scientific scrutiny as other ideas, and so they decreased in prominence. This commitment to scientific knowledge has not come without its costs. Historian Julie Reuben, who chronicles the rise of the modern university, argues that efforts to create a scientific objectivity that was value neutral ultimately failed, leading instead to a complete separation of facts and values. This means that fields like science, considered completely based on fact, are separated from more humanistic fields such as English and history. Scientists are left, then, with little vocabulary for thinking about the moral implications of science or what kind of public translation of science works well.[6]

The connection between religion and science was a central concern of what sociologist Christian Smith calls the movement to secularize the academy. The people behind this social movement used language to their advantage, effectively equating science with reason, and religion with an irrational faith not worthy of intellectual consideration (at least not within a university context). As the major state research universities developed, the Ivy League schools increasingly secularized. Princeton University, with roots in the Presbyterian Church, and Harvard University, named after the minister John Harvard, loosened their religious ties. Smith has argued that this institutional shift in the model of the modern university—a shift, in other words, in what universities *ought* to be—came complete with funds and institutional leaders who wanted to bring about a more secular education. The efforts of professional associations (such as the American Sociological Association) and benefactors (such as Andrew Carnegie) were a huge success: religious concerns were redefined as irrelevant to the educational mission of universities.[7] As a result, religion was pushed to the outskirts of university life, to take place only in chapels, divinity schools, religious studies departments, and specialized campus ministries. And religious ideas, theology, and moral frameworks lost their place as central to the university's mission.

But change is afoot. Religion scholars John Schmalzbauer and Kathleen Mahoney contend that religion is coming back to the academy through burgeoning social movements that are concerned about revitalizing campus religion. After years of researching university and college ministries across the country, they find "strong evidence [that] indicates a new story needs to be told about religion in the academy, one that recognizes the resilience of the study of the sacred in a secular institution." These scholars discovered that at least "fifty religious scholarly associations foster the integration of faith and learning, while newly created centers for the study of religion can be found at Columbia University, the University of Virginia, Princeton University, New York University, and a host of other institutions."[8] Just as previous funders supported the demise of religion in the academy, new institutions are supporting its rise. Philanthropic trusts such as the Lilly Endowment, the Pew Charitable Trusts, and the John Templeton Foundation[9] have funded interdisciplinary centers for research and programming in various disciplines that examine religion. In addition, the social sciences disciplines are taking the study of religion more seriously. The American Psychological Association (APA), the American Sociological Association (ASA), and the American Political Science Association (APSA)—some of the organizations Smith argued were part of the deliberate social movement to secularize American higher education—all now have large sections devoted to examining the place of religion in modern society. And foundations such as the Teagle Foundation have committed resources to the specialized mission of developing models of character in higher education.[10] Princeton University scholar of American religion Robert Wuthnow, in a 2003 article in the *Chronicle of Higher Education*, argued for more "scientific studies of religion."[11] And the Metanexus arm of the Templeton Foundation has created more than 200 discussion groups on religion and science around the country, funding many of the U.S.-based and international centers that study religion and foster scholarly conversations on its connections to science. Plainly, scholars are making a place for religion.

And so are students. Scholars of higher education such as Helen and Alexander Astin show that an increasing number of students (and faculty) are practicing traditional forms of religion or are interested in broader ideas of spirituality.[12] In general, religion is meaning more to today's undergraduates, say religion scholars Conrad Cherry, Betty A. DeBerg, and Amanda Porterfield. According to their study of religion among students at four major U.S. universities, religion is "alive and well" among American college students.[13] Although their faith isn't as officially linked to the university as it used to be, students are likely to utilize religion when they are not in church, as when praying before sporting events or as a motivation to volunteer in their communities.

And Boston College political scientist Alan Wolfe has written about the "welcome revival" of religion in the academy.[14]

If there is indeed a resurgence of religion on campuses, it might have more traction in some geographic locales and in some types of universities than others. Universities like Duke and Emory might be more open to integrating religion into the curriculum because they are located in the South, in the midst of a populace that is more likely to be religious (the "Bible Belt"). And sociologists Neil Gross and Solon Simmons show that faculty at regional universities and teaching colleges might be more religiously similar to the general population than are those who teach at the kinds of flagship state research universities and Ivy League schools that I included in my study for this book.[15]

MODELS OF UNIVERSITY LIFE

Although there is strong evidence that religion among students is returning to top university campuses, I did not find as dominant a group of science professors who advocated public expression of religion on campus or scholarly conversations about religion and its role in public science. This lack of commitment among scientists to talking about and responding to religion on their particular campuses comes—for both religious and nonreligious faculty—from particular *models* of the university. Remember that models are understandings of what *ought* to be. We all subscribe to certain models, and they influence our actions, even if we're not totally aware of them. If I hold a model, for instance, that elementary schools should be safer, then I might endorse the hiring of security guards there and criticize a perceived lack of fire alarms. In the same way, elite scientists subscribe to models of what life at their universities ought to look like. And through analysis of interview transcripts, we are able to identify some of these models, which I discuss below as Opposition, Secularism, and Pluralism. When a university is seen as a place that should be religion-free, the result is an institutional separation of religion from the rest of intellectual life and, in some cases, actual suppression of religion.

Irving,[16] a psychologist, told me that the university is a place for the "generation of knowledge rather than the generation of faith." For him, to accept religion in university life would be to support opinions that he sees as dangerous to the mission of science in the university. Scientists like Irving are stuck. Many wonder how they can stay true to their commitments to science and to their universities while still responding in good conscience to religion and religious people on their campuses.

In this chapter and the next, we're moving beyond scientists' abstract views about religion and science to discover what place they think religion ought to occupy on their particular campuses as well as in universities more generally. This is important, in part, because flagship institutions such as Harvard and Berkeley form a collection of universities that accept and produce similar types of students and knowledge. How scientists at these schools perceive the proper model of the university is consequential for the broader institution of American higher education and the place of science (and religion) within it.[17] If the scientists at elite universities fail to successfully engage with religion on their campuses, other American universities might follow suit. And if the current resurgence of religion on college campuses collides with persistently antireligious models of university life, might a collision or an explosion of some sort be inevitable?

In this chapter, we delve into the views of scientists who think that religion is irrelevant or even dangerous to the mission of science within universities. In chapter 7, we explore the models scientists have for how religion and science might usefully intersect. It is not my intention here to encourage scientists to recover a previous and more religious vision of the university but rather to help them understand how the more modern models of the university have influenced how they respond to issues of religion. Before we look at the three main secular models of modern universities, we'll explore a belief that clearly underlies each of them: that religion is a viable and dangerous threat to science in the university setting.

Why Is Religion Seen as a Threat?

As I traveled the country talking to scientists at the nation's top schools, I asked them what role they think religion ideally ought to occupy in institutions like theirs. Many scientists believe that religion has no legitimate place in the modern American academy; 54 percent mentioned the dangers that religion could bring to universities (in particular, to science) when it goes wrong. A large minority of scientists I talked with (about 36 percent) have a model of university life that does not allow *any* positive role for religious people, institutions, and ideas on their campuses.[18] They have few models for how scientists (with or without faith) might sustain productive interaction with or even respond to religious people and ideas. In their models of the university, such people and ideas exist primarily as a threat to science.

In one sense, scientists appear to have good reasons for these views. According to one recent national survey, "more Americans approved than disapproved of instruction about three explanations of the origins of life (evolution, intelligent design, and creationism) in public school science classes,"[19] and the great majority of scientists only endorse evolution as actual science. Scientists at elite universities can come to see the academy as the only remaining American institution that is safe from the encroaching impact of religious conservatives on their life's passion, science. Scientists also come to their views about religion in the midst of what they see as religiously based opposition to their freedom of speech—movements led by David Horowitz and others who argue that universities are overrun by liberal academics hostile to religion.[20] Given the decrease in public funding for science, the need for greater science literacy among the general public, a growing fear that faculty will be attacked if they appear to malign religion, and recent court cases that threaten to give religion more place in public life, scientists feel they have good reasons for thinking that religion might threaten science education. And since elite universities are the places that train the next generation of top scientists, it makes sense to some scientists that they should do all they can to constrain or marginalize religion.[21]

As explained before, however, religion still appears to be advancing. More structures on university campuses than ever before are currently aimed at developing an intelligent interface between religion and science. Increased discussion about religion at major U.S. research universities is seen in an increase in the number of religious studies departments, societies for the scholarly study of religion (in a variety of disciplines), and scholarly institutes devoted to dialogue between religion and science. But because of the busyness of their work as scientists (the hours worked per week for research university professors has steadily increased) and/or their inherent lack of interest in religion, elite scientists do not know about such structures.[22] In addition, because religious scientists often have a closeted faith (as discussed in Chapter 3), their nonreligious colleagues might find little reason to question their assumption that there is simply no place for religion in the academy. This is too bad, because scientists who fear religion generally fear narrowly understood fundamentalist forms of it. And since their fellow scientists with religious views are reluctant to talk openly about their own convictions, such stereotypes are rarely dispelled.

We turn now to the models that guide these scientists in how to respond to religion on their campuses. Understanding what scientists believe universities ought to be can provide an explanation for the reluctance and resistance I sometimes found among them to enter into dialogue about religion and science or to ascribe to religion any value at all.

THE MODEL OF OPPOSITION: RELIGION OUGHT TO BE VIEWED IN OPPOSITION TO SCIENTIFIC REASONING

Some scientists think that universities are inherently focused on reason and rationality, and little else. They believe that the most important part of university education is teaching students the reasoning skills they will take with them into other spheres of occupational and personal life. Drawing on the best tools of reason inherent in specific disciplines, then, universities ought to be sites of research that discover new knowledge about all spheres of the natural and social world. These models of university life seem to overlook departments in the fine arts, well-funded athletics departments, and some humanities departments, all of which have ideas and ideals separate from the pursuit of this form of rationality.

And there is disagreement about what relationship religion truly has to reason. Different from the social movements to bring religion back to universities (as discussed by Schmalzbauer and Mahoney), the largest group of scientists that I talked with endorsed Enlightenment thinking, arguing that reason is the primary authority and tending to privilege science over other forms of knowledge.[23] Such a model derives in part from these scientists' acceptance of the conflict paradigm—that science and religion endorse fundamentally different and completely incompatible ways of knowing. Religion, then, would be necessarily dangerous to science. These scientists see an important struggle being expressed in social conflicts over religion and science. In the most extreme cases, they see themselves fighting a culture war on their university campuses, with only religion *or* science as the possible victor.[24]

Scientists mentioned their fear that the public school court cases over intelligent design might be replicated in universities. A chemist,[25] an assistant professor at an Ivy League school, explained that what is happening with intelligent design in the United States has pushed things precariously close to the edge of religious involvement: "I don't like it if science is influenced on a level that it shouldn't be by religion . . . this evolution and intelligent design debate comes in." This chemist went on to explain that any science that "has as a backdrop ideas related to philosophy or religion might . . . become tainted."

Noted scholars argue that the connection between religion and science is shifting from a war to a dialogue, citing as evidence, for example, the development of hundreds of science-and-religion courses.[26] Yet the majority of scientists at elite schools did not show much of a willingness to engage in dialogue about the topic. And those who thought religion was a dangerous threat to science did not seem to know about the efforts at their own universities to engage students in discussion about these topics. Their lack of interest in or even negativity toward religion was not because of an absence of institutional supports at their particular universities. Indeed, at the universities where I interviewed scientists, I found over 120 courses on "science and religion" or "science and society" that specifically discussed religion and science. But it wasn't the scientists I interviewed who were teaching them, of course. The courses were rarely, if ever, housed or even cross-listed as part of science departments. The courses were more likely to be taught in history, religious studies, or American studies departments.[27]

According to one economist,[28] "there is absolutely no place for religion in science or in the university." Another economist[29] explained the big differences he sees between the natural and social sciences:

> Especially social sciences—they're not too much at the front lines. But . . . the *real* sciences like physics, chemistry, biology, I think they need to do scientific, objective research. And those are the areas [that have] the most direct conflict with religion. And for the sake of scientific progress, there should be protection against religious interference.

For this social scientist, religion and specifically "religious interference" is something from which natural scientists and science need to be protected. A chemist[30] explained that science departments absolutely need to be kept separate from religion. This assistant professor said that the "chemistry department is not a place where we want to teach anything about religion or spirituality whatsoever." He went on, apparently concerned that he might offend me because of my disciplinary home in sociology: "So you might not be happy to hear this. . . . I'm not asking to talk about carbon and hydrogen in your department, am I? No. . . . Irrelevant. Just leave it to the church or individuals. University is no place." He softened a little as he went on to suggest the possible validity of a "department of religious studies, like your department and students there or such who are enrolled in the classes you are offering. But other than that, no place. Don't even bring it in." He ended his heated monologue by providing an analogy to the music department at his university. "We don't ask them to teach or discuss chemistry at all," he said. As with this chemist, the majority of faculty saw a place for teaching about world religions in a religious studies department, but they felt strongly that religion should never be discussed in the same breath with science.

These scientists particularly feared that religion could lead to irrationality and poor-quality science if it were included in science education in any kind of institutional way. Some scientists wondered aloud what might happen if there were religious individuals with certain perspectives in their departments. If these religious individuals were in power—department chairs or full professors—they might allow religion to enter their decision-making, which would have the eventual result of tainting the supposed purity of science. An associate professor, who is a microbiologist[31] at a large state research university in the Midwest, explained that he has no problem with universities sponsoring religious services for students, although he has no intimate knowledge of these services: "I'm sure there are religious groups that are official student organizations here on campus, and I have no problem with that." What this microbiologist would find problematic is if religion appeared in his department. "Let's say the head of my department was a fundamentalist Christian of some kind and that started to influence the scientific content and decisions that were being made in microbiology. That would be inappropriate," he explained. Interestingly, this biologist didn't offer any "appropriate" ways that religion might surface in department life, and he defaults to describing what he calls "fundamentalist Christianity," the form of religion that scientists find most dangerous to scientific progress.

Scientists also mentioned that religion might be dangerous to reason and to science if it entered departments at the level of hiring. A sociologist,[32] a named-chair professor who teaches at a large state research university in the Midwest, talked about the dangers of considering religion in hiring decisions. He mentioned his son, who is an academic in a field where it is extremely difficult to get a job. Difficulty in finding academic employment has led his son to apply widely for jobs, even (he mentioned with some chagrin) those at religious colleges. At some of the religious schools where his son has applied, he was asked how "your personal relationship with Jesus Christ will affect your daily work in teaching." The sociologist found "that kind of thing really quite revolting." He would certainly "draw the line" at having "religious tests for faculty" be a part of the academic environment.

Those scientists who mentioned being fearful that religion might come into hiring decisions did not mention a corresponding fear that religious applicants might be discriminated against. And their examples were always related to confessional religious colleges and universities having "litmus tests" for hiring faculty; there were no examples given of a secular research university—the kinds of institutions where the scientists I interviewed taught—doing the same thing. Further, since most faculty at elite research universities who are religious keep their faith commitments secret, it would be unlikely that their faith would have the kind of impact that this sociologist feared.

It seemed difficult for faculty who thought that religion was dangerous to the life of the mind, to reason, and to science, to resolve their views with the fact that many of their universities have religious roots and some have active divinity schools and chaplaincy programs. Their universities were, in some ways, clearly taking religion seriously, and this caused them obvious dissonance.

Irving, the professor of psychology we met at the beginning of this chapter, explained that for him religion is inherently "supernatural," and nothing supernatural can be discussed in a university setting. Irving is deeply interested in spirituality, but he never discusses personal ideas about spirituality with his colleagues. In the course of his entire career (he is 60), he has only known "a couple" of religious colleagues, and he does not know of any religious individuals in his current department. He differentiates himself from his "religious compatriots" in that he does not invoke notions of the "divine" or "supernatural" to answer questions that have to do with the meaning of life. He was religious for part of his childhood and was even briefly "born again." During this time, he was particularly enamored of Billy Graham. This only lasted for about a year and a half, however, after which he "became a secularist" and has "been there ever since." Irving abandoned religion because it just did not "make any intellectual sense" and seemed like a "superstition." He responded to my question about what place, if any, religion ought to have in universities by saying, "I don't think frankly religion should be at the university."

He paused to reflect a bit more and then explained that in reality, the place religion ought to have at universities "is a tough question, because most universities . . . started as a school of divinity. This university has a very powerful, old, and highly respected divinity school." He finally concluded, "I see the university as a center for the generation of knowledge rather than the generation of faith or the protection of faith." Notice here that Irving assumes in his narrative an opposition between faith and knowledge. And for him, "knowledge" doesn't include religious knowing; likely, it would be limited to the scientifically verifiable.[33] In the end, he is "not at all certain that religion should be at the university other than as an object of study." In this line of reasoning, divinity schools are not legitimate.

A physicist[34] who teaches at a university with a well-known divinity school took his views a step further than Irving's. An atheist who grew up in a household that he described as ethnically Jewish but "vehemently and almost violently antireligious," he told me that he thinks divinity schools are ultimately dangerous. "Divinity schools sort of blithely assume that . . . clergy is a neutral term, which it is not," he said. This physicist thinks that divinity schools tend to see themselves as just training professionals, similar to the way a law school might train lawyers. He feels that "it is simply not the same." In his words, "For a divinity school to say that training pastors is just like training any other professional is similar to a law school saying that it would be neutral to train grassroots labor activists." By this he meant that any good law school would not train lawyers to have an inherent agenda about the law just as a good university should not train students to have an inherent agenda about religion. He links what he sees as the dubious legitimacy of divinity schools to his idea that the "place that religion is allowed to fill in most American universities is really detrimental to the mission of the university, which is to educate." He takes his views from what he calls "all kinds of Enlightenment junk, to educate people in human knowledge, of which religion is certainly a part." He makes a strong distinction, though, between just teaching people religion as an object of study and "building a university around religion, like a Methodist college. . . . I'm not comfortable with this aspect of things at all. And I think it leads to problems." This physicist believes that some knowledge of religion and religious traditions is required for a broad liberal arts education, in which one can accord "religion the respect you accord French baroque literature," for instance. His phrase that this is part of "all kinds of Enlightenment junk," however, indicates some underlying cynicism. He is sure that to have divinity schools or confessional faith be part of the university environment, or to take any kind of stand on religion—as those do who teach and study at divinity schools—should not be allowed. To do so would mean that religion might be allowed to oppose the reason of science.

THE MODEL OF SECULARISM: UNIVERSITIES OUGHT TO BE BASTIONS OF SECULARISM

The group of scientists discussed above think universities ought to be committed to reason alone and that the most sincere expression of such reason is science itself. Other scientists have a somewhat different, yet related, model of the university; they see within the purpose of the university a mission to be distinctive from religious institutions. Instead of relying on rhetoric of science as embodying the supreme form of reason, they generally employ the rhetoric of separation of church and state. This view is predominant among both social and natural scientists and does not seem to be concentrated in one discipline more than another. These are the professors who contribute both actively and passively to the social movement to secularize the academy. Scientists who talk extensively about the separation of church and state argue that there are enough places in the broader society where religion has taken hold and that universities should be places where knowledge is protected from its grip.

An outgrowth of viewing research universities as bastions of secularism is that these scientists think that students who are interested in religion would be better off at universities and colleges with a specifically religious mission. One sociologist[35] explained that he is an agnostic and a "scientist wannabe, [who] lives, for the most part, in a very positivistic, scientific world." On one hand, he said, "you probably can't be ardently antireligious [here] in the sense of driving out believers, which is a good thing . . . because [I am] actually ambivalent toward believers." He does, on the other hand, hope the academy will remain "a bastion of secularism to the degree humanly possible." A political scientist[36] who described himself as ethnically Jewish without any religious beliefs added that being at a state university helps him to definitively answer the question of what place religion ought to occupy in university settings:

> Because it's a state university, an arm of the state and bound by constitutional principles, I feel quite strongly that it would be utterly inappropriate for the university to do anything to suppress, discourage, or denigrate religion. It would be equally inappropriate for the university to do anything to promote a particular religion, or religion over irreligion.

Most scientists do not have views about the separation of church and state that are as well thought out as this particular political scientist's, which is based on his study of constitutional law. Others did have views that were similar, however. An economist[37] said, "It would be hard for me to envision a conflict [between science and religion], because it's hard for me to envision what it would be like being religious." He teaches at a large state research university in the West and explained that because he teaches at "a state school, this essentially precludes any religious part of the actual faculty, I guess." He especially assumed that any sort of proselytizing on the part of faculty was not allowed, since religion posed a threat to secular education and should be separated from the intellectual life of the university.

The reality of university life does not match these scientists' ideal. For example, most universities—even state schools—do have a chaplaincy service and a public chapel on campus. Student ministries of many sorts are active on campuses, from evangelical Christian to Muslim to New Age—ministries that bolster students who do raise religiously motivated concerns in classrooms. For instance, the ethical (and religiously based) implications of genetics testing and human genetic engineering would certainly crop up in a genetics seminar.[38] Those who continue to express a view of the university that argues for an exclusion of religion are not able to respond adequately when religion inevitably does enter the campus.

THE MODEL OF PLURALISM: UNIVERSITIES
OUGHT TO FOSTER PLURALISM

At the dedication of Cornell University in 1868, cofounder Ezra Cornell displayed his commitment to plurality—both of academic disciplines and of people. He proclaimed, "I trust we have laid the foundation of [a] university, 'an institution where any person can find instruction in any study.'"[39] Cornell was one of the few private universities founded without commitment to a specific religious mission. Most major American universities were founded as Protestant, Catholic, or in a small number of cases, Jewish.[40] But as a result of recent immigration and world events, plurality is gaining preference over specific religious affiliation. According to one survey recent immigrants are five times more likely to practice a faith outside of a Jewish or Christian tradition than are the native-born (20 percent, compared to 4 percent).[41] Just as the proportion of persons of different faiths increases in the United States, so does their representation on university campuses, where the weekly Protestant service in the chapel has been supplemented by Friday prayer services sponsored by the local mosque and a midweek Buddhist meditation. This seems fitting. The mission of most universities is to be representative of the universe of knowledge, which includes accommodating those of many faiths.

But it seems, ironically, that those scientists I interviewed who most prize the vision of the university as committed to plurality are actually the most opposed to the entrée of diverse religious views into the fabric of the intellectual life of universities. In particular, it is difficult for these scientists to figure out how they will engage with religion without appearing intolerant of one and supportive of another. In their experience working on university campuses, students, faculty, and university programs can be irritatingly partisan—wanting to argue for their particular religious view. Talking about religion at all, then, just invites a fight. Scientists wondered aloud how, if religion is to be brought into the university, it could ever be discussed in a civil manner.

A sociologist[42] said that he was trained by a scholar who thought that "religion was an opiate of the social sciences. If you suffered from it, you couldn't possibly be a critical scholar," making a play on Karl Marx's famous quote that religion is the "opiate of the masses."[43] This professor, who teaches at a large private research university, cautioned that as a faculty member, one needs to be "very careful that if one gives an affirmative answer [about religion] that one doesn't come off as privileging a particular faith." He explained that to do so might risk a "slippage [that] becomes very great." He explained that it's not "violation of the relationship between politics and religion, but politics and a particular form of Christianity." In other words, this scientist and others find danger in talking about religion in university contexts because of the possibility of especially evangelical Christian proselytizing and its detriment to the mission of science.

Another professor, who holds a named chair in economics[44] at a large state research university in the Midwest, is also fearful of bringing religion into a discussion in a university setting. To do so, he believes, would risk proselytizing, a possibility so dangerous that it would be better to leave religion out altogether:

> Another downside of [bringing religion in] is that the university is supposed to be a place that is welcoming to everyone, and I would be somewhat afraid that it would become this place for a dominant set of religious beliefs. That's a very negative kind of feeling, because it suggests that you can't [discuss] those beliefs and express them personally in a way that is at the same time pluralistic. . . . And I'm absolutely dead set against proselytizing.

SECRET, SEPARATE, SUPPRESSED: THE CONSEQUENCES OF THESE UNIVERSITY MODELS

Margaret,[45] a chemist, is deeply religious yet keeps her faith private on her campus. She is also one of the more memorable scientists I interviewed. She wore a blue T-shirt, khaki pants, and sandals. Her office met my stereotype of a serious scientist. Bookshelves full of lab notebooks, three-ring binders, and science textbooks lined the walls from floor to ceiling so that she could see everything at once. Indeed I needed to walk through a maze of papers to get to the one empty chair at the other side of her desk. She motioned for me to sit down and then asked about the study. But before I could get too deeply into my explanation, she began to tell me how important her faith is to her personally. She talked about teaching an adult forum class at her Episcopal church; she had been working on it when I entered her office. She seemed a little nervous about the interview, telling me that she wondered if she would say the right things. As we talked, it became clear that Margaret is keenly interested in discussing issues related to her faith, especially those involving science. She put considerable thought into her often lengthy answers.

Margaret explained during our discussion that she "knows God is out there" and that "he has a plan for me." Her faith is deeply relevant, but it's not always public. In the course of her department life as a scientist, she generally remains quiet about her involvement in her congregation, since she is convinced there are very few scientists in her department or broader university who are also religious. However, she had a lot to say about the ramifications her faith has on her life as a scientist, such as her ethos of teaching and mentoring. Margaret told me exactly how religion influences her interactions with students and colleagues. It helps her to respond to what she called "the games people play" in the academy. Unlike many of her colleagues, she tries to provide all those who work with her clear insights into how the research process works and the kind of information they need, whether they are undergraduates, colleagues, or even potential competitors outside the university. Among elite scientists like Margaret who have a religious tradition, 53 percent see their religion or spirituality influencing their interactions with students and colleagues (compared to 25 percent of scientists with no religious tradition).[46]

Even though Margaret is herself religious, her model of the university also could fall under the Model of Opposition—not because she finds religion or science dangerous, but because to her, religion is inherently private and science is public. When I asked Margaret how religion comes up in her department or in the broader university, she would instinctively turn the conversation to the private aspects. She knows that some of the people she works with—graduate assistants and postdoctoral fellows—are religious, because these individuals will sometimes talk about their religious practices. But there are no deep conversations about the content of religion. When I pressed Margaret further to answer my question about the role that religion ought to occupy in universities, she had no ideas:

> I can't think of scientists really being spiritual. Maybe I just don't see that aspect of my colleagues. I don't see it so much in the workplace. I mean I see people who have ethics, who are imaginative with respect to their work, but their spiritual side . . . [she trailed off]. We just don't talk about it.

Margaret then wondered aloud how they *would* talk about science and religion together. She was deeply thankful that religion had not come up publicly in her own work as a chemist, expressing some relief that at least those in her field of chemistry "haven't been faced with creationism or anything like that, at least not in the classes or in the lab settings so much." In general, she told me that she tries to keep the personal, which includes religion, out of her lab. She explained, "I've had some Baptist students. I mean those are the most conservative ones I can think of, and I knew [that one researcher in my lab] went to Bible study . . . but so did I." Even though she and this researcher encountered each other in the same Bible study, they never discussed religious ideas at work.

I asked Margaret what the bottom line is for how her faith commitments influence how she lives her life. She replied, "I guess . . . [I am] a little bit more understanding or forgiving perhaps than some of the others." Again, her answer dealt mainly with the personal aspects of her faith.

Implicitly, Margaret's views of religion as private and science as public (and so, in a sense, opposed) match those of many of the scientists I talked with who have very negative attitudes toward faith. So their models can be called similar. But the reasons behind them are very different. Margaret spoke of inconvenient or troublesome controversies that can result from religion, not the possibility that religion is dangerous to science. The controversies and awkwardness she fears, however, are undoubtedly connected to the fact that others around her *do* see religion as a threat. In her own way, then, she shares and reinforces their Model of Opposition—most notably through her closeted faith (see Chapter 3).

Like Margaret, the scientists who subscribed to the university models of Opposition, Secularism, and/or Pluralism dealt with religion by privatization (keeping their own religion secret), separation (keeping religion out of the classroom), and, to a lesser extent, suppression. Different from discrimination (and not illegal), suppression can manifest as anything from disparaging remarks to aggressive confrontation.

Surprisingly, both the highly religious and the highly secular among scientists had a difficult time thinking of ways that a scientist might productively interact with religion on a university campus. Those who found religion personally irrelevant or dangerous considered engagement not worth the risk. And for those like Margaret, who have a difficult time imagining how religion would intersect with science, it would be hardly worth the trouble.

Nonreligious scientists who practiced separation said that they worry about offending their highly religious students and colleagues—mostly students, since both religious and nonreligious scientists did not suspect their colleague scientists to be highly religious. A chemist, for example, doesn't talk about religion or matters related to religion in university settings because he is afraid of offending others. He told me in no uncertain terms that he is simply "afraid of retribution" from those who are religious, mentioning that society does not look favorably on individuals who do not have a religious tradition or belief in God. His feeling has some empirical grounding; the nonreligious—and atheists in particular—are among the social groups from which other Americans most wish to distance themselves.[47]

A psychologist[48] who, when pressed, described himself as an agnostic, said he personally gives very little thought to religion. Private things (his sense of what religion is) do not generally come up in his department:

> You can talk about kids. You can talk about movies. . . . But mostly we talk about
> science and what we do, because there are not all that many people . . . who are
> going to be interested in what you do. And so when you find somebody who is,
> you spend most of the time on that.

He went on to describe what to him is the almost euphoric experience of going to a conference, where "basically . . . 24 hours a day, [we] just eat, drink, sleep, breathe [research]." While he doesn't tend to comment on religion, the debates about teaching intelligent design in public school classrooms have caused him to become more vocal. He says it is "crystal clear" that there is an "absolute lack of evidence" for creationism and intelligent design. This is consistent with his view that, strictly speaking, science does not conflict with religion but rather conservative religion conflicts with science. He explains, "I view it as religion perceiving there to be a conflict when there really isn't."

This psychologist maintains a "completely neutral stance" on the existence of God. He has "a hard enough time with questions . . . in the science stuff." He does not want to waste time thinking about unanswerable religious or spiritual questions. When asked about the meaning of life, he answered, "It beats me. I have no clue." Part of the reason he never thinks about these issues is because of the pressures of academia. When asked whether he engages in any spiritual practices, he responded, "I'm mainly trying to just get the stuff done that was due two weeks ago." His views are similar to those of other nonreligious scientists who subscribe to the Model of Secularism: The only questions worth asking are secular ones. Their departments and the broader university exist for the purpose of forwarding knowledge, and religion is not an important type of knowledge.

Although this psychologist and Margaret the Episcopalian chemist have very different underlying motivations, both think that the best way to handle faith is to keep it private. Science and religion are kept in separate boxes, religion in a closed box within the closet and science in an open box outside it, and this practice is largely due to assumptions about what the university ought to be. This compartmentalization is not violated until there is an event that forces open the closet; this happened for our psychologist when intelligent design cases gained in prominence.[49]

One way of separating religion is to put literal institutional barriers around it. Some scientists proposed that science could be protected from religion by confining it to divinity schools or religious studies departments. For some, religion should be further restricted to only specifically religious institutions, where students could go if they wanted to learn more about faith. A Nobel

Prize–winning physicist[50]—one of six Nobel Prize-winners who were part of the study—explained that while he does not think the religious community should be barred completely from the university, he also does not see a place for religion being "favored in the university context." According to him, religion is "just different":

> It's not what the university is all about. It was at one time, of course. Even at places like Cambridge University, where its origin was to prepare people for the ministry. . . . It's still pervasive [at Cambridge], the services and the music and the chapels and so on. It's charming in a way, but I don't think we want to go back there.

Scientists who think that religious studies departments and divinity schools should exist still often believe that these departments and institutes ought not to be given the same legitimacy or resources as science departments. Our Nobel Prize winner explained that the reason religion should not be a central part of knowledge making in universities is because we have more advanced forms of inquiry now:

> In some ways, when that tradition was founded, it was the most advanced, incisive view of the way the world works. So it would've been very unnatural to separate it off from inquiry at the forefront of knowledge. But that's not the case anymore. These [religious traditions] can be treasured and practiced for what they are but not as the vanguard of knowledge.

For this physicist, there is no room for religion as a living force in people's academic lives, but it can hold a minor place as an object of study and sentiment. It is difficult for him to imagine that faith might play an active role for students, staff, or faculty on university campuses.

A named-chair professor in political science[51] at an Ivy League school could see some place for religion in divinity schools. But he did not think that those who pursued divinity degrees tended to be engaged in rigorous study or to have advanced intellect, compared to their scholarly peers:

> I think the days of theology departments as such are probably numbered in most places—most serious places. Talented people don't go into those kinds of departments anymore. I mean, I do recall as an undergraduate that if you wanted to go to Oxford and you were lazy, and you did not do that much work as a high-school student, the best strategy was to apply to the theology [program], because it had the highest rate of acceptance. And then, having done a year or so of theology,

you would try to transfer to another discipline with a slightly higher degree of respect. And so, broadly speaking, although smart people can be religious, they're not considered smart because of their religious convictions.

Generally, scientists who endorse institutional separation of religion within the university are not all that convinced that religion is a legitimate subject of study to begin with. They surmise that those who do want to study religion should leave mainstream educational institutions and go to divinity schools. How they waste their time when they get there is their own business.

When Separation Becomes Suppression

There is a small group of scientists (less then 5 percent of those I interviewed) who go beyond privatizing religion or separating themselves from it to actively suppressing its expression. Because of their vocal bent, this group can appear much larger than it really is. They have been outspoken about the irrelevance and danger of religion as well as the need to suppress it where possible, and their work and views have received a lot of public press because of their contrarian nature. Suppression is most likely to be displayed by scientists with no religious tradition and who hold most rigidly to the Model of Secularism.

Insights from the highly influential anthropologist Mary Douglas—who was herself a Catholic—are curiously related to this group of suppressors. She explains that in what she calls more primitive cultures, individuals use religion to overcome ideas of dirt and pollution in their societies, calling things that are dirty or dangerous "sin," for example. Building on the ideas of Émile Durkheim, Douglas explains that religious rites provide societies with rituals that separate the sacred from the profane.[52] To scientists who suppress religion, religion *is* the profane, dirtying the waters of science's rational transmission of knowledge. These scientists do not see religion as benign, so privatization and separation are insufficient—even cowardly—alternatives. They assert that something ought to be actively done to get religion out of universities, because it is so dangerous to their educational mission.

When asked for his definition of religion, Arik,[53] the physicist whom we met in Chapter 1, explained that there are two different, "logically distinct" types of religion. One is merely cultural. The other involves belief based on "zero evidence" and is often used as "a convenient tool to exert power in political or social spheres." Arik said that "logic plays no role" in religion except as "an opportunity for a sort of scorn and mirth." He explains that religion ought to "be the target on the dart board" and that "it has absolutely no role" in university life. Arik is on the far end of the spectrum of scientists who hold negative views about religion, because he actually thinks it should be expunged from universities completely.

Unlike his colleagues who think that religion is only threatening if discussed publicly, Arik believes that even the personal practice of religion could have the dangerous consequence of eroding reason in the practitioner. He specifically singled out campus ministries, saying that he is "disgusted by the number of religious organizations that buy properties around campus." In Arik's opinion, these ministries are dangerous to the cause of teaching reason, because they pull "little, fragile people, . . . vulnerable people away from home, people whose immune systems, sociologically speaking, are low, and ensnare them." He thinks of these organizations as sinister and is "disgusted by the way they [advertise] by putting signs that make their buildings look like they are parts of the university." He finds the mission of such organizations antithetical to a "genuine institution of higher learning." He is not even sure why universities *have* departments of divinity, and he commented, "I think they should be in the pathology department," as religion is actually a disease. He tells me passionately that he would "resign if there were any violation of the establishment clause that [his] institution sanctioned." Interestingly, Arik sees no inconsistency between his quest for rational, empirical scholarship and his volatile response to religion on campus.

CHAPTER 7

God on the Quad

Making Room for Faith on Campus

I would like to introduce the reader to Ian Hutchinson, professor and head of the Department of Nuclear Science and Engineering at the Massachusetts Institute of Technology. The intricacies of his work on the magnetic confinement of plasmas would not be understandable to someone without specialized training, but his research might eventually lead to new forms of energy production. Hutchinson also specifically tries to reach out to a larger community of scientists beyond his discipline. He often gives talks about the relationship between religious faith and science. I attended one such lecture for graduate students and faculty at Cornell University titled "Science: Christian or Atheistic?" Hutchinson started his talk by relating how Nobel Prize-winning physicist Steven Weinberg, in a commencement address to students at Bates College in 2002, set out to "welcome students to the Enlightenment, explicitly disparage all religions as superstition and medievalism . . . while praising science."[1] In contrast, Hutchinson set out to help his audience move beyond the popular view that science is inherently atheistic. He argued that the image of science at war with religion, though often fed by high-profile scientists, is not supported by history. Hutchinson urged the 50 or so graduate students and faculty gathered that evening from a variety of disciplines and faith traditions to look at the evidence. He argued that a remarkable fraction of history's great scientists have been convinced that science and Christian faith are compatible—such as Scottish physicist James Clerk Maxwell, who did foundational work in electromagnetism and the kinetic theory of gases.[2] Hutchinson also discussed the importance of understanding that science is a particular kind of knowledge, with the characteristics of reproducibility (other scientists will get the same results if an experiment is done again) and clarity (any rational scientist will agree on the results of an experiment).[3] Hutchinson then compared science to other kinds of knowledge, such as history (which deals with unique events), the arts, and law. He rejected the philosophical belief known as scientism (which asserts that the only meaningful knowledge is scientific and that scientific knowledge has authority to interpret all other forms).[4] After giving other kinds of evidence, he ended his talk with the assertion that science is closer to being Christian than to being atheistic. After the lecture, many of us remained to press Hutchinson for more information. Some of us left satisfied and some did not, but he encouraged the students to probe further. While the content of Hutchinson's lecture is important in its own right, this event is most relevant to our current discussion because of what it exemplifies: a sincere and brilliant scientist translating ideas about science and religion to a broader audience.

While Hutchinson speaks to science on behalf of religion, others, such as physicist Sylvester James Gates Jr., speak on behalf of science, addressing religion when necessary. In 2008, Gates gave a public lecture at Rice University entitled "Einstein's New Millennium Legacy."[5] Like the science that Hutchinson engages, Gates's work as named professor and director of the Center for String and Particle Theory at the University of Maryland is hard for the non-specialist to understand. As if sensing the possible intimidation factor, Gates began his talk by putting the crowd at ease with the words, "If you see anything you think is physics, you are hallucinating." Easygoing, Gates quipped that when scientists found background radiation in the universe, they said, "My God, ET has nuclear weapons!" Gates then transitioned to the theme of his lecture: "What is the nature of science?" According to Gates, "Science does not depend on us; it is always there. It is up to us to figure it out." At one point in the lecture, Gates remarked that science is different from other human beliefs:

> This is because, with science, we can abandon at the drop of a hat beliefs that we have held dear for centuries, once we have new information. Science cannot be a threat to anyone's religion. Science is about measuring things. It is not about truth, but it is about reducing the falsity of our beliefs.

The package Gates was delivering was an increase in the acceptance of science. But helping the audience to understand how science and religion connect was one of the vehicles he drove. In the question-and-answer portion of the session, Gates said, "If we as a society are worried about moral issues coming out of science, we must have the public involved." When someone in the audience asked what scientists could do to better transmit science to the broader public, Gates remarked in the course of his answer that "scientists must be open, honest, and sincere with the public." In an informal period after the lecture, students pressed Gates further about the connection between religion and science, and he did not shy away. He encouraged the remaining small group of students to go directly to the writings of the scientists themselves, rather than to a "man of the cloth" (a religious leader). Gates mentioned that "Einstein, while not being religious in a conventional sense, was definitely not antireligious." He pointed out that James Clerk Maxwell and Isaac Newton were deeply committed Christians. Gates reminded the students that we must try to understand the nature of the universe with the tools and techniques we have. Science is about what can be measured (and is limited to measurable answers), and faith is not measurable. Therefore, he said, the two cannot conflict.

Hutchinson and Gates have both attained an elite status among scientists, and for good reason. They are exceptionally accomplished in their fields. No one can claim that they aren't *real* scientists, and they are clearly interested in more than proselytizing. But they are also different from one another. Hutchinson holds Christian convictions, but Gates's religious perspective is not clear from his lecture; he seems most concerned that the general public—religious or not—remain scientifically literate.[6]

What makes them both boundary pioneers is that they break down the walls of separation between science and religion, introducing to us new ideas for reconciliation. As pioneers, they are also able to lead others to navigate the rubble and cross over the areas where the walls once were.[7] Both of these men are able to handle just about any question thrown at them, because they have spent some amount of time thinking deeply about this issue. And for Hutchinson, coordinating the intersection of his work and his faith involves more than treating students and colleagues well. He spends part of his energy engaging his peers about ways that these two worlds might reasonably connect.

Over 40 percent of the scientists I asked believed that religion could play some positive role on university campuses.[8] Analyzing their collective thoughts provides us with new models of how religion could be part of university life in a way that stimulates discovery, enriches students, and benefits the eventual public transmission of science.

NEW UNIVERSITY MODELS FROM THE VOICES OF SCIENTISTS

Scientists' models for how religion could be part of life on campuses vary in the level of legitimacy and necessity ascribed to religion. Those who think religion should be engaged mainly in a private way see the role of universities as funding chapels, campus ministries, and other resources to support students' personal expressions of faith.[9] This model springs from an understanding of the university as a place that provides emotional care for students.

Another way that religion can be considered legitimate is as a subject of study. This view is generated from a model of the university as a place where anything that influences the physical or human world is worthy of investigation. Even for these scientists, however, there are academic boundaries within which religion ought to remain. If religion is an object of study, it should be studied only in religion departments.

A minority of scientists (less than 20 percent) think that religion can meaningfully intersect with their particular research and with the education of their students. They see religion as important to science ethics and as potentially helpful in guiding research questions. This model comes from a view of education and research as having multiple knowledge sources, including religion as one of these sources. A perception of discrimination can also accompany this view; those scientists who think religion is both important as a form of knowledge and as a compelling belief system say they sometimes experience bias in their universities.

THE MODEL OF NURTURE: UNIVERSITIES OUGHT TO NURTURE STUDENTS—INCLUDING SPIRITUALLY—IN THEIR FORMATIVE YEARS

Most of the 42 percent of scientists I interviewed who thought there could be some positive role for religion on campuses specifically mentioned universities supporting the private expression of religion. Their examples of support ranged from tolerance (not standing in the way of personal religious expression) and symbolic support, to universities providing money, space, and personnel to the organizations that undergird religious life on campus. This latter view relates directly to a model of university life that stresses the role of universities as providing care for their members in arenas of life not directly related to scholarship. The rationale endorses exercise facilities, for example, to take care of the physical body, as well as chapels and religious programs to care for students of faith.[10]

Those who feel strongly that religion ought to be an important, personal part of people's lives also support universities going to great lengths, including financial support, to make sure that there is an active religious life on campus. This might include supporting student religious organizations; allowing students to have religious holidays off; providing centers, chapels, and chaplains; and making sure that the legal structure of the university enables individual faculty and students to follow their moral religious convictions.[11]

A psychologist,[12] a Quaker with some Buddhist practices for whom belief in God is not central, remarked, "Universities are charged with taking care of students in their formative years." Clearly something of a bibliophile, he talked with me about Hermann Hesse's *The Glass Bead Game*, a novel about an elite group of intellectuals who play an elaborate game that relies on cultural and scientific knowledge. He mentioned that "[Hesse] talks about the academy being a sort of priesthood or a spiritual pursuit where everyone is seeking, and they are turning it all toward scholarly endeavors." This scientist agrees that this is what the university should be. Religion ought to be included—and even to some extent protected—in university life, because it is an important source of comfort and meaning for students and faculty.

A physicist[13] I spoke with perhaps best captured this view of religion as a legitimate private pursuit deserving of nurture. A named-chair associate professor at a private school in the Northeast, she said that religious expression in universities ought to be protected at the same level as other "lifestyle things that we as a university do. . . . We provide an athletic facility for the athletes; we should provide some religious outlet for the religious or a safe space for the gay and lesbian students. I think it's in that realm." A political scientist[14] echoed these views, emphasizing the still-tender ages of university students: "Part of what a university does is serve as a parent to the children involved. . . . That might [mean] accommodating various formal religions."

THE MODEL OF LEGITIMACY: UNIVERSITIES OUGHT TO EXTEND LEGITIMACY TO RELIGION AS A SUBJECT OF STUDY

Nearly all of the scientists who think there is some legitimate place for religion on university campuses (and even many who don't) mentioned the specific role of religious studies departments and the legitimacy of religion as a subject of study. They find it important to provide education about the world history of religion or religious traditions within the United States.

A chemist,[15] a conservative Jew who believes in God as a "very far away entity," suggested that religion could be taught "from a number of different angles, from a historical, social developmental, from a philosophical analysis of the . . . ethical frameworks presented by different religions, from a literary perspective—I think it's great that all of these possibilities are available." A biologist[16] had a similar perspective but also cautioned that religion must not become more than a subject of study. This Unitarian, a distinguished named-chair professor at a state university on the East Coast, thinks that religion is a very important topic of study for a broad understanding of society. In his words, "I consider it a quite legitimate topic for academic study—no doubt about that. It's impossible to understand [the] history of the world or society without taking a close look at religion. It's got a huge effect on all kinds of things."

The Model of Legitimacy, however, is not without consequences to religion. Historian Darryl Hart and sociologist Nancy Ammerman argue that by relegating the study of religion only to religious studies departments, those in other disciplines are often allowed to ignore the relationship of religion to their own disciplines.[17] And I found evidence to support this scholarly assertion. Some of the scientists I interviewed clearly thought that religion ought to be a subject of study in religious studies departments in order to insulate it from science. In one sense, they hold religion legitimate enough to warrant its own department. In another sense, as with some of the colleagues we met in the last chapter, they generally consider religion dangerous to the free intellectual pursuit of science on university campuses. So while they don't see religion as totally without value, it's a value they want absent from their own departments.

A chemist[18] explained that he certainly thinks religion ought to be a subject of study in universities—and also surrounded by rigid boundaries. This scientist, who is a professor at a large midwestern state school, is very interested in issues of public science and mentioned writing an op-ed piece against the teaching of intelligent design in schools. He would "like to see [religion] constrained to a defined field of study":

> Just like intelligent design should be taught in religion classes, there should be a department of religion on a campus, and they can teach sophisticated classes on all aspects of religion and spirituality. I don't think it has any place . . . in science departments. I suspect that religion intersects with . . . humanities and social sciences, and that ranges from [the] field of sociology all the way to art. Religion and having courses related to religion is very important in those fields, but I just don't see a need for religion in the science curriculum at all.

THE MODEL OF CONNECTED KNOWLEDGE: UNIVERSITIES OUGHT TO SUPPORT THE CONNECTION OF RELIGIOUS KNOWLEDGE TO OTHER FORMS OF KNOWLEDGE

About 10 percent of the scientists I interviewed who see a positive role for religion on campuses also think that faith insights can meaningfully connect with their own actual scholarship. Some believe they have a responsibility to talk about these connections in broader university contexts. Because they study human behavior, the social scientists are more likely than are their natural-science peers to think that religion ought to be part of their particular discipline. A political scientist[19] who is a Catholic said, for example, that religion often has an impact on the kinds of phenomena examined in her discipline. She goes to a Catholic church about once a month and is more attached to the overall values and community of the church than its biblical tenets. In her opinion, religion "should be discussed. . . . As social scientists, we're talking about how individuals interact and how societies form, how politics work, and religion is a defining force." This view echoes the ideas of historian George Marsden, who in his somewhat controversial *The Outrageous Idea of Christian Scholarship* argues that faith-informed scholarship should have more of a place at the table of dialogue within the American university. Marsden urges Christian scholars to take bold initiative in connecting their beliefs to their specific disciplines while at the same time playing by the rules of their particular guilds. While a few of the social scientists I talked with struggled with what it might look like to follow Marsden's suggestion, it was nearly impossible for the natural scientists to figure out what it would mean to have their faith traditions or ideas about spirituality influence what they do as scientists. (Those who said their faith influences their science or the transmission of their science were adamant that they do not have different ideas than their nonreligious colleagues about the scientific method.) But a plurality of scientists think religion might be helpful in dealing with complex ethical issues, citing examples that ranged from avoiding misrepresentation of data to human genetic engineering.[20]

Ethan[21] is a biologist. I talked with him in his office in a cancer research center attached to a hospital on his campus. Filling the building of elaborate corridors and stark white walls were people in hospital scrubs and white lab coats. Ethan had the door to his office open, and I could see him typing on his computer. As I knocked and entered, he quickly stood up and reached out to shake my hand. I was immediately struck by how casually Ethan was dressed, given all of the white coats I had just seen. He was wearing khaki shorts, a batik-print shirt, and fisherman sandals. His long hair was pulled back into a pony-tail. Taped to the wall directly above his computer were three postcard-size pictures of Jesus Christ. One was of a painting of the Christ child, another was Christ with the disciples, and another was Christ with Mary. Children's artwork was also taped on the walls, and several works of fiction—including *The Brothers Karamazov*—had found a place amid lab notebooks and biology texts. Ethan had a somewhat cynical and reticent tone at the beginning of the interview, but as we talked, he loosened up considerably.

Ethan thinks that religion can help scientists deal with controversial issues. In his role as a professor, he is interested in teaching graduate students "how to think about what science is and how to do science." He compared his approach to science education at his university with that of some of his colleagues, indicating that his approach is different from just "distributing facts to [students]," which his colleagues seem to focus on. He went on: "Because it's not really that difficult to find any sort of fact you want nowadays. Anybody can go learn about a topic pretty quickly on their own, but actually thinking about the discipline and what you're supposed to be doing in science is a very difficult problem." Ethan gave the analogy of an engineer who wants to build a bridge. The engineer, if he has the plans, the materials, and the people to help him, knows when he is finished. But the work of a research scientist is different; it's extremely open-ended. There are no clear-cut blueprints for building a bridge. There are not even exact bridges in need of building. Instead, science at a university involves teaching students to think beyond their own research. For Ethan, this includes teaching them how to apply science, how to communicate it to a broader audience, how to think about science from "some sort of moral and ethical standpoint."

But the biology department where Ethan works does not seem so interested in these broader issues of public science. He thinks his department ought to change and make faculty take more responsibility for teaching students about communicating science to the public. But because he is only an assistant professor, he feels particularly constrained, unable to give his true opinions. He tries instead to effect change in more subtle ways. For example, he will not directly give students or colleagues his opinions on embryonic stem cell research. But he might direct them to a lecture on campus, perhaps by a law professor who deals frankly with the issue. When I asked Ethan why he feels so constrained, he said that it's because his campus is an "amazingly homogeneous environment." When I asked Ethan what he meant, he responded rather emphatically: "Everything. Politically. Religiously. Everything. It's amazing. It really is. I never would have believed it, but it really is. You certainly have pockets of people [who are different] on any big campus, but overall, particularly at the faculty level, the homogeneity is just amazing." Ethan talked about being in a faculty meeting and other faculty making comments about politics or religion with "just the assumption that everybody there absolutely agrees with them, and they really have no idea."

So instead of rocking the boat, Ethan simply invites his colleagues and students to attend lectures about public science with him: "It gives the students a chance to see how some of the real basic research has very big policy implications." Ethan cares a lot about helping students understand the different perspectives on controversial issues such as embryonic stem cell research. As we spoke, he gave an indictment of his colleagues: "Scientists are notoriously bad about caring anything about this. . . . The vast majority of them don't think there's any issue with stem cell research. It's just inconceivable to them that there could be any sort of important philosophical or ethical questions." He commented that this kind of attitude can have dire consequences, saying it's "the same mind-set that developed the atomic bomb."

Informing Choice of Subject Matter

The natural and social scientists in my sample differed sharply on the question of whether religion should or even could actually inform the choice of subject matter in universities: what faculty taught, how they did experiments, and the kinds of research questions they engaged. Even social scientists who were not particularly religious said that religion sometimes informs their subject matter. One sociologist,[22] whose religious activity consists of going to synagogue on special occasions, nevertheless thinks that religion could easily inform the choice of subject matter in the social sciences. He said that choices of subject matter rarely proceed logically from existing social research—as he perceives they do in the natural sciences. In his opinion, something has to motivate a choice of topic, and social scientists ought to be more self-conscious about such motivating factors: "The reason we study things, choose things to study, has to be motivated by something. And probably [for some], what motivates it is religious faith." He brought up Max Weber, one of sociology's founders, and his ideas about choosing research questions. According to Weber, what a social scientist chooses to study has to be ultimately based on values, though the methods of the study should be value-neutral and uniform within the discipline. A religious reason would be just as good as any other reason for choosing a subject of study.[23] A political scientist[24] who described himself as a cultural Jew who attends services regularly said that beyond religion being a subject of study, religion might inform how individuals decide what is important to them in "guiding the research" they do. According to him, a distinction ought to be made between how religion might be "informing what we study but not the conclusions that we come to." Such social scientists think that reflecting on how the choice of research topic is informed by a researcher's personal values is all part of doing good research. And they think that discussions about such values should happen more often than they do. These scientists who want to reflect on how their values inform their work would benefit from the increasing number of interdisciplinary centers for the study of religion on many campuses.

Structural Supports for Interdisciplinary Study of Religion

Religion scholars John Schmalzbauer and Kathleen Mahoney argue that the social movement to bring religion back to the academy involves increased social and institutional supports for religion. And one sign of this trend is the growing presence of cross-disciplinary centers that engage in discussion about religion.[25] Examples include the Center for the Study of Religion at Princeton University, the Center for Religion and Civic Culture at the University of Southern California, and the Center for the Study of Science and Religion at Columbia University. A sociologist[26] who finds himself occasionally "tapping into spiritual power" mentioned that the active presence of such a center at the university where he teaches helped him to realize how central religion is to many people's lives—and just how much those in academia have generally ignored it. Some directors of centers that focus on the academic study of religion in the social sciences are, in many ways, boundary pioneers through the work they do to foster interdisciplinary dialogue about religion. And more and more, this dialogue involves natural scientists as well. Still, recognition of the centers' legitimacy can be slow in coming. For example, although I interviewed numerous scientists at Columbia University, which houses a center specifically devoted to dialogue about religion and science, I can count on one hand the number of scientists who mentioned Columbia's center or any other center or initiative to foster discussion about the topic.[27]

PERCEPTIONS OF RELIGIOUS DISCRIMINATION

Grammy Award-winning rapper Kanye West sings "Jesus Walks":

> They say you can rap about anything except for Jesus
> That means guns, sex, lies, video tapes
> But if I talk about God my record won't get played Huh?[28]

Although a world away from the lives of most scientists at top universities,[29] West's lyrics characterize the tension some scientists say they face in the world of academics. The relatively few scientists who are open with students and colleagues about their faith lives said that they sometimes experience discrimination. It is important to discuss these perceptions of religious discrimination and how to address it, since fear can limit the extent to which faculty are willing to talk about issues related to science and faith. For example, about 8 percent of natural scientists I surveyed said that they had at some point been discriminated against because of their religious beliefs. And about 12 percent of social scientists gave the same answer. About 43 percent of all scientists disagreed to some extent with the statement, "The scholars in my field have a positive attitude towards religion."[30]

Geraldine[31] is a sociologist who thinks there is some religiously based discrimination on university campuses. She has a bachelor's degree in math and became interested in the social sciences during her college years. At the time, she was involved in Vietnam War protests and issues of social justice. She wanted to use her math background to improve what she viewed as some very poor social science research.

Geraldine said that although she does sometimes experience religious discrimination, she also has positive informal discussions about religion with students. Students know that she is a Catholic and so will sometimes come to talk to her about religious issues. For example, a non-Catholic graduate student who was engaged to a Catholic once scheduled a meeting to talk with Geraldine about her faith. One of her colleagues is an ordained Baptist minister, and they have often discussed how angry the religious right makes both of them. Additionally, her department chair is a nonreligious Jew, and Geraldine has occasionally had discussions with him about religion.

But based on her interactions with colleagues, Geraldine has concluded that "in academia in general, . . . there is substantial hostility against people who are religious and especially against Catholics." She explained that at a cookout for her research institute, the wife of one of her colleagues gave her a "look of horror" when she discovered Geraldine is a practicing Catholic. Her faith became known broadly among her colleagues, however, when her husband died and they attended his Catholic funeral.

Prayer and belief in God are both very important to Geraldine. She is a Eucharistic minister at her church, but she does not find it necessary to adhere to all of the Church teachings; she is even somewhat critical of both the previous pope and the current one. She is a member of an organization called Voice of the Faithful, which attempts to grant laity more influence in the Catholic Church, and she speaks highly of a statement released by Catholic members of the House of Representatives that expressed a need to address issues of poverty and social justice. Her commitment to these issues and her reasons for researching them are influenced by her religious faith. The discrimination Geraldine experiences is informal, such as when a colleague expresses disdain for her strong religious views, so in her case it could be better described as suppression. It does not seem to make Geraldine want to abandon all discussions about faith while she is at work.

Others mentioned more systemic and institutional forms of discrimination, however. A psychologist[32] I interviewed "grew up in a very scientific household" in Salt Lake City, Utah. Even though the city was largely Mormon in influence, religion wasn't present in his life, and he became somewhat hostile to Christianity because of the hypocrisy he saw. His academic parents talked about religion mainly in terms of "Jesus was a good man, and some people think very highly of him." He explained that being a religious person is not looked upon favorably in the world of science, and it can result in dire consequences. After all, colleagues hostile to religion often have the ability to bring about professional sanctions. "There is this perception that if you are doing research and you are a religious person that you are probably biased to some extent," he explained. "Being religious is perceived as being flaky, at least in the field of psychology." This psychologist raised an important issue: How do those who want to be more open to university dialogue about the connections between religion and science—particularly those who are religious—overcome the perception that their science is tainted? Such a concern was particularly acute at the beginning of my study because of the backlash against religion in the academy brought on by the intelligent design movement. Even those I interviewed two years after the *Kitzmiller v. Dover* intelligent design court case in 2005 thought that what their colleagues perceive as antiscience sentiment from religious people makes it more difficult for religious scientists to talk about their own faith.

A psychologist,[33] a practicing Jew who teaches at a private school, mentioned in different ways throughout our discussion that his connection to God plays an important role in his life. But at his particular university, he sees "some stifling antireligious stuff on occasion." For him, this backlash is as upsetting as "people trying to proselytize in the classroom." Stifling discussions about religion is academically dangerous, he believes, because there are "plenty of topics where [religion] really is relevant, and we ought to be able to go into detail, even if you're not in religious studies." As one whose scholarship deals with how people recover from drug addictions and abuse, he finds that religion and spirituality are often key to how those in recovery understand their process toward wholeness. Thus it ought to be a central part of what he teaches in his classes. This psychologist contrasts himself with many colleagues in his field, who ignore religion's obvious influence in this research setting because of their personal bias. "Plenty of people teach classes like that and don't discuss it at all, and I just feel like there's so much fear about, 'Oh, I'm going to insult someone or be accused of teaching religion.'" He went on to say that "anything . . . beyond empirical approaches is taboo in the classroom." He blamed some of this lack of discussion on those in his field "who think all religion is irrational."

As discussed in Chapter 2, many scientists have a restricted code based on shorthand stereotypes of religion and religious people.[34] The sociologist[35] mentioned above (the one whose religious activity consists of going to synagogue on special occasions) explained that when his faculty colleagues say negative things about religion, they are not really outraged by religion per se so much as they are concerned about "religious political movements that they see as the enemy." He elaborated:

> People will talk about, "Oh those crazy fundamentalists are doing such and such," and the threat that poses, and "are they seeping into trying to control the university," or "are they trying to control the government," or "are they taking over the world?" So it's not that they're religious, it's just that they're seen as being from an enemy religious movement.

Sadly, to have a conversation like the one this sociologist described be the only one that occurs in a science department about religion can mischaracterize all religious people as being "crazy fundamentalists."

And scientists with faith said that such stereotypes about religious people sometimes make it difficult to be open on their campuses about matters of faith. True to character, however, the boundary pioneers find ways to specifically overcome this difficulty in the broader university. In *People of Faith*, sociologist John Schmalzbauer documents the various ways that religious elites in the social sciences and journalism (two professional arenas that scholars view as particularly secular) maintain a distinctive religious identity and a commitment to their profession. While acknowledging the obstacles Catholics and evangelicals face in expressing religious convictions in professional arenas, Schmalzbauer also challenges the claims of secularization theory and argues that even the "quintessential enlightenment professions"[36] of the media and social sciences are more open to religious expression than previously realized.

Similarly, I talked with a chemist[37] who is a fairly outspoken Christian on his campus, having converted to Christianity in his mid fifties. He said he maintains his religious identity in both subtle and overt ways. For example, he makes it comfortable for a student to talk about a religious vocation, mentioning that some students have come up to him and told him that they want to go to seminary after they finish their undergraduate work. Another student decided to leave graduate school to work with an organization that creates translations of the Bible for indigenous people who don't have it in their own language. And he told a story of a woman with breast cancer, a colleague, who came to visit him, and they prayed together. He is involved in a religious group for faculty and staff, and his openly religious presence seems to foster more open thinking and talking about religion in his department. He gave me one such example: "Our Nobel Prize winner . . . said as we were walking along not too long ago, 'I say daily prayers every day just before I go to bed, just like my mother taught me.' He's not a believer." He laughed, "As far as I could tell before that moment!"

This chemist is, however, greatly troubled by the way religious opposition to science is sometimes handled on university campuses. He agrees with those who think that intelligent design theory is "not good science," but he says that religious challenges to science "really frighten university professors, and then they respond in a way that is anti-intellectual." After struggling with his words for over 12 seconds—a long time in a personal conversation—he said, "At times they are really anti-Christian or anti-Jewish as well, or anti-Islam." While he did not think those on his campus are overtly antireligious, religion seems to be acceptable only as long as no one talks about it, as long as it remains closeted. He thinks of it as a kind of "don't ask and I won't tell you" policy. He then mentioned that if you do talk about your faith, "people think you're nuts, actually—a lot of people—if you really step out." He does talk about issues of faith whenever he can, however, because "you can't deny who you are." He explained that is why he wants to be associated with other Christians on campus.

Like this chemist, other scientists also thought that antireligious sentiment—and particularly anti-Christian sentiment—could be rectified on campus if faculty were more willing to talk about their own beliefs. A biologist[38] who, although he considers himself Catholic, attends a nondenominational church with his family, told me that he thinks most of his colleagues are nonreligious and even hostile toward religion. On a few rare occasions, a colleague in the sciences has tried to convince him to reject his faith. He said with a tone of laughter in his voice that it's a "sort of a fun kind of activity for them, you know, to try to put religion down and then to get me to renounce it." He thinks that religion is almost uniformly viewed as something conservative, and because most of his colleagues are liberal, he reasons, they might be more reluctant to talk about religion or their attitudes toward it. From his perspective, "the academy in general is biased in a negative way toward religion. Students are a lot less biased toward religion than faculty. And, you know, the faculty bias in general kind of bothers me." He sees this bias as detrimental to learning. In his words, "At the academy, we're supposed to be open-minded—as open-minded, as objective, as possible. And that's not always the case."

Both religious and nonreligious scientists mentioned that when antireligion biases make their way into public arenas on university campuses, students might feel fearful of talking about religion in academic settings. According to a physicist[39] with no religious identity, "Getting students to talk about religion is an important part of their instruction in a university setting." He considers religion so fundamental to the larger academic purposes of the university that "it ought to be something everybody talks about—personally and even professionally. . . . That is our job—to get our students to think and evaluate. And religion has to be a part of that—not just their own, but other people's." To ignore or suppress religion on university campuses, he believes, means denying students the possibilities of learning firsthand about a variety of religious traditions through the religious students, faculty, and staff in their midst. (This physicist is portraying perfectly here the Model of Connected Knowledge described earlier.)

Janice,[40] the physicist at a prestigious East Coast university whom we met in Chapter 3, believes in a personal, relational God. She believes God brings people together and that simple words like "I'll pray for you" can create an amazing connection between people. "I haven't found anybody who didn't appreciate that," she said gently. Janice also thought that religion ought to be more "freely discussed [on university campuses] than it is." But the recent controversies over intelligent design have made Janice even more reluctant to discuss religion with science colleagues. She explained, "I think academia is not always an accepting environment. And I think this intelligent design thing has made it a lot worse. It has made it really hard to be a religious academic, because they have polarized the public opinion such that you're either religious *or* you're a scientist!" Janice went on to say that to let others know that you are religious might undermine how colleagues view your academic work. When I asked her if she personally has experienced this sort of discrimination, she quickly added that she has not, because most other physicists do not know about her faith. But she wasn't content with this arrangement:

> I certainly don't think anybody should be preaching from the classroom. I certainly don't think anybody should be trying to convert anybody, but it's really a shame that [religion is] so taboo, because I think a lot of people are searching, and it would be much nicer if the students could see that the faculty are human and do have their various traditions. . . . There are probably quite a few more [religious people] than I think. . . . But everybody keeps it so quiet. And that's really unfortunate, especially from the point of view of the students who are trying to figure out who they are. . . . They have virtually no role models who are successful academics and religious.

When I asked her what she would do if she could change things, Janice thought for a while and then said, "There are a few brave souls who will give talks that show that they're religious." She mentioned with a degree of cynicism, "It's so funny, because I think for students we have all of these diversity-type programs or cultural awareness programs or be-nice-to-your-neighbor programs, and I almost feel like the faculty needs one. I think there's not a lot of respect for religious diversity among the faculty. . . . If those of us who are religious weren't so afraid of the disrespect of our colleagues, maybe it would be easier to be an outward role model." But she finds this to be particularly difficult for faculty who are not yet tenured (and thus lack job security), because for them, the approval of their colleagues is all the more important. So, perhaps a future boundary pioneer, Janice continues for now in her closeted faith.

WHAT'S AT STAKE?

In Chapter 6, we examined three dominant models of elite university life: Opposition, Secularism, and Pluralism. We saw that some scientists (particularly religious ones) have felt pressured by these models to keep their faith secret or at least separate, and sometimes even suppressed. In this chapter we have heard the voices of the significant minority of scientists who are religious—and of their sympathetic nonreligious colleagues—who harbor a vision of what could be instead: the models of Nurture, Legitimacy, and Connected Knowledge. But, we discovered, even these models have serious consequences for universities. Relegating religion to the personal sphere (Nurture) or to only a distinct department (Legitimacy) has actually been counterproductive for dialogue between religion and science, providing scientists ample reason to ignore religion altogether. Religion becomes something outside what sociologist Andrew Abott calls a "professional jurisdiction," the framework by which professionals decide which topics are relevant to their work. It is left entirely to university chaplains and campus ministers rather than being part of the purview of scientists themselves, especially those who are not religious.[41] This smoothes things over for a while but finally leaves scientists without rhetorical or other resources to engage with religion in diverse university settings where it inevitably comes up publicly.

Consequently, while some scientists think that universities ought to provide support for students to practice religion privately, such as through a functioning chapel or a dean of religious life, they often know amazingly little about the resources that their universities already employ along these lines. The scientists are themselves generally uninvolved in campus religious life. Though religious scientists tended to be involved in faith communities outside their universities, this does little to foster dialogue on campus for the good of science—and of the students of science.

A plurality of scientists think that to shy away from discussing religion on university campuses is to risk educating students improperly. Like proponents of the Model of Pluralism, they believe that universities should promote inter-cultural understanding and tolerance. But they stress that teaching students how to openly talk about the connection between religion and science is part of the university's mission to promote these pluralistic values, and so they more accurately fit the Model of Connected Knowledge. Tobin,[42] an economist we have met before, said that he would like to think that the university is moving in a direction where the actual "antagonism between religion and academics goes away." He mentioned that at his university in the Southeast, they "say a lot about diversity and an appreciation of diversity, but there is this underlying sense that religion is a sort of fiction to be explained by science." Tobin thinks that such views lead to the stifling of religious students and scholarly discussions about religion: "A lot of students certainly sense that if they are religious, they'll be viewed as not as smart as their nonreligious colleagues." When asked about the place that religion ought ideally to occupy in universities, he said that schools such as his "ought to be respectful of religion and open in more than words to the possibility that one can be both religious and a scientist or an intellectual."

A conversation with a political scientist,[43] who described herself as a cultural Jew, provides some instruction for Tobin and other scientists about how to move forward in having conversations about religion on campus. For her, talking about religion is similar to talking in a civil manner about other topics. She provides her students with tools for discussing any controversial issue that people might take personally, and she takes teaching time to do so. She explains, "People have to take responsibility for the ways in which their beliefs and values affect other people." She advocates having "discussions and debates about how we might better address the kinds of things that religion brings up," because this would be better for science and the academic world in general.

When it comes to building arenas and providing forums, it might be important for elite schools to lead the dialogue on where it is actually useful for religion and science to intersect and where it is less so. As sociologists of science have demonstrated time and again, *elite* scientists have the distinct role of creating the contours of science for the next generation. According to Bruno Latour, scientists at the top of their professions are the ones with the power and the resources. They are the ones who are building the labs, forming the networks that guide science, and publishing the seminal works that other scientists read.[44] As such, scientists who work at top universities have the ability to chart public discussion surrounding religion and science for the other universities in their organizational field and within the institution of higher education at large.

Some of the scientists I interviewed even thought that public funding of universities could be at stake if individual scientists do not learn how to better interact with religious people and religious ideas on their campuses. A physicist[45] who is a nonpracticing Jew said, in an echo of the views of Sylvester Gates Jr. quoted at the beginning of this chapter, "The academy is really doing itself a big disservice in the way it interacts with religion." He remarked that the "hostility of the academy to people of religious beliefs, at least particular certain subsets of people with religious beliefs, is bad. . . . In the long term, it's damaging for the academy." I pressed him to elaborate, and he continued: "People in the academy want to be listened to. They want their opinions to amount to something." This physicist said, however, that some of the work that is being done by academics in the name of scholarship is not really worth funding, and such work makes universities less appealing to the general public. He gave the example of Peter Singer, the Ira W. DeCamp Professor of Bioethics at Princeton University. Mentioning perhaps Singer's most extreme view, he said that Singer has "been saying infanticide is acceptable under some circumstances.[46] I mean maybe an academic can justify that, because he can write that in a fancy paragraph. But to any level-headed human being, it doesn't matter what kind of paragraph you can write. It's simply wrong and that's the end of it." Singer's views, according to this physicist, are indicative of why the public might lose faith in the academy. Before he went on, he stopped to ask, "Are you a disciple of Singer's, by the way?" After saying that I do not know Singer personally, I asked, "Do you have any solutions or any sort of working ideas about how scientists or academics in general can better translate their work to a broader public?" He did not seem to be able to answer that specific question but went on, "I think the risk that the academy puts itself in is that people will stop supporting [the aspects of it] that they don't like." In his sense of things, the best way to avoid such a withdrawal of support from the general public is for the academy to better reflect the diversity of thought that exists in the country, saying, "the only diversity they [academics] don't like is intellectual diversity. The other diversities are fine." He ended this part of our conversation by giving me something of a thought experiment: "So in the end, I could imagine 10 years from now that citizens of [my state] are even further fed up than they are now and they vote to run the referendum. They'll try to govern the university." This scientist brings up the important role that the general public plays in funding universities and connects this public power to the need for scientists to take the broad variety of religious views of the public more seriously.

Is there room for meaningful dialogue about religion and science on the campuses of our nation's elite universities? Nearly 50 percent of academic scientists have a religious identity, and the majority are interested in spirituality. These scientists are potentially crucial commentators and mentors to students who are searching for ways to make meaningful connections between religion and science. But most religious scientists see their faith mainly manifesting through their willingness to spend more time caring about students' personal needs. Although positive, such a role is a limited and even secretive one. So such scientists are only rarely engaging students in meaningful dialogue about their faith, to the point where students often cannot even tell that these scientists are religious. And this suggests a split religious or spiritual identity (along public and private lines), where scientists perform one way outside the university and another way within it.[47] Because of their unwillingness to talk about their own views on religion and spirituality, scientists with faith could be partly to blame for uninformed conversations about religion and science on university campuses. To go forward with such a split identity can lead to religious scientists abdicating their unique and important role in the lives of their religious students of science.

One task of all science professors is to educate citizens who are capable of using their knowledge in a variety of public environments. A particular calling for religious scientists might be to foster dialogue about religion and science more broadly on their campuses, encouraging students to think through and reevaluate the frameworks with which they were raised, equipping them as ambassadors of scientific knowledge within their own faith communities. Such an initiative would be a forceful step toward waging peace on the science-and-religion battleground and advancing the public transmission of science.[48]

CHAPTER 8

What Scientists Are Doing Wrong That
They Could Be Doing Right

What concerns me about this perception . . . of science and religion going head-to-head . . . . It's like there's two monologues going on. I don't really feel like it's a dialogue between scientists and people who want to see . . . religion taught in a science class. There are just two monologues. People are not talking to each other very well.

—A forty-year-old chemist

Astronomer Carl Sagan, author of *Cosmos*, wrote in a 1989 article in *Parade* magazine, "Ignorance of science threatens our economic well-being, national security, and the democratic process. We must do better."[1] Twenty years later, how are scientists confronting this national ignorance that Sagan warned us about—especially when it comes to engaging a largely religious general public? In this chapter, we move beyond classrooms and universities to examine how scientists see themselves as addressing religion-science controversies in their interactions with the rest of the U.S. populace. After 275 interviews with scientists, I found that their responses fell along a continuum from nonintervention to active outreach.

Most nonreligious scientists view religion as a generally negative force in society. Some think scientists should not waste their precious research time talking about issues of science and faith with the public, that religious America will never be won over to science and scientific understanding. Many talk cynically about religiously committed Americans, whom they see as a threat to scientific research and science education.

Others are eager to connect with the public about religion and faith but disagree about how best to do it. And those who think that imparting better scientific understanding to members of the American public is a central goal for scientists are sometimes at a disadvantage. That over 50 percent of scientists currently identify with no religious tradition means they have little ongoing interaction with religious people and communities. As discussed in Chapter 5,

127

this lack of experience leaves some without any cultural script and others with a negative cultural script when talking about the connection between religion and science. In other words, they either don't know what language to use in discussing religious issues or the language they do use ("crazy fundamentalists!")[2] is hardly productive.

Enter the other half of scientists at elite research universities, those who do identify with a religious tradition in some way. The ones who are the most religious sometimes see themselves as having a special responsibility to help religious people better understand that religion and science do not *have* to be in conflict. Even those who want to pursue this role sometimes still lack a language to build bridges with nonscientists who share their faith. After talking with scientists about these issues for over three years, I've concluded that such a language is urgently needed.

Here I synthesize the voices of scientists themselves as they comment on this role in shaping public understanding of the relationship between science and religion. If that is a goal, scientists first need to develop a more intricate language and set of frameworks for religion and for the relationship between religion and science—regardless of whether they personally identify with a religious tradition. Here we both examine the impediments to scientists taking a role in shaping public understanding of possible science-religion intersections and shed light on some of the best practices in which individual scientists are already engaged.

FEAR OF RELIGION IN PUBLIC SCIENCE

One serious impediment to fostering more open dialogue on questions of science and religion is the current fear among scientists about how religion might endanger science. To the extent that they talked about how scientists ought to respond to religion in the public sphere at all, some 75 percent of scientists mentioned specific ways that religion could have a negative impact on science and science education. A majority of scientists mentioned the role religion has played in popular resistance to the teaching of evolutionary theory in the public school systems.

Whereas scientists have not traditionally had to talk much about religion at work, conditions of environmental push—that is, positive or negative pressure from outside the university on the boundaries between religion and science—have caused many social and natural scientists to begin to discuss religion fervently. For example, a psychologist[3] who works in physiology and human biology at his university mentioned that religion generally has not come up much in his field. But with the increase in debate around intelligent design and other public issues related to religion and science, scientists have started to talk about religion a lot more. In his words, for religion to come up, it has "to be prompted by something, so recently there's been a flurry around the intelligent design issue." He does not think that religion will "ever go away." He continues to find this disconcerting in some ways, because for him and other scientists, "who are just astonished at the progress of science and how much we learn every day about science, to see that there's basically been no movement in the general population in this country is disconcerting. It says we're doing something wrong."

Scientists generally discussed the public impact of religion on science in unfavorable terms. Many hope that they will develop workable strategies not to engage science with religion but to protect science from it. I asked another psychologist,[4] who was raised Jewish although is not currently an observant Jew, what he thinks about the place of science in American society and whether he sees religion as generally a negative or positive force. His response was automatic: "I think negative." Another psychologist[5] said that religion seems to stifle free inquiry and be a serious impediment to the advancement of science. He also mentioned that those in his department have similar views: "You know we're the sort of standard godless bunch." Moving on to his perception of the impact that religion has on the advancement of science, he said, "One example is the stunning resistance to science that you find in many Americans." He thinks that such controversies move well beyond debates about earth origins, remarking that there is actually a "serious percentage of people in the United States who believe the sun revolves around the earth." He is concerned that many nonscientists do not seem to "take science as a serious force." Instead, he lamented, "they are socially cued into believing in matters of faith. And science is just nothing to them." Conversations about intelligent design seemed to make scientists feel downtrodden about their efforts to reach a broader public with science and about science education. Intelligent design and other controversies have made them much more hostile to the idea of religion rearing its head in any public setting.[6]

As scientists become more afraid of religion in the public sphere, they become insecure about their abilities to reach out to a religious public. For those like a biologist[7] who teaches at a private school (in a state where the majority of the citizens go to church more than once per month), it can be difficult to know how to respond well to religious challenges to science. He sees himself as an atheist, mentioning that there is "constant debate amongst all of us who are fighting creationism. It is true that most evolutionists, at least at the higher level of the sciences . . . are atheists, and the question is, do we hide our views?" He went on to say that the situation becomes particularly acute if part of scientists' role in the public transmission of science is to engage with religious people. "Suppose we don't have any respect for people who are religious, like I don't, for example," he pondered. He wondered aloud whether he ought to claim to have respect for religious ideas anyway, for the sake of public science. He wonders how he would respond in good conscience if people were to ask him if evolution and religion are compatible. On the one hand, he postulates that he could simply say, "Well, many people find them compatible, and that shows that they're compatible." On the other, if he were to be completely honest, he would say, "I think they're incompatible. You can hold them [both] as views, but I think you're being a hypocrite if you do that." At the end of the day, "There are two ways that you can answer that question. One of them will win you friends; the other one won't. But the second answer to me is more honest." This biologist brought up a serious impediment to engaging the general public with issues related to religion and science: If as a scientist you think that religion is the enemy and that religious people have nothing to offer, how can you then enter into productive dialogue with them? His colleagues might suggest that this scientist should at least develop a nuanced idea about religion. He is right that when compared to those in the general population, more of his fellow biologists at top research universities are atheists and are not a regular part of religious communities. He is mistaken, however, that there are almost no theists among his colleagues. (Over 30 percent of biologists at top universities actually have a firm belief in God.)

As discussed previously, scientists often have a limited vocabulary for talking about religion. This is evident in their unsubtle lumping together of the variations in religious belief. It is clear, for example, from listening to this biologist—and indeed most of the scientists who see religion as having a negative impact on science—that the religious threat they fear refers to a specific type of religion, fundamental Protestantism. For example, a chemist[8] mentioned that his babysitter is a "born-again Christian." He said that he and his colleagues talk often at conferences about the potential threat of this type of Christian (presumably he means fundamentalist) to the broader dissemination of science. Although he was raised a Catholic and is currently raising his children Catholic, this assistant professor, who teaches at a prestigious midwestern state university, explained that "these new Christians are a little too extreme. . . . They're pretty fanatical, and that's what worries us the most, that the sciences are going to have so many constraints that, for example, even funding for stem cell research" will be at risk. This chemist is a religious scientist himself, yet he did not offer another way—a more Catholic way, for example—of seeing the connection between religion and science. Instead, an "us versus them" mentality leaves little room for variations in religious belief.

WHAT SCIENTISTS ARE DOING WRONG

If scientists believe that religion in general and some forms in particular might be a threat to the advancement of science in the United States, then what are they specifically doing to engage with religion so that it does not halt the advancement of science? Now we hear from scientists (even some not religious) who—in response to their colleagues who are fearful of religion's threatening encroachment—would argue that the onus is ultimately on scientists themselves to advance the cause of public science through a more thoughtful dialogue with members of the general public.[9] They are quick to point out what their colleagues are doing wrong in this regard. And from listening to these public-minded scientists, we can develop a set of best practices that could change the toxic dynamic of current discussions.

Just Doing Science

Public-minded scientists criticized their colleagues, in particular, for being focused too much on "just doing science" rather than seeing as part of their job the spreading of science to a broader public, particularly a religious one. Their most common complaint could be typified by an excerpt from my discussion with a biologist,[10] who, when I asked him if he had any advice for scientists who want to reach out to a broader public, said, "I think scientists should be doing science." Some scientists I talked with would say rather critically that a biologist like this one should be using his position (at an Ivy League school) as a platform for convincing the general public about the value of science and science education.

A minority of the scientists I interviewed criticized their colleagues in a general sense for doing little to interact with the local and national communities outside their universities. They feel that scientists talk mainly to *one another* about issues of public science, leaving them with little direct familiarity with members of the public and little ability to relate to those outside of academia, especially when important religion-and-science issues come to the fore. The following is an example of what these public-minded scientists typically criticize: A biologist[11] I interviewed immigrated to the United States over 20 years ago, but his experience of living here since then has largely been restricted to "the academic community, the scientific community." His words shed light on the fact that often, scientists have little ongoing experience with the world outside the academy and with religion in particular—especially if they are not religious themselves. In addition, nearly 28 percent of natural scientists and 25 percent of social scientists are first- or second-generation immigrants. And about 16 percent of each group are not U.S. citizens. Cultural barriers and lack of experience with American religion make it much more difficult for them to get involved in U.S. politics or to be advocates for public science.

Some scientists think that they have essentially been left out in the cold by colleagues who are not willing to be involved in transmitting science more broadly. Another biologist[12] said that political debates are influencing his own discipline of biology, and the apathy on the part of other scientists really angers him. He said rather strikingly that he is "really pissed off at [his] colleagues for behaving like scientists, for behaving so arrogantly in response to [religious challenges to science]." Then I asked him to tell me what specifically he thinks his colleagues could be doing better:

> I would want them to try and sell science on its true merits, which is the skeptical improvement of all knowledge. That's what science is all about—resting it on the evidence. And the evidence is never perfect. Every fact can be overturned, and we all know this. But when it comes to talking publicly about creationism, . . . suddenly evolution is a fact, Darwin is completely right.

By this he means that scientists should be honest with the public about the uncertainties of science but that many aren't. "So they don't sell us, they don't put our best foot forward," he went on. "I think we should at least appear open-minded if we're not. That's the only way that you are going to win hearts and minds." Another biologist[13] virtually echoed these views with a sense of urgency in his voice: "We all feel some kind of need to communicate with the general public more than perhaps we have in the past. I think people are less willing to shy away from dealing with these issues now. . . . So it's a good idea that people are talking about it more." Scientists criticized their colleagues in very specific ways, challenging them to reorient their sense of what it means to be a scientist in a university setting and what their responsibilities are to the public.

We have heard the voices of scientists who think that religion in the general public is dangerous to science. We have heard the voices of those who think that scientists themselves ought to be doing more to engage nonscientists about issues related to religion and science. But what exactly should scientists be doing? Now we'll hear from some who have ideas about what their colleagues could do better to advance the cause of science among a religious public.

WHAT SCIENTISTS COULD BE DOING RIGHT

Contrary to the predictions of some, religion does not seem to be going away.[14] It has a tremendous ability to affect the public perception of science and is something about which all scientists should develop nuanced views. We might think of the dialogue scientists enter into with the public about issues of religion as having distinct stages—not hierarchical stages, wherein all scientists ideally proceed from one to the next, but stages where scientists might choose to enter and remain or to progress from one to the next, depending on their own backgrounds and propensities. These stages of dialogue might be named as follows:

Recognizing religious diversity. This base stage would be for scientists to recognize that there is a diversity of religious traditions and that different traditions intersect with science in distinct ways.

Recognizing the limits of science. In this stage, scientists could develop a willingness to discuss what science is and what it is not.

Active engagement. The third stage—especially for scientists who are religious—would be a willingness to talk publicly about the connections between their own faith and the work they do as scientists. This engagement would provide models for religious members of the public who might be otherwise unwilling to trust and endorse.

Recognizing Religious Diversity

While elite scientists have a very elaborate vocabulary for the subjects they deal with in their own particular fields and subfields, those without a religious identity (over 50 percent) have limited experience or limited ongoing interaction with religion and religious people. (Thirteen percent of scientists were raised with no religious tradition, and those who were raised in a religious home often saw religion practiced only weakly.) The first stage of effectively engaging religion and science, then, is to recognize the diversity in religious thought and practice. Just as not all biologists study the same biological system, not all religious people have the same beliefs or apply their beliefs in the same way. In addition, academic scientists will have to broaden and deepen their ideas about religion because of the increasing diversity of their own student populations. And it will be especially important to open a dialogue with the broader public about issues of religion and science because of the increasing diversity of the nation as a result of recent immigration. (More Hindus, Muslims, and Buddhists are coming to the United States, and Christian immigrants are changing the racial and ethnic composition of established American Christianity.)[15]

But these scientists who have little personal experience with religion often characterize it as what they see on the front page of the *New York Times* or *USA Today*. In their sense of things, religion equals white, Protestant fundamentalism. And their religious colleagues are critical of them for not recognizing the diversity in religious perspectives that exists both in their midst and within the broader public. Much antireligious sentiment, of course, comes from exposure to media coverage about the public challenges to science voiced by some branches of American evangelicalism. But public-minded religious scientists, in particular, think their colleagues still need to understand the variety of religious traditions that are in the broader world and stop promoting stereotypes about religious people.

Geraldine,[16] a sociologist we met in the last chapter, talked at length about this. She gave a story as an example of just how politicized she thinks public discussion of religion is:

> I think that in a social discourse, religion's place is extremely politicized, and it reminds me of this Algerian scholar I was talking [with] who was a very religious Muslim. He did a survey in Algeria [where] he was measuring Muslim religiosity by looking at whether people said they prayed five times a day. . . . He was looking at this related to other attitudes and political views about Islam. He found quite strong evidence that being a militant Islamist political-type person was not related to Muslim religiosity at all.

Geraldine's point was that because of political forces, many people misjudge the most militant Muslim as the most religious or devout, committed Muslim. She suspects that this same politicization might be happening in the United States: "There are a lot of people using religion to back their political views, and these folks may not be the most religious. This kind of religion may not be what it really means to be religious in the U.S." She thinks there needs to be more discussion in the public arena about religion. Such discussion would help her colleague scientists know that there is real diversity of thought among people of sincere faith.

A psychologist[17] I talked with would agree with Geraldine's sentiment. He thinks that those in his scholarly community also need to look at religion in a more nuanced way and that doing so would help them better translate their scholarship to a broader public. He mentioned that he is involved in a "lot of lefty groups" and described his discontent with some others in these groups.

> There's a lot of perception of fundamentalist folks, particularly in Texas actually [laughs], taking hold of the government and trying to impose religious views on others and things like that. . . . Organized religion is depicted as narrow-minded, intolerant. . . . So it really gets this bad rap, when in fact, folks I know who are connected to organized religions of almost every type are actually very warmhearted. . . . These generalizations end up hurting us.

An economist,[18] talking about the place of religion in the broader American public, explained that there are certainly places where it's a "negative force, but there are millions and millions of people who try to do good, and partly the reason that they do so is because of their religious teachings." He hoped that over time, these day-to-day genuine acts of kindness would have more impact than do the negative headline stories about religion.

Scientists thought that more ought to be done to dispel misconceptions that some in the general public have about the incompatibility of religion and science. A chemist[19] who is in her early forties and married to another chemist said that what is happening between science and religion in the broader public is troubling. She thinks that scientists need to do more to dispel the idea that religion and science are in conflict, which she called "defeatist" thinking. It makes her "cringe when [she] hears it": "I can't bend the observational facts that we see, but I can certainly find ways to interpret it that wouldn't be an anathema to what people believe in their faith." She calls herself spiritual but "can't say that I worship in a church or synagogue and that particular worship to a God is important to me." She is open-minded to religion and thinks that this is important, compared to "some flavors of religion and some people [who] interpret language that's 400 years old as though it were a complete and absolute truth." She thinks that an essential part of the work scientists must do to reach out to the religious in the general public is to help them know that there are scientists involved in religious communities, such as those she knows of who have managed to integrate their faith with their work as scientists. She mentioned, for instance, the Los Alamos National Laboratory, where there are many scientists who actively participate in worship communities. In her words, "There can be ways to bridge the gap. . . . Part of this is recognizing that there are various religious traditions with various approaches to science. And scientists and those in the general public need to recognize that science is not in conflict with all religious traditions." Bridging the gap, she believes, includes trying to "be as tolerant as possible to views that are unlike your own":

> [I talk] about it in my nonscience-major class, by offering views of how other people have learned science even when it conflicts with something maybe stated in a holy scripture and . . . provide students examples of how they've managed to do that. . . . I think we need to have more of a dialogue of how we resolve what's religion and what's science and how they are the same. I think we should talk more about how they are the same, but also how they're different.

Some feel that for social scientists in particular, not to take religion seriously is to fail to take seriously the subjects whom they are studying. A political scientist[20] had thought so much about the relationship between religion and science that I found it difficult not to abandon the role of researcher entirely and simply "just talk" about these issues. He thinks that in general, those in his field have not done a good enough job engaging with religion and that this is actually damaging to their research and to the cause of their discipline: "A failure to engage with religion, and failure to know religion, inhibits people who want to do serious work in certain areas. I suspect that people that don't take religious belief seriously can't possibly know the objects of their study."

Other scientists think that part of recognizing religious diversity is drawing attention to the positive role some religious institutions have had in society. For example, a physicist (astronomer)[21] in his late fifties who is not personally religious and has no firm belief in God mentioned that there are specific positive aspects of religion that include "social structures for people, engagement, belonging." His sense of the positive things that religion can offer also translated to religious communities: "Depending on the church, also, it can be a good intellectual self-evaluation, self-fulfilling experience." Echoing a similar kind of perspective, another physicist,[22] a professor in his late forties with two young children, remarked, "I've got a much more positive view I think than the average reader of *The New Yorker*." He works on an urban campus, and at one point, he had lived "downtown in a big, older, urban apartment," where he noticed firsthand the crucial role that religion can play in the infrastructure of a city. In his words, "organized religion is the only thing that has kept the big cities from completely burning down years ago." Recognizing the positive role of religion can act as something of an antidote to religion's less positive role. This physicist believes in Einstein's conception of God as one who "reveals Himself in the lawful harmony of the world,"[23] and said there is certainly "a lot of negativism about religion that focuses on extremists and misses its fundamental role in organizing." Other scientists, too, adopted the view that religion had things to add to American society. Such a view might help them more effectively engage with the broader public on issues concerning religion.

Religion also provides some scientists with important ethical guidelines, and they believe that being open about them might help the general religious public understand how some scientists utilize religion in thinking about the implications of their work. Although he does not believe in God, a biologist[24] I spoke with thinks that the "social aspects of religion" can "be very important." Another biologist,[25] who is not from the United States, said that religion often provides important ethical principles. "It is a positive force when it is used . . . as a guideline to make sure that people follow good ethical rules." This biologist had been strongly influenced by the Roman Catholic Church, and although he does not describe himself as Catholic, he does believe in God and that his actions and the way he lives his life are extremely important and will determine his fate after he passes. He thinks that "all religions . . . when interpreted the right way, have actually the best form of teaching for ethics, ethical behavior . . . which is probably one of the most important things that everybody should follow, especially in an academic environment." He contrasted this "best" form of religion with the way that religion is sometimes used in U.S. society as a way for religious people to "impose themselves, as opposed to a way to basically follow good ethical rules." He said that "unfortunately, very often the most vocal people are the ones who are the most influential."

In sum, publicly minded scientists believed that their colleagues' ignorance of religion, religious communities, and the potentially positive societal role of religious institutions complicates efforts toward positive interactions with religious people. They think that scientists who lack this understanding of the diversity within religion miss vital chances to create alliances that would mitigate the influence of extremist religious groups and increase public acceptance of science.

Recognizing the Limits of Science

Philosophers of science and scientists themselves have discussed what they call *scientism*, a disciplinary imperialism on the part of scientists that leads them to explicitly or implicitly assert that science is the only valid way to knowledge and that it can be used to interpret all other forms of knowledge.[26] Scientists who want their colleagues to do more to advance the public transmission of science—particularly those who think their colleagues are already doing an extremely poor job in this regard—mentioned rejecting scientism and developing a more publicly acceptable philosophy. Religion is of significant consideration in this view, because true scientism potentially disregards religion altogether. But scientists often feel that their colleagues should see religious ways of knowing as separate and even valuable distinctions from scientific ways.

I asked a political scientist,[27] a Catholic who teaches at an Ivy League school, whether he sees an inherent conflict between religion and science. He told me that he had invested a great deal in thinking about these issues and in particular, the relationships between religion, science, and the cultural transmission of science:

> I certainly don't think that there's any conflict between science and religion. I think . . . science aims at understanding the facts of the physical world. It has no direct concern with whatever lies beyond the physical world, the spiritual world. . . . I'm saying that science cannot establish certain key premises that are needed to navigate ethics.

His advice for scientists and others interested in the public transmission of science is that "science [should] not pretend to be able to solve spiritual or ethical problems and not pronounce on things that it has no authority to pronounce on." Because he has clearly thought about such things extensively, I asked him to explain what he means by limiting the expanse of science. He said he really wants to see people "reject the scientistic mentality as opposed to the scientific":

> Critics of this thing, scientism, define it as the idea that the only truths are those truths that are apprehended by the application of scientific methods, by empirical work. There are a lot of reasons why that can't be true, including the fact that it's self-defeating to assert it. That is, if the assertion of it is true, it can't be true on the basis of scientific methods, because scientific methods can't establish that. . . .. I want to be very critical of scientism, but I also want to be very science-affirming.

He wants everyone to see "science not as an enemy but as the truest of true friends. Even if the facts disclosed by science are uncomfortable." His words evoked a major philosophic criticism of those who try to say that scientific truth is the only truth. Such a claim, he insists, is one that science unaided by other forms of knowledge simply cannot make.[28]

Biologists, in particular, talked about having a responsibility to expound upon the limits of science and the proper place of science in relationship to religion, since their discipline often garners the most public criticism. A biologist[29] who teaches at a private university explained that he has a deist view of God and believes that a "watchmaker God . . . set everything up running by a set of rules and then stood back." A question I asked him regarding whether he believes there is a conflict between science and religion sparked him to talk about his efforts to dispel this very notion through his teaching. He thinks that, even outside the classroom, scientists should do more to talk about the limits of scientific knowledge with the broader public. He knows many good arguments for the idea that science and faith do not have to be at odds with one another. And he "can see where . . . religion is going to be built on an inherent level of faith, regardless of how much science you know, and it always has been, and it always will be." And he doesn't "see where science necessarily chips away at that at the end of the day." To him science and faith are separate kinds of endeavors. This plays very much into Stephen J. Gould's ideas of science and religion as nonoverlapping magisteria, that scientific thinking and practice are in one realm while religious thinking and practice are in another.[30]

Scientists talked about the ways in which science is deficient in helping to answer questions concerning the meaning of life. Another biologist,[31] in her mid thirties, addressed the limits of science when I asked how she would answer questions about the meaning of life:

> [Religion and science have] different operational values, but they are not at all incompatible. I mean the point of science is to select hypotheses and test them and try to reject them, and much of religion is actually about faith and applies to things that are not necessarily testable at all. So they seem to be really different realms of knowing to me.

Going back to the question of the meaning of life, she explained that this is indeed where "biology falls a little short." Pregnant with her first child, she felt that the purely biological answer to life's deepest questions was simply insufficient:

> We're here to make more copies of our genes, but I also believe that we—as humans with big brains and other capacities for ethical thought—have a much bigger responsibility than that. In fact, making as many copies as we can is probably just about the worst thing that we can do for our global responsibilities.

For this biologist, who teaches at a school in the West, there are other forms of knowledge besides science that need to enter into developing answers to questions on the meaning of life. She explained, "My ethical position on why we are here is . . . to make the world a better place. That's almost a direct quote from my grandfather."

Another biologist,[32] who said that he is not particularly spiritual but is a "sympathetic agnostic," explained that he has been "active on [his] own campus and in outreach in [his] community" to try and bring better science education to a broader public. He thinks scientists need to collectively "get before the public, that we need to teach good science and not cloud together science and religion." But part of this public science mission is to address concerns about the connections between science and religion sensitively. In particular, when he is teaching an introductory biology course, which includes teaching evolution, and students come up to him with religious concerns, he always tries to "handle those questions that they have as sensitively as possible." In his words, "I'm not interested in destroying anyone's faith."

ACTIVE ENGAGEMENT: TOWARD
BEST PRACTICES

Scientists advocating successful dialogue between religion and science need charismatic public spokespersons. Such spokespersons for successful dialogue could chart an agenda to let the American public know that science and religion need not conflict. These individuals must be legitimate in the scientific community yet outgoing and savvy enough to connect with nonscientists. Scientists I talked with used these individuals, whom I have called boundary pioneers,[33] as inspiration for how to successfully cross the boundaries between religion and science. Scientists said that those with religious faith could be especially crucial commentators when pushing for better dialogue between religion and science. Through witnessing the efforts of these boundary pioneers, a collective set of "best practices" can be developed for better engaging the general public on this topic. Here we examine some of the emerging practices that scientists themselves commend their colleagues for doing to promote better dialogue between scientists and members of the general public.

The biologist[34] mentioned just above, who was expecting her first child, said that "one of the greatest challenges of being human is to be faithful and also to be critical about science." She lamented that "there's so much . . . controversy . . . because there are people who can't find common ground." Scientists like her, who also think that their colleagues should do more to find common ground with the religious American public, feel that it could often be done by simply finding ways to interact more with religious people and religious structures. This is a particularly important practice for scientists who are themselves religious. The general public might better apprehend science if they know there are scientists with the same kinds of faith commitments that they have.

Involvement with Religious People and Communities

Although uncommon, a few of the scientists I talked with—especially those who are themselves very involved in religious communities—mentioned their own efforts to do more to engage with religion and religious people in intelligent ways. The biologist[35] described above explained that her work has a lot to do with nature, and for her, this has spiritual components: "One of the main reasons that I am actually in the discipline has to do with a deep and abiding sense the earth is precious and unique and that there are a lot of really wonderful and awesome things that humans are influencing, maybe without even realizing it." Her motivations, she believes, have more to do with religion and spirituality than with science. And her work sometimes gives her the opportunity to interact with religious people. "A lot of the work that I'm doing now is actually in a pretty rural area, and folks there . . . are more likely to be associated with religion than the urban academics who I spend my time with," she explained. She would like to become more involved with a "church community and have the opportunity to talk about the natural world and human effects on it. Certainly there are lots of precedents for religious organizations . . . to be fairly outspoken in terms of human stewardship [of nature] rather than just using it, to protect it for future generations." So this biologist's connecting of religion to her scientific work on the environment leads her to want to help religious people better understand—through their own lens—why they should care for the natural world.

Scientists also mentioned the need to reflect on the myriad ways that research and scholarship could be made relevant and accessible to the broader public. Some thought that being in better dialogue about religion and science was a part of this broader mission of public scholarship. A sociologist[36] who is an Ivy League professor mentioned that there is essentially a lot of lip service paid to making sociology more accessible to the public but that there is not much real reflection in his particular discipline about what a public sociology would look like or how to convince the broader public of the relevance of sociological research. He observed that "public sociology has not been very self-introspective. . . . I don't think we [have] gotten our principles down very well, and we don't argue about them at all." He quipped, "We just declare ourselves public sociologists. [Then] we go do whatever we want to do." This social scientist, who has no religious or spiritual identity and is not sure whether or not there is a God, seemed almost surprised at himself when he said, "I think we ought to really start thinking through how we can become a light in the darkness." (He quickly followed with a laugh: "How do you get away from the Christian metaphors anyways?")[37] A better translation of social science research to a religious public would be part of this "light in the darkness."

As if to address this issue, some social scientists mentioned that interacting more with religious people might provide them with unique opportunities to gain credence for their particular disciplines. A political scientist[38] explained that as a Jewish person, she is not just a "political scientist but a member of a minority religious group." (It is important to note here that although she is a member of a minority group in the broader American society, she is not a minority in the academy, where nearly 16 percent of scientists have some form of a Jewish identity and account for the highest proportion of religious natural and social scientists at elite universities.) She mentioned, uncritically, the assumption that religion entering into public dialogue necessarily refers to Christian religion. And although this overemphasis on Christian religion scares her to some extent, she thinks that it is ultimately her responsibility and that of other religious academics to bring more diversity of religious tradition to such discussions.

Interacting with the Media

A political scientist[39] with an endowed chair thought that scientists should be doing more to interact with the media and direct intellectual discussion around certain topics on which they are experts. He said that inside the university, true religious discussion rarely happens and that scientists should move beyond facile banter about what is "regarded as foolish religious convictions in the public domain." Such discussion might lead scientists outward and make them less reluctant about having what he called "adult conversations in the public media." This could be a real addition, he thinks, "to American television [and its] abysmal treatment of any complex moral questions." Presently, though, he sees academics doing nothing to rectify the situation: "I think American academics seem to think it's partially an inappropriate conception of their role to profess their discipline in public." If other university scientists are to apply the advice of this professor, they might need more training in how to talk about their research and how to address the public's religious concerns about science in media-savvy ways.

When I asked a physics[40] professor in his mid sixties to describe his perception of the role religion is playing in the public sphere, he mentioned that it is "kind of troublesome as it relates to religion and science kinds of issues." I pressed him further by asking if he had any recommendations for what scientists should be doing to interact in the public realm over issues related to religion. This professor, a Quaker who only occasionally attends Friends meetings, explained that he and other scientists should be getting out there and "writing things." He said with conviction that American science is in a difficult place when competing on the international stage, making it important for scientists "to step up and point out when some of these issues come up and particularly in misunderstandings." He then showed me a newspaper clipping with the title, "The U.S. Needs to Hold On to its Scientists." Reluctance on the part of scientists "to get involved with political debates or public debates on a lot of these things," he thinks, could be costly to the international standing of American science. To the extent that misguided views about religion or the relationship of religion to science keep people from entering science careers, then, scientists need to be doing more. In his sense of things, there are simply too few scientists who are ready to go out and say what science is and what it is not. Scientists "should be doing more of this," even if this means taking time off from research: "To some extent, we've allowed a lot of these ideas [that challenge science] to propagate without correcting it from the very beginning, which would have caused a lot less grief . . . than allowing [it] to spread far and wide and then trying to stop it."

Addressing Religious Challenges to Evolution

As we have seen throughout this book, even when I did not mention them, religious challenges to evolution were brought up the most often of all issues when considering the public relationship between religion and science. I interviewed many of these scientists during a time when Kitzmiller v. Dover was in session involving teaching intelligent design in U.S. public schools. And although historian of science Ronald Numbers shows in his extensive volume, *The Creationists*, that such challenges are hardly new, religious and nonreligious scientists were almost uniformly negative about such curriculum changes in U.S. science classes.[41] They were divided, however, about how scientists ought to handle the public issues raised by the debate. Sociologist Amy Binder has done extensive research on what she calls the "movement to teach creationist perspectives in public schools." Using insights from social movement theory, Binder argues that "vigorous repression of challenger demands often leads to a growing sense of solidarity and moral obligation amongst challenging groups like creationists." So the zealous response the scientists have given creationism might even be lending more power on the part of this fringe movement (as Binder sees creationism), given the enormous cultural authority of science.[42] Few of the scientists I interviewed, however, would agree with Binder's idea that it would have a minimal impact on science curriculum and the teaching of evolutionary theory to introduce (even minor) discussions about intelligent design.

Some scientists are making very real curricular efforts to address intelligent design and to say more about religion and science more broadly. A biologist[43] who teaches at an elite midwestern state school provides a model for how scientists could actively and productively respond to those who have religious views that appear to contradict and sometimes even stand in the way of science. This respondent was raised in a home that was actively Catholic, but he does not hold any particular Catholic religious beliefs at this point (aside from perhaps basic ethics). He still identifies with the tradition, however, remarking, "Once a Catholic, always a Catholic," and compared his attitude toward Catholicism to that of a cultural Jew toward Judaism. About five years ago, he taught a class to undergraduates called "Creationism," during which he presented a variety of different philosophical and scientific arguments for and against the theory of creationism in order to help students understand how to analyze scientific texts and not just take what scientists say for granted. Over time he became convinced that views about creationism and science are formed in grade school, and he continued his efforts by developing a graduate seminar on the topic. The graduate students in his seminar have addressed the "25 or 30 standard creationist arguments that have been coming up with great regularity for the last 50 years at least" and developed simple scientific responses that can be put on a web site or given out to high school biology teachers as a handout. He doesn't think of himself as having an agenda for the study of creation; he has a desire to have students learn how to think more critically. In his sense of things, scientists should be engaging more with the public about issues related to religion and the public transmission of science, and he feels that educating high-school science teachers is a good place to start. By accomplishing this through a graduate seminar, he is also teaching a new generation of scientists how to talk about issues related to science with a broader public.

This biologist disagrees adamantly with his "activist atheist" colleagues who say that science is inherently in conflict with religion. To have such views, he thinks, is to ignore the empirical evidence that there are scientists who are both at the top of their given fields and who have serious religious commitments. He believes instead that science and religion can coexist quite happily and that the only kind of religion that is in conflict with science is very narrow religion that, for example, requires a seven-day creation in order to be true. In his own tradition of Catholicism, he finds little if any conflict between religion and science. "My personal agenda," he said, "which is shared by a lot of people around here, is that the scientists who are using evolutionary biology as a club against religion are really doing a lot of harm. I think the activist atheists . . . they are quite visible, and I think they do a lot of damage." Like some of the other scientists I mentioned earlier, this biologist thinks that other university biologists should be doing more. In his opinion, most biology departments "pay no attention whatsoever" to the connections between religion and science. What this biologist is doing is also helping to create a sense of best practices for dialogue between religion and science that others can learn from.

Moving Beyond the Headlines

While issues related to intelligent design were certainly prominent in the media when I conducted many of these interviews, scientists who wanted to see their colleagues do more to interact with the religious public had a broader approach than dealing only with the hot-button topic of the day. Scientists mentioned the need to help members of the public talk more effectively about the religious concerns related to embryonic stem cell research, human genetic engineering, genetic testing, and population control, to name just a few. One biologist[44] said that "religious beliefs seem to prohibit stem cell research, which, you know . . . has enormous promise for curing some of the most difficult diseases. But because of that religious belief, many people couldn't study stem cells." This biologist thinks that more should be done to bring better understanding of embryonic stem cell research to religious people.

Social scientists, in particular, mentioned that they thought their colleagues ought to be more involved in questions that have to do with public policy and religion. This might mean speaking out either against or in favor of religious issues that also influence public policy. A psychologist,[45] for example, said that the United States is, as a nation, "making decisions now that have long-term harmful effects." And in his words, "one of my biggest concerns . . . is the overwhelming [evidence] that humans must regulate their populations. We can't leave this to chance." This psychologist thinks that religion might be dangerous to the survival of the world population:

If you have a religious view that opposes any kind of family planning, that turns out to be an extraordinarily cruel—I would even say a vicious—policy. So that's an example of how a religious view that was probably completely reasonable at a time when there were a million people on the face of the earth is now, at a time when we have over six billion, no longer a tolerable idea.

According to these publicly engaged scientists, their colleagues need to think more about the big-picture implications of their work, particularly those related to religion. Ethan,[46] a biologist we first met early in Chapter 7, thinks that scientists ought to be more critical when thinking through the ethics of their research and that sometimes this involves religion. He explained that "there are some very relevant and important moral issues associated with stem cell research that should be addressed by the scientific community, and that is not occurring." He thinks that "the scientists involved in that work have an obligation to articulate their reasoning and rationale for proceeding along that path, and scientists don't do that. Basically, if you *can* go down the path, they'll go down the path." To become involved in these issues is somewhat problematic, especially for Ethan, who was an assistant professor at the time I talked with him, because "it takes a lot of energy, and it doesn't really contribute to what I'm trying to do with my own research, so I haven't." Ethan's sentiments help us segue to talking about a main impediment to scientists getting involved in issues concerning religion and public science: It is outside the main concern of a scientist's personal goal of achieving tenure at his institution.

Implementing Best Practices

Even religious scientists—those we would think would be the most invested in seeing their coreligionists think more about the connections between religion and science—also mentioned doing little in the way of outreach efforts. Scientists simply cannot or will not make time for it. After his talk, Ian Hutchinson (the MIT physicist from the beginning of Chapter 7) sat down to talk with me about how his faith informs his work as a scientist. He explained that there is a supportive community of other committed Christians at his university. The group is very interdisciplinary, although it's mainly composed of natural and social scientists. For him, the group is a place to talk about the specialized challenges to people of faith in the academy. The biggest challenges that scientists with faith face, he said, do not have to do with reconciling science and religion, because most elite scientists seem to have reconciled these well before they came to their current posts. Rather they struggle with how to balance work demands with the rest of life. And having time to address religious matters might seem to some colleagues like a sign that they're neglecting their work. Busyness, on the other hand, might be worn as a badge of courage.

The biologist who teaches a class on religion and science also said that he gets some flak, either formally or informally, from his colleagues in the biology department—although his tenure offers him a protection from this that Ethan, for instance, does not enjoy. Still he feels the pressure of their disapproval:

> In fact, some of my colleagues think I'm crazy for devoting any time to this at all in two courses over the period of six or seven years. It doesn't have anything to do with getting grants, publishing papers, hiring new faculty, obtaining tenure. It's just totally irrelevant to anything we do.

What does this biologist say to those colleagues who think he is engaged in something not worth the precious time of a high-level science researcher? He responds that "the strategy of just ignoring [the religious public] is not working, especially since the new generation of creationists is more sophisticated and has more money and more political clout. So I personally am willing to devote some energy to this!"

CHAPTER 9

Shattering Myths, Toward Dialogue

I began this book with the story of Galileo. Many of the scientists I talked with gave Galileo's torture at the hands of the Inquisition as a central piece of evidence that religion and science are in an entrenched conflict. But really, Galileo was never tortured; that's a myth.[1] Misconceptions about religion and science abound.

The best research is often deeply surprising, because it dispels common myths that we believe about ourselves and the world around us. Research cannot tell us how to live. But, interpreted through our own values, it can help free us up to live in ways that more closely align with our own view of the world. So far, we have listened to the voices of myriad scientists. We have discussed statistics revealing what scientists think about religion and religious people and how scientists incorporate religion into their own lives.

But here I trade in my scholar's hood for the robe of an arbitrator. My goal is to see religious nonscientists and scientists (both religious and nonreligious) engage in more productive dialogue. I would like to see their conversations lead to more acceptance of some parts of science among people of faith and, among scientists, toward a better understanding of the diversity of religion. So I would be remiss if I did not directly point out how some of the assumptions of the present religion-science debates simply do not hold up under the weight of research data. I then offer possible recommendations for other scientists and religious people who share my goal of productive dialogue.

MYTHS RELIGIOUS PEOPLE BELIEVE

Both scientists and religious nonscientists have been to blame for the misconceptions that have fostered the antipathy of the religion and science debates. For some religious people, atheists are held at arm's length as the complete "other," those who are mostly interested in attacking religion and religious people. Religious people might think that atheists are misguided, but it is equally misguided to have a wrong impression about who atheists really are.

Atheists are always hostile to religion. Indeed, there are certainly some atheists who—like Arik,[2] a physicist we met earlier—made it clear that they are completely hostile to religion. Their sentiments are that religion should not exist at all.

But the majority of atheist scientists and agnostic scientists I talked with were not hostile to religion. Indeed, only five (!) of the atheist scientists I talked with were so hostile that they were actively working against religion. I discovered many spiritual atheists, those who think that key mysteries about the world can best be understood spiritually. Other atheists and agnostics were parts of houses of worship, completely comfortable with religion as moral training for their children and for alternative forms of community. If religious people understood the full range of atheist practice and the way that, for some, it interfaces with religion, they might be less likely to hold such negative attitudes towards scientists who are atheists. Richard Dawkins aside, many atheist scientists have no desire to denigrate religion or religious people.

Spirituality doesn't matter. Whether efficacious or detrimental, this sense of being able to pick and choose from various traditions in a syncretistic fashion is what some scholars think makes spirituality—when compared to traditional forms of religion—so appealing to so many people and so compatible with American individualism. Americans cherish their freedom of choice, and, scholars have argued, they desire to extend it into the creation of their own spirituality. Implied in these conceptions is the assumption that the search for spirituality in general is necessarily disconnected from the larger search for ultimate truth and often from actual religious practice.[3] Consequently, a religious person who is deeply involved in a house of worship might find this sense of spirituality thin and misguided.

Yet there is clearly a group of scientists who are neither traditionally religious nor completely secular. And a significant minority (about 40 percent) of the interviewed scientists who considered themselves spiritual tried to integrate their spirituality with their science. For some of them, spirituality and science were actually linked through their search for truth. Spirituality allows for searching because it is broader than religion—not broader in the sense of being relativistic but more tolerant of genuine inquiry. It's not institutional, so in their perception, not trammeled—as religion is—by boundaries called doctrines.[4] Those in the general public who adhere to certain forms of religious practice might find this group of scientists more open to conversation than they had thought, especially to discussions about how science might offer spiritual insight or the possible connections between religion and science ethics.

Science is the major cause of unbelief. It is important to remember that many scientists forgo religion for reasons that have little to do with science per se, such as an argument with God or a lack of childhood experience with religion. It is not always science that has pushed God away. Understanding this has pointed implications for how intellectual religious people might enter into dialogue with scientists. Religious leaders need to listen more carefully to scientists. The most effective intuitive middle ground between science and religion for many scientists might be the same ground that we all face: the struggle for purpose, the search for meaning, the disenchantment of a childhood where religion was handled poorly, and struggles with the problem of evil in the world. Scientists like Evelyn[5] have had bad experiences with religion or none at all; their main exposures to faith are the national headlines, such as the portrayals of fundamentalist Christianity and fundamentalist Islam in the *New York Times*. Given this, it should come as no surprise that scientists often react negatively toward public, institutionalized religion, wanting to turn instead to spirituality.

There are no religious scientists. The survey I conducted among scientists revealed that nearly one in five is actively involved in a house of worship, attending more than once a month. This means that top scientists are sitting in the pews of our nation's congregations, temples, and mosques. And just as religious scientists have (usually) a closeted faith within their science departments, they sometimes closet their science within their religious communities. So their colleagues don't know they're religious, and their fellow believers don't understand their scientific convictions.

Dispelling stereotypes of atheists, reaching out to the spiritual-but-not-religious scientists, and mentoring and involving scientists within faith communities would mean that leaders within houses of worship would need to do a better job of integrating science and scientists within congregational life. Provide scientists with a forum in their religious communities to discuss the connections between their faith lives and their work as scientists. Invite them to be leaders in adult religious education and to have other public roles that will provide them a more prominent voice in their religious communities. They must not be required to leave behind their identities as scientists when they come to the altar.

And religious scientists must take the lack of scientific understanding found among some in their religious communities as a wake-up call. They might have a special calling to be boundary pioneers for science within their religious communities. Cognitive scientists mention the specific power of *stories* in the development of cognitive schema (interpretive frameworks, such as a scientific understanding); when concepts and ways of thinking are bundled within stories, they are easier to believe, apprehend, and remember.[6] From a faith perspective, we would call these stories *testimonies*. Religious scientists from various traditions may thus need to do a better job of telling their own stories or testimonies of how they personally reconcile being a scientist with being a person of faith. Scientists opening up about how they resolve the connections between religion and science will go a long way in opening dialogue between scientists and members of the general public.

One biologist in the Midwest (introduced in Chapter 3), whose mother was a choir director in a Presbyterian church, had given lectures at his church about the compatibility between science and religion. He spoke positively of the experience, explaining that this was a time for scientists within his church to come together in sane dialogue. He wishes that these discussions would happen more regularly, because the lack of consistent discussion puts him out of practice: "I'm not perhaps articulating to you as well as I could if I had these conversations on a regular basis." Increased discussions will not only help scientists with faith to connect with one another, they will also provide the nonscientists in their congregations with role models for working out a peace between faith and science. Just as scientists might be more likely to respect religious individuals who are also scientists, nonscientists within religious communities might be more likely to accept scientific ideas from fellow parishioners. So as religious scientists are more outspoken in their religious communities, the people in the pews will find a place for scientific ways of knowing within their understanding of truth.

MYTHS SCIENTISTS BELIEVE

Ignore religion, and it will go away. As we have discussed, there are 14 times more evangelicals in the general population than among top scientists. And only 9 percent of scientists are Catholic, compared to 27 percent of the general population. More than 50 percent of Americans agree that "we depend too much on science and not enough on faith" and that "scientific research these days doesn't pay enough attention to the moral values of society." And according to a recent national survey, nearly 25 percent of the American public thinks that scientists are hostile to religion.[7] Religion and (more important) the intersection between religion and science cannot be ignored by scientists who care about the public's knowledge of science and its propagators. These scientists should set forth an agenda for dialogue and bringing discussions about religion out of private confines and into the open, an agenda that emphasizes a more nuanced view of religion and a more realistic view of the limits of science.

Yet as we have also seen, those who *want* to talk with members of the general public about science face something of a language deficit. Since they did not learn a religious vocabulary as children, they find themselves without the right tools with which to engage religion. (What does Genesis really say about the earth's origins anyway? Does Qur'an 21:30 describe the big bang?) Such scientists do not need to become religious believers to have more productive discussions about science with people of faith. But they do need to know more about religion—at least basic facts about the variety of the world's traditions—so that they might more effectively engage with a variety of religious people in a way that advances science, perhaps preserving some of its public funding.

All religion is fundamentalism. It is true that in some ways, religious fundamentalism has posed the biggest threat that science has ever faced. We have recounted this many times. And so have the nation's major newspapers. The plethora of articles published about the perceived threat of religious fundamentalism to science can lead scientists to think that there are many more people with these views than there really are. Yet fundamentalism is not all there is in the great scheme of religion. Scientists who do not believe and those who have little experience with religion must be careful not to build caricatures of religious people based only on the loudest current religious voice. Besides, your respected colleague just one office over could be a closeted person of faith and you don't even know it. Scientists who wish to speak meaningfully about topics related to religion and science could learn more about the diverse ways in which different religions approach science by reading the works of religious philosophers and poets whose higher purpose and sense of religious meaning have borne up under science.

And basic stereotypes about religious people should be dispelled. For example, generally speaking, religious people have as much education as nonreligious people. And they're not all Christians. The majority of recent immigrants *are* part of Christian religions, meaning that they are changing the character of American Christianity.[8] But there has been extensive increase in the number of non-Christian religions, too, such as Buddhism, Hinduism, and Islam, as a result of recent immigration. Understanding how different religious traditions approach matters of science and faith can go a long way toward dispelling stereotypes from both sides. Scientists should take the time to recognize diversity among religious traditions in their approaches to science, just as there is diversity among scientists in their approaches to religion.

Such understanding might even compel scientists to reach out to religious leaders, looking for allies in unexpected places. Scientists may even play a supporting role in the efforts of religious activists who are sympathetic to science. For instance, Jim Wallis, head of Sojourners, an evangelical Christian ministry focused on social justice, has worked to dispel the idea that science and religion can't get along in what he calls a "post–religious right America."[9] Leaders like Wallis could be crucial support in helping scientists reach out to large groups of religious people for the sake of science.

In the classroom, scientists who do not hold a personal faith still have a responsibility to interact respectfully with religious students and not require them to hide their worldviews on philosophical, moral, or aesthetic issues. But many scientists adopt a dismissive or pejorative stance toward religious students, even suppressing discussion of religion altogether. Recall Raymond,[10] a physicist we met earlier, who said that the views of religious students should not be considered because "they're in the big time now." Bear in mind also the implications of those sentiments expressed by the social scientist[11] who tells her students to put aside their religious beliefs if they want to succeed in her class. She seems to assume that studying religion from a scientific worldview is necessarily at odds with having personal faith—as if faith somehow dilutes or softens the brain—so much so that one's religion must be put aside in order to engage in analytic and systematic science. If she wants her students to abandon religion in favor of science, her approach is counterproductive. Her nonreligious students will simply be encouraged to buy into the myth of science-religion conflict, and her religious students might abandon certain important scientific tenets (such as evolution) in an effort to maintain their faith.

These negative ways of approaching religion in university classrooms often stem from lack of understanding of the diversity of religion. As pointed out in Chapter 2, a substantial portion of scientists have little present positive exposure to religion. We may even go so far as to call some religiously illiterate. One step toward religious literacy would be to find out more about the various faith traditions of their students. The levels of religious commitment among their students most often will mirror those of the general public, since religious and nonreligious persons now generally seek higher education at the same rate.[12] I am not saying that scientists need to advance religion or religious causes they disagree with. Rather, they should *be open* to learning about the perspectives from which their students come. Other approaches to religious literacy might include exploring the ways in which various religions relate to science, or the role that religion has played historically in the academy. And still another way to broaden religious literacy would be to make efforts toward dialogue between secular and religious scientists.

A broad benefit of religious literacy will also be scientists reaching the general public—most of whom are religiously involved—with the results of their research. The religious demographics of the American public leave scientists with a responsibility to consider how they engage with religious individuals.

In fact, many grants from the federal government now require that scientists devote part of their funding to public science—that is, engaging the American public with their research. And to communicate well with this public, scientists need to be able to speak their religious language.

All evangelical Christians are against science. Scholars are also finding that evangelicalism is not as detrimental to gaining scientific knowledge as they once thought. Evangelical Christians—those who believe in the authority of the Bible and salvation in Jesus Christ alone—are quickly catching up to and surpassing other religious groups in terms of education levels. Evangelicals and members of other traditional religions now graduate from college at the same rate as most other groups of Americans. And those who call themselves "evangelical" come from a variety of Christian denominations, most of which are *not* advocates of all aspects of a "religious right" political agenda.[13] Further, there are several scientists, such as Francis Collins, who are engaged in massive public efforts to help a Christian constituency understand that they don't have to choose between their faith commitments and science.[14] Secular scientists might not agree with the religious premises of such arguments, but they can share with their religious peers the larger goal of transmitting science to as broad an audience as possible. And to this end, they might draw on the resources of the religious scientists in their midst.

Philip E. Hockberger and Richard Miller are engaged in exciting and novel efforts at Northwestern University through a course on science and society they teach to biology graduate students. Among other topics, the course provides a brief overview of the historical debates between religion and science, the lives of religious and nonreligious scientists, public challenges to science, and how to discuss science with a believing American public.

More than 60 Northwestern University graduate students attended an event where Hockberger presented findings from my study about approaches to faith among university scientists. This relatively high attendance at a nonrequired lecture shows the interest in these issues among students pursuing advanced degrees. The next day, I led a roundtable discussion with some of the students who had attended the lecture. We talked about why religion persists given what we know about science, about various ways that religion might influence science ethics, how to translate science to a largely religious American public, and a host of other issues. Courses and events like these would be a popular addition to social and natural science curricula in undergraduate and graduate programs. Although such courses are already being taught in some science-studies departments, they would be just as relevant to the fields of biology, physics, and chemistry.

Well-trained young scientists who can lead thoughtful religious dialogue might well be our nation's next great science breakthrough.

The Study

The data for *Science vs. Religion* comes from the Religion among Academic Scientists study (RAAS), a broad study of religion, spirituality, and ethics among university scientists at twenty-one elite research universities in the United States, conducted over a four-year period between 2005 and 2008. Scientists included in the study were randomly selected from seven natural and social science disciplines at universities that appear on the University of Florida's annual report of the "Top American Research Universities."[1] The University of Florida ranked elite institutions according to nine different criteria, including total research funding, federal research funding, endowment assets, annual giving, number of national academy members, faculty awards, doctorates granted, postdoctoral appointees, and median SAT scores for undergraduates. Universities were ranked and selected according to the number of times they appeared in the top twenty-five for each of these nine indicators.[2] The universities included in the sample are

Columbia University
Cornell University
Duke University
Harvard University
Johns Hopkins University
Massachusetts Institute of Technology
Princeton University
Stanford University
University of Pennsylvania
University of California at Berkeley
University of California, Los Angeles
University of Chicago
University of Illinois, Urbana Champaign
University of Michigan, Ann Arbor
University of Minnesota, Twin Cities

University of North Carolina, Chapel Hill
University of Washington, Seattle
University of Wisconsin, Madison
University of Southern California
Washington University
Yale University

When looking at this list, it is clear that there is not significant geographic diversity in the population of universities where I studied scientists. By surveying and interviewing scientists at Ivy League and top research universities we are missing many universities in the American South and the "fly-over" states in the middle of the country, places that are highly religious and that form important voting blocks when it comes to issues concerning science. Their predominant location in the Northeast and on the West Coast may also explain why some scientists underestimate the strength of religion in the United States.

In this understudied topic, an examination of scientists at *elite* institutions was initiated because elites are more likely to have an impact on the pursuit of knowledge in American society. As sociologist Randall Collins persuasively argues, top scholars are a kind of elite who contribute to knowledge creation in the broader society. If scientists at elite universities are at the forefront of the newest ideas in our society, studying their views broadens our understanding of the academy and the way it affects other major institutions in this country.[3]

There is no research to date that examines the attitudes toward religion and spirituality (using comprehensive indicators of religion and spirituality) among natural and social scientists who teach and do research at top U.S. research universities and that uses both survey and qualitative interview data. Even so, I benefit from two major studies on topics closely related to this one. Most recently, sociologists Neil Gross and Solon Simmons did a 2006 survey on the political and religious views of American faculty at different types of universities and colleges, also replicating questions from the General Social Survey. My work is different from theirs in that I focus specifically on natural and social scientists, and particularly those who work at elite research universities. Further, the RAAS study involves a broader survey of religiosity among this population of scientists. Their survey provides an important comparison, showing that at less elite institutions, social scientists are less religious than natural scientists, a finding that is not upheld at the kind of elite universities I studied.[4] I have also benefited from the work of historian Edward Larson and journalist Larry Witham.[5] In 1996, they replicated psychologist James Leuba's exact early twentieth-century questions about belief in a personal god, belief in human immortality, and desire for immortality among 1,000 scientists (biologists, physicists, and mathematicians) randomly selected from the current edition of *American Men and Women of Science,* which includes those in the public sector and in the academy. Larson and Witham provide an important comparison through examining a group of elite natural scientists and comparing their views on religion to those of the general population. The RAAS study differs substantially from this study as I examine scientists who work in top U.S. research universities and include those from seven different disciplines, including social scientists as well as natural scientists, and explore much broader contours of religiousness that are more representative of those among the general population as well as discover new forms of religion and spirituality among scientists.

The RAAS study began during a seven-week period from May through June in 2005, when 2,198 faculty members in the disciplines of physics, chemistry, biology, sociology, economics, political science, and psychology were randomly selected from the universities in the sample. Although faculty were randomly selected, oversampling occurred in the smaller fields and undersampling in the larger fields. For example, a little more than 62 percent of all sociologists in the sampling frame were selected, while only 29 percent of physicists and biologists were selected, reflecting the greater numerical presence of physicists and biologists at these universities when compared to sociologists. In analyses where discipline is not controlled for, data weights were used to correct for the over- or undersampling. Table A.1 describes the sample and weighting in greater detail.

Initially, I wrote a personalized letter to each potential participant in the study that contained a fifteen-dollar cash preincentive (i.e., I sent fifteen dollars in cash to each of the potential respondents regardless of whether they decided to participate in the survey). Each selected scientist received a unique identification code with which to log in to a website and complete the survey. After five reminder e-mails the research firm commissioned to field the survey, Schulman, Ronca, and Bucuvalas, Inc. (SRBI), called respondents up to a total of twenty times, requesting participation over the phone or on the web. The preincentive raised quite a bit of controversy among some scientists and admiration from others. For example, one psychologist said, "as soon as I opened that up I thought, 'Oh my God. I've got the bills now. I have to do it [*laughs*] . . . It was just brilliant."[6] Other scientists called the study "harassment" or even "coercion." For example, a well-known sociologist wrote me an email saying, "It is *obnoxious* to send money (cash!) to create the obligation to respond."[7] It is important to note that the study received full human subject's approval by Rice University and later by University at Buffalo, SUNY.

TABLE A.1. Sampling and Data Weights

	Number Sampled	Number of Respondents	Response Rate (%)	Percent of Sample	Number in Population	Percent in Population	Data Weight	Weighted Number of Respondents	Weighted Percent of Sample
Physics	328	241	73	12.9	1123	19.56	1.305894	315	19.6
Chemistry	300	214	71	11.5	719	12.53	.942092	202	12.5
Biology	372	289	78	15.5	1278	22.26	1.23932	358	22.3
Sociology	300	228	76	12.2	478	8.33	.58785	134	8.3
Economics	300	207	69	11.1	705	12.28	.954518	198	12.3
Political Science	300	225	75	12.0	718	12.51	.894604	201	12.5
Psychology	300	205	68	11.0	719	12.53	.983452	202	12.5
Other[1]	–	36	–	1.9	–	–	1	36	–
Refused	–	1	–	.1	–	–	1	1	–
Total	**2200**	**1646**	**74.8**	**100**	**5740**	**100**		**1646**	**100**

[1]When asked to specify, the most common "other" disciplines were subfields of the core disciplines, such as "molecular biology."

As economists and political scientists have already discovered, the preincentive does work. Six and a half percent of the respondents completed the survey on the phone and 93.5 percent completed the web-based survey. Overall, this combination of methods resulted in the response rate of 75 percent or 1,646 respondents, ranging from a 68 percent rate for psychologists to a 78 percent rate for biologists, a high response rate for a survey of faculty.[8] For example, even the highly successful Carnegie Commission study of faculty resulted in only a 59.8 percent rate.[9] Many of the scientists who chose not to participate wrote to tell me why. I received 132 personal emails or letters from those who did not wish to participate (out of 552 total nonrespondents). Their reasons for not participating were systematically coded. In total, the scientists provided thirteen discrete reasons for not participating in the survey. Dominant reasons included "lack of time," "problems with the incentive," "traveling or away during the survey" and simply "do not wish to participate." I also did demographic analyses of the nonrespondents and found no substantial differences along basic demographic indicators between those who responded and those who did not (such as gender, age, discipline, race).

The survey asked some questions about religious identity, belief, and practice, which were replicated from national surveys of the general population, such as the General Social Survey and other questions on spiritual practices, ethics, and the intersection of religion and science in the respondent's discipline, some of which were replicated from other national surveys and some of which I developed for this study.[10] There were also a series of inquiries about academic rank, publications, and demographic information. A complete survey guide is included in Appendix B.

At certain points in the manuscript I have compared the scientists in my survey to those who responded to the 1969 survey of American faculty sponsored by the Carnegie Commission, in order to make comparisons over time. For that survey, information was collected from a mail survey of faculty members who were employed by two- and four-year colleges and universities in the United States. Faculty members were asked questions about various social, political, and educational issues, demographic information, as well as several questions on religion. Among the 2,300 colleges and universities in the United States at that time, 43 universities were indicated as elite or high quality.[11] Only faculty members who were employed by institutions that the Carnegie Commission indicated as "high quality universities" were used for analysis when I compare the Carnegie data to the RAAS survey. To roughly match the academic scientists from the 2005 survey, the Carnegie sample was further narrowed to include only those from the same natural and social science disciplines. The complete demographics of the RAAS survey population is included in Table A.2.

TABLE A.2. Demographics of the Sample

	Natural Sciences				Social Sciences				
	Physics	Chemistry	Biology	Overall	Sociology	Economics	Political Science	Psychology	Overall
Academic Rank									
% Full Professor	70.5	66.4	58.5	**64.6**	55.7	61.4	54.2	54.1	**56.4**
% Associate Professor (with tenure)	13.3	10.7	17.0	**14.2**	16.7	7.2	16.9	19.5	**15.0**
% Assistant Professor	15.4	19.2	22.8	**19.3**	25.9	29.0	26.7	24.9	**26.7**
% Associate Professor (Without Tenure)	.0	.9	.3	**.3**	.0	1.9	1.8	1.0	**1.2**
% Other Ranking	.8	2.8	1.4	**1.5**	1.8	.5	.4	.5	**.7**
Mean Age	51.3	49.9	49.8	**50.38**	48.6	46.6	48.3	49.4	**48.25**
% Currently Married	85.4	84.8	85.4	**85.2**	80.4	81.5	82.2	75.2	**79.8**
Mean Number of Children	2.20	2.18	2.46	**2.30**	2.33	2.11	2.27	2.19	**2.21**
% White	85.3	85.7	83.9	**84.9**	82.6	85.9	84.1	87.4	**85.2**
% Black	.4	1.0	1.1	**.8**	4.6	1.0	2.3	4.0	**2.8**

% Hispanic	.9	1.0	1.8	**1.3**	4.6	3.5	5.5	1.0	**3.5**
% Asian	12.5	9.4	12.9	**11.9**	4.6	9.1	5.0	6.0	**6.3**
Citizenship Status									
% Non-Immigrant, U.S. Citizen	46.8	61.7	63.4	**57.0**	69.6	40.4	63.6	71.4	**60.7**
% 1st Generation Immigrant, U.S. Citizen	20.3	15.3	11.6	**15.6**	8.5	12.3	9.3	9.9	**10.1**
% 2nd Generation Immigrant, U.S. Citizen	5.5	5.7	4.9	**12.2**	4.9	3.9	8.0	3.0	**13.5**
% Non-U.S. Citizen	17.7	12.9	14.4	**15.3**	10.3	35.5	9.3	6.4	**15.7**
% Female	9.2	12.0	26.1	**16.7**	35.3	13.3	27.1	34.5	**27.0**

While surveys provide us with broad contours, the relationship between religion and science among scientists themselves is so complex that basic statistics can never tell us the whole story. To this end I thought it necessary to employ a method that would allow discovery of new categories for how scientists structure meanings of religion, science, spirituality, and the relationship between these in their public and private lives. Many of the assertions in the book revolve around the in-depth interviews I conducted with natural and social scientists. (A final interview guide is included in Appendix C.) For the interviews, 501 of those who completed the survey were randomly selected and asked to participate in a longer in-depth interview. At least fifty individuals were selected from each of the seven fields. Over a three-year period between July 2005 and November 2007, 275 interviews were completed in person or over the phone. I completed 245 of these interviews personally and 30 were completed by research associates. These in-depth interviews (using a semi-structured interview guide) ranged from twenty minutes to two and a half hours and were all completely transcribed with the help of twelve undergraduate research assistants at Rice University, where I was a postdoctoral fellow at the time when much of this research was completed. Respondents were asked specifically how they understand the terms "religion" and "spirituality." They were also asked if religion or spirituality have any influence on their specific discipline or their particular research as well as how they perceive the relationship between religion and science.

The student research team and I worked on coding the interviews. In light of previous research we developed some codes a priori for testing existing theories about interdisciplinary and interfield (natural and social science) differences in views about the relationship between religion and science as well as definitions of religion, spirituality, and science.[12] For straight definitions and interview questions that I developed to respond directly to other research I am able to provide frequencies of answer categories and do so in the text.

Other questions on the interview guide, however, were added after I had interviewed several or (in some cases) large numbers of respondents. I added these questions when themes emerged from the interviews that needed to then be systematically explored in the rest of the interviews. Once the interviews were sorted according to these categories, we then used a modified form of the inductive coding scheme[13] to develop grounded categories about the range of ways academic scientists viewed religion, science, and the relationship between these. We then systematically recoded the interviews. I wanted to make sure that the same passage would be coded the same way by different research assistants. To that end, the final coding scheme was tested for inter-coder reliability and achieved a reliability statistic of .90. When a passage from an interview transcript was not coded the same, then a code was revisited and changed to achieve consistency.

In addition, between 2005 and 2008, I (or research assistants) attended thirteen different lectures and events around the country where prominent scientists spoke about the connection between faith and science or how to better translate science to a broader audience. These lectures were coded for how scientists approached these topics. And discussions of several of these lectures appear in the text of the book.

Web and Phone Survey

Thank you for participating in this ten-minute web survey sponsored by Rice University. I emphasize that this is a research study and all information you provide is protected by law and will be kept strictly confidential. Your identity and that of your institution will not be disclosed in any findings that are disseminated about the study. If you have questions, or want to confirm the legitimacy of this research, SRBI National Public Policy Research Center can be reached toll-free at 1-800-772-9287. Please ask for study #3472. For concerns about human subjects, the chair of Rice University's Institutional Review Board may be contacted. For any other questions about the study, please email me directly at ehe@rice.edu. Thanks again for your participation.

Sincerely, Elaine Howard Ecklund

First some questions about your academic career.

1b. Which one of the following best describes your academic rank?

1) Assistant Professor
2) Associate Professor, with tenure
3) Professor, with tenure
5) Other, please specify_____
6) No answer

2b. Which one of the following comes closest to your main academic field?

1) Physics
2) Chemistry
3) Biology
4) Sociology
5) Economics
6) Political Science
7) Psychology

8) Other, please specify_____.

9) No answer

3b. In your entire academic career, about how many scholarly books or monographs have you published or edited, alone or in collaboration?

1) None
2) 1–5
3) 6–10
4) 11–15
5) More than 15
6) No answer

4. In your entire academic career, about how many articles have you published in academic or professional journals?

1) None
2) 1–10
3) 11–30
4) 31–50
5) 51–70
6) 71–90
7) 91–110
8) 111–200
9) More than 201
10) No answer

Now some questions about your own views on spirituality and religion.

4a. To what extent do you consider yourself a spiritual person? Are you

1) Very spiritual
2) Moderately spiritual
3) Slightly spiritual
4) Not at all spiritual
5) No answer

4b. In the PAST SIX MONTHS have you engaged in any of the following? [PLEASE CHECK ALL THAT APPLY]

1) Private meditation
2) Private prayer
3) Yoga
4) Relaxation techniques
5) Reading a sacred text

6) Other spiritual exercises please specify _____.

7) I do not engage in any of these

8) No answer

5. Which one of the following statements comes closest to your views about religion?

1) There is very little truth in any religion.

2) There are basic truths in many religions.

3) There is the most truth in only one religion.

4) No answer

6. Which one of the following statements comes closest to expressing what you believe about God?

1) I do not believe in God.

2) I do not know if there is a God and there is no way to find out.

3) I believe in a higher power, but it is not God.

4) I believe in God sometimes.

5) I have some doubts but I believe in God.

6) I have no doubts about God's existence.

7) No answer

7. Which one of these statements comes closest to describing your feelings about the Bible?

1) The Bible is the actual word of God, and it should be taken literally, word for word.

2) The Bible is the inspired word of God, but not everything in it should be taken literally.

3) The Bible is an ancient book of fables recorded by men.

4) No answer

8b. To what extent do you consider yourself a spiritual person? Are you

1) Very spiritual

2) Moderately spiritual

3) Slightly spiritual

4) Not at all spiritual

5) No answer

9b. In the PAST SIX MONTHS have you engaged in any of the following? [PLEASE CHECK ALL THAT APPLY]

1) Private meditation

2) Private prayer

3) Yoga

4) Relaxation techniques

5) Reading a sacred text

6) Other spiritual exercises please specify _____.

7) I do not engage in any of these

8) No answer

10. Compared to most Americans, where would you place your RELIGIOUS views on a seven-point scale, with 1 being "Extremely Liberal" and 7 being "Extremely Conservative?"

1) Extremely liberal

2) Liberal

3) Lean Liberal

4) Moderate

5) Lean Conservative

6) Conservative

7) Extremely Conservative

8) I do not hold religious views

9) No answer

11. Compared to most Americans, where would you place your POLITICAL views on a seven-point scale, with 1 being "Extremely Liberal" and 7 being "Extremely Conservative?"

1) Extremely liberal

2) Liberal

3) Lean Liberal

4) Moderate

5) Lean Conservative

6) Conservative

7) Extremely Conservative

8) No answer

Next a series of questions about your own religious background.

12. In what religion were you raised? Was it Protestant, Catholic, Jewish, some other religion, or no religion? (If you were raised in multiple religious traditions, please indicate the SINGLE tradition that was most significant in your childhood home.)

1) Protestant—Go to Q13

2) Roman Catholic—Go to Q14

3) Jewish—Go to Q14

4) Other, IS THAT —Go to Q12b
5) None, IS THAT —Go to Q12c

Q12b

1) Mormon
2) Buddhist
3) Hindu
4) Another Eastern Religion, please specify_____.
5) Muslim/Islam
6) Eastern Orthodox
7) A Native American Religion
8) Another religion not listed above, and could you tell me what that religion was?_____.
9) No answer

12c

1) Atheist
2) Agnostic
3) No answer

13. In what specific Protestant denomination were you raised? Baptist, Methodist, Lutheran, Presbyterian, Episcopal, or another Protestant denomination?

1) Baptist—go to Q13-1b

Q13-1b—In what specific Baptist denomination were you raised, if any?

1) American Baptist Association
2) American Baptist, USA
3) National Baptist Association
4) National Baptist Convention, USA
5) Southern Baptist
6) Another kind of Baptist, please specify_____.
7) Baptist, but I am not sure which kind
8) No answer

2) Methodist—go to Q13-2b

Q13-2b—In what specific Methodist Denomination were you raised, if any?

1) A.M.E. Church
2) A.M.E. Zion Church

    3) United Methodist

    4) Another kind of Methodist, please specify_____.

    5) Methodist, but I am not sure which kind

    6) No answer

3) Lutheran—go to Q13-3b

Q13-3b—In what specific Lutheran Denomination were you raised, if any?

    1) American Lutheran

    2) Lutheran in America

    3) Missouri Synod Lutheran

    4) Wisconsin Synod Lutheran

    5) Evangelical Lutheran Church in America

    6) Another kind of Lutheran, please specify_____.

    7) Lutheran, but not sure which kind

    8) No answer

4) Presbyterian—go to Q 13-4b

Q13-4b—In What Specific Presbyterian Denomination were you raised, if any?

    1) Presbyterian Church, USA

    2) United Presbyterian

    3) Presbyterian

    4) Another kind of Presbyterian, please specify_____.

    5) Presbyterian, but not sure which kind

    6) No answer

5) Episcopal

6) Non-Denominational Protestant

7) Another denomination not listed above, please specify_____.

8) Protestant, not sure which kind

9) No answer

14. How important was religion in your family while you were growing up?

    1) Very important

    2) Somewhat important

    3) Not very important

    4) Not at all important

    5) No answer

15. For classification purposes only, what is your *current* religious preference? Is it Protestant, Catholic, Jewish, some other religion, or no religion?

    1) Protestant—Go to Q16
    2) Roman Catholic—Go to Q18
    3) Jewish—Go to Q19
    4) Other, IS THAT —Go to Q15b
    5) None, IS THAT —Go to Q15c

Q15b

    1) Mormon—Go to Q19
    2) Buddhist—Go to Q19
    3) Hindu—Go to Q19
    4) Another Eastern Religion, please specify_____?
        —Go to Q19
    5) Muslim/Islam—Go to Q19
    6) Eastern Orthodox—Go to Q19
    7) A Native American Religion—Go to Q19
    8) Another religion not listed above, please specify_____?
        —Go to Q19
    9) No answer

15c

    1) Atheist—Go to Q19
    2) Agnostic—Go to Q19
    3) No answer

16. What specific Protestant denomination is that? Is that Baptist, Methodist, Lutheran, Presbyterian, Episcopal, or another Protestant denomination?

    1) Baptist—go to Q16-1b

    Q16-1b—In What Specific Baptist Denomination is that, if any?

    1) American Baptist Association
    2) American Baptist, USA
    3) National Baptist Association
    4) National Baptist Convention, USA
    5) Southern Baptist
    6) Another kind of Baptist, please specify_____.
    7) Baptist, but I am not sure which kind
    8) No answer

2) Methodist, is that—go to Q16-2b

Q16-2b —In What Specific Methodist Denomination is that, if any?

1) A.M.E. Church
2) A.M.E. Zion Church
3) United Methodist
4) Another kind of Methodist, please specify_____.
5) Methodist, but I am not sure which kind
6) No answer

3) Lutheran—go to Q16-3b

Q16-3b—In What Specific Lutheran Denomination is that, if any?

1) American Lutheran
2) Lutheran in America
3) Missouri Synod Lutheran
4) Wisconsin Synod Lutheran
5) Evangelical Lutheran Church in America
6) Another kind of Lutheran, please specify_____.
7) Lutheran, but not sure which kind
8) No answer

4) Presbyterian—go to Q 16-4b

Q16-4b—In What Specific Presbyterian Denomination is that, if any?

1) Presbyterian Church, USA
2) United Presbyterian
3) Presbyterian
4) Another kind of Presbyterian, please specify
5) Presbyterian, but not sure which kind
6) No answer

5) Episcopal
6) Non-Denominational Protestant
7) Another denomination not listed above, please specify_____.
8) Protestant, not sure which kind
9) No answer

17. [IF PROTESTANT—those who answered Q16, IF Q15=1] When it comes to your religious identity, would you say you are a fundamentalist,

evangelical, mainline, or liberal Protestant, or do none of these describe you?

1) A fundamentalist
2) An evangelical
3) A mainline Protestant
4) A liberal Protestant
5) None of these (please specify) _____.
6) No answer

18. [ASKED OF ROMAN CATHOLICS, IF Q15=2] When it comes to your religious identity, would you say you are a traditional, moderate, or liberal Catholic, or do none of these describe you?

1) Traditional
2) Moderate
3) Liberal
4) None of these, please specify_____.
5) No answer

19. In the last 12 MONTHS, how often did you attend religious services, not including weddings, baptisms, and funerals?

1) More than once a week
2) Once a week
3) 2–3 times a month
4) Once a month
5) 6–11 times a year
6) Fewer than 6 times a year
7) Not at all in the past year
8) No answer

Thinking now about your faith or spiritual perspective and your professional life, For each of the following statements, please indicate if you STRONGLY AGREE, SOMEWHAT AGREE, HAVE NO OPINION, SOMEWHAT DIS-AGREE or STRONGLY DISAGREE.

20. There is an IRRECONCILABLE conflict between religious knowledge and scientific knowledge.

1) Strongly agree
2) Somewhat agree

3) Have no opinion

4) Somewhat disagree

5) Strongly disagree

6) No answer

21. My spiritual or religious beliefs have an influence on how I interact with colleagues and / students.

1) Strongly agree

2) Somewhat agree

3) Have no opinion

4) Somewhat disagree

5) Strongly disagree

6) No answer

22. Evolution is the BEST explanation we have for the development of life on earth.

1) Strongly agree

2) Somewhat agree

3) Have no opinion

4) Somewhat disagree

5) Strongly disagree

6) No answer

23. In general, I feel that the scholars in my field have a POSITIVE attitude towards religion.

1) Strongly agree

2) Somewhat agree

3) Have no opinion

4) Somewhat disagree

5) Strongly disagree

6) No answer

Turning now to some questions about your personal experiences at your university: At your current university, how often have you felt discriminated against based on the following:

24. Your religious beliefs?

1) Very often

2) Fairly often

3) Rarely
4) Never
5) No answer

25. Your racial or ethnic group?

   1) Very often
   2) Fairly often
   3) Rarely
   4) Never
   5) No answer

26. Your gender?

   1) Very often
   2) Fairly often
   3) Rarely
   4) Never
   5) No answer

And turning now to some other questions:

27. In the last SIX MONTHS, please indicate if you have done any volunteer work or community service with a group or organization devoted to any of the following . . . [CHECK ALL THAT APPLY]

   1) Volunteering for activities in your church
   2) Helping the homeless
   3) Political activities (including helping political parties, political movements, election campaigns, etc.)
   4) Distributing food to the needy
   5) Helping abused women or children
   6) Doing AIDS related activities
   7) Doing environmental projects
   8) Building houses for the poor
   9) Volunteering for activities related to schools (such as PTA)
  10) Helping through another volunteer organization, please specify_____.
  11) I have given money to a community service organization in the past six months.
  12) I have not done any of these in the past six months.
  13) No answer

And finally some background questions:

28. Which of the following best describes your marital status? Are you now married or living with a partner, widowed, divorced, separated and NOT living with a partner, or have you never been married?

    1) Now married
    2) Living with a partner, but not married
    3) Widowed
    4) Divorced
    5) Separated
    6) Never married
    7) No answer

29. If you have children, how many dependent children under the age of 18 currently live with you?

    1) I have NO children under the age of 18.
    2) I have children, but none are under the age of 18 and currently living with me.
    3) I have ONE child under the age of 18 currently living with me.
    4) I have TWO or THREE children under the age of 18 currently living with me.
    5) I have MORE THAN THREE children under the age of 18 currently living with me.
    6) No answer

30. Is your salary, on a full-time basis before tax and deductions for the current year below or above $100,000?

    1) Below (GO TO 30a)
    2) Above (GO TO 30b)
    3) No answer

        30a. (before tax and deductions)Below, is that

        1) Below $40,000
        2) $40,000–49,999
        3) $50,000–59,999
        4) $60,000–69,999
        5) $70,000–79,999
        6) $80,000–89,999
        7) $90,000–99,999
        8) No answer

30b. (before tax and deductions)Above, is that

    8) $100,000–109,999
    9) $110,000–119,999
   10) $120,000–129,999
   11) $130,000–139,999
   12) $140,000–149,999
   13) $150,000–159,999
   14) $160,000–169,999
   15) $170,000–179,999
   16) $180,000–189,999
   17) $190,000–199,999
   18) Above $200,000
   19) No answer

31. And what is your age?

    1) Record age, _____.
    2) No answer

32. What is your gender?
    1) Female
    2) Male
    3) No answer

33. Which of the following describes your race/ethnicity?
    [PLEASE INDICATE ALL THAT APPLY]

    1) White
    2) Black, African American
    3) Mexican, Mexican American, Chicano
    4) Puerto Rican
    5) Cuban
    6) Another Spanish/Hispanic/Latino not listed above, please specify_____.
    7) American Indian or Alaska Native
    8) Asian Indian
    9) Chinese
   10) Filipino
   11) Japanese
   12) Korean
   13) Vietnamese
   14) Another Asian group, not listed above, please specify_____.
   15)   Pacific Islander, *please specify*_____.

16)   Another race/ethnicity not listed above, please specify_____.
17)   No answer

34. And which of the following BEST describes your US citizenship status?

1) I am a citizen of another country, not the US.
2) I was not born in the US, but I am a US citizen.
3) I was born in the US, but one of my parents was born in another country.
4) I was born in the US, but both of my parents were born in another country.
5) I was born in the US and both of my parents were born in the US.
6) No answer

On behalf of Rice University, thank you for participating in this survey. When the study is completed you will be provided with a summary of results. Thank you again for your time.

Long Interview Guide

ACADEMIC AND RESEARCH BACKGROUND

1. To start, could you describe briefly how you decided to become a [insert type of scientist]?

2. And in a few sentences, could you describe the general topic or questions you address in your central research?

VIEWS ON CONNECTION BETWEEN RELIGION, SPIRITUALITY AND SCIENCE

I am specifically interested in what you think about religion [and spirituality] and how they relate to your work, if at all.

3. I'm going to use the words "religion" and "spirituality" interchangeably here, recognizing there is a lot of public discussion about the differences between these terms. Could you say a bit first about how you understand the terms "religion" and "spirituality"?

4. How do religion and spirituality come up, if at all, in the course of your discipline?

5. How about in teaching, do religion or spirituality come up at all in interactions with students or teaching? If so, in what kinds of ways? (If relevant, how do you think religion should be talked about in the classroom?)

6. What kinds of informal ways do people in your field talk about religion (hallway conversation, mealtime conversation)?

7. How about in conversations related to politics or public policy? Does religion come up then?

8. Can you describe a colleague in your field for whom religion and spirituality is very influential? How do you know religion is important to this person? How does it play out in their life?

9. I'm also interested in the relationship between religion and your work as a scientist. How does religion (or spirituality) influence the work you do as a scientist?

10. On the other hand, how does being a scientist (social scientist) influence how you think about or view religion?

11. Some say there is a "conflict between science and religion." How would you respond to such a statement? Do you hear people say this? What do you think these people mean?

ETHICS IN THE WORKPLACE

Switching now to the topic of ethics more broadly, what kinds of ethical situations have come up for you in the course of your work? (research, teaching, administrative responsibilities) What kinds of principles have you used to make decisions about these topics?

12. To what extent were religiously informed perspectives a part of your decisions?

PERSONAL RELIGIOUS/SPIRITUAL HISTORY
AND FAMILY LIFE

Now, I have just a few questions about your own religious history.

13. In what ways was religion a part of your life as a child? How was religion talked about in your family setting?

14. As a child, were there ways you thought about the connection between science and religion?

15. How about your family now, if you have a family, are there ways in which religion/spirituality come up? [Even for those who are not religious] How do you talk with your children about religion?

CURRENT RELIGIOUS IDENTITY, BELIEFS, AND PRACTICES

16. How about now for you personally, how would you describe the place of religion or spirituality in your life?

17. What religious or spiritual beliefs do you hold? (religiously or spiritually speaking)?

18. If you have a religious tradition, in what specific way does being part of that religious tradition influence your life now? What kinds of things do you do to practice being part of that religious tradition?

19. [If says spirituality is important], are there specific spiritual practices in which you engage?

20. If you no longer practice a religion, what were some of the factors involved in your decision to stop practicing? [Alternatively, was there a time when you experienced a dramatic religious shift? What was part of that shift?]

21. If you have a religious tradition/spiritual perspective, how did you come to this particular set of beliefs?

22. How do you answer the big questions of the meaning of life, such as why we are here, what is the meaning of my life? (If respondent just can not think of an answer, ask, "what kinds of things give you purpose on a day-to-day basis?")

23. Are there ways in which you discuss your personal thoughts about religion or your religious/spiritual beliefs with your colleagues, either in your field, or among those more broadly at your university?

24. What do you think the place of religion in the academy ought to be? (Also, do you think the place of religion in the academy should change?)

25. Do you find religion to be a generally positive or negative force in American society?

26. Last, did anything I asked [or didn't ask] spark anything else you wanted to mention?

27. Just for the record, could I ask some questions about your demographics? What is your academic rank? How old are you? How would you describe your ethnic group? Are you married or in a long term partnership? How long have you been married (try to find out if first or second or more marriage) If so, what does your spouse do for their work? Do you have children? (try to find out gender of children) If so, how many? What are their ages?

Thank you again for your time. All results are confidential and a report of the research findings will be sent to you after the completion of the study.

NOTES

Chapter 1

1. I have chosen two women and one man to represent the different approaches scientists have to matters of faith. The reader should not infer from this that women are overrepresented among scientists at elite universities. The demographics table included in Appendix A shows that women are vastly underrepresented in the natural and social science departments at these elite universities.

2. See Peter Machamer, *The Cambridge Companion to Galileo*. This volume contains a special focus on Galileo's relationship to the church. In addition, Maurice A. Finocchiaro persuasively dispels the misconception that Galileo was incarcerated and tortured for his scientific work. See Finocchiaro, "Myth 8." It should be noted here that Richard J. Blackwell has argued that this view is an "oversimplified and false view . . . [when] the church had understandable reasons for refusing to reinterpret the Bible in Galileo's favor" (Ferngren, *Science and Religion*, 105). There is a growing literature that challenges the conflict narrative. See, for example, Giberson and Artigas, *Oracles of Science*, Evans and Evans, "Religion and Science," and Collins, *The Language of God*.

3. It's important to remember that White was in favor of what he saw as "rational religion" and against "revealed religion." White spoke in positive terms about religion as he defined it. See White, *A History of the Warfare of Science with Theology in Christendom*. See also Noll, "Science, Religion, and A. D. White."

4. See a short history of Cornell University at www.cornell.edu/visiting/ithaca. See White, ibid.

5. Leuba, "Religious Beliefs of American Scientists," 300.

6. His seminal work was Leuba, *The Belief in God and Immortality*. See the following for a replication of his work many years later: Larson and Witham, "Scientists Are Still Keeping the Faith" and "Leading Scientists Still Reject God." Other research also examines the religiosity of scientists compared to the general public, revealing that scientists are generally less religious (when examining traditional indicators of religion) than are other Americans. See, for example, Stark, "On the Incompatibility of Religion and Science." Stark has since recanted this earlier work, arguing that some forms of religion have been particularly supportive of the development of science. See Stark, *For the Glory of God*.

7. Psalm 93:1, King James Version of the Holy Bible.

8. The "God gene" refers to the idea that part of the reason why religious people are religious is that they are genetically hardwired to be so. See Newberg, D'Aquili, and Rause, *Why God Won't Go Away*. See also Hamer, *The God Gene*. Some have responded to public debates about religion and science by arguing that the two areas are in different philosophical domains, what evolutionary theorist Stephen Jay Gould has called nonoverlapping magisteria. See, for example, Gould, "Nonoverlapping Magisteria." For more information about intelligent design, see Behe, *Darwin's Black Box*. For a wonderful overview of nearly everything about creationist challenges to evolution, see Numbers, *The Creationists*. For broad statistics about levels of religious belief and practice in the United States, see Gallup and Lindsay, *Surveying the Religious Landscape*. For information about how levels of religiosity influence educational levels, see Eckberg and Nesterenko, "For and Against Evolution," and Ellison and Musick, "Conservative Protestantism and Public Opinion toward Science." Also see Pruett, "Silent Scientists," for a discussion of why scientists have remained largely silent on issues having to do with the connections between religion and science.

9. See Dye, *Who's Running America?*

10. Throughout the book, I introduced several different "characters." Though their names are changed, these individuals are actual scientists whom I interviewed. Each one is also representative of a group of scientists who held similar views. So quotations from the interviews, although direct quotes from a specific respondent, are also exemplary of sentiments used by a group of scientists.

11. While Arik, Evelyn, and Margaret are actual scientists I interviewed, they also represent dominant groups of scientists and the way they approached religion. The nuances of these groups will be discussed later in the book.

12. Weber, *The Sociology of Religion*, 131–32.

13. For more discussion of concepts related to boundary work, see Lamont and Fournier, *Cultivating Differences*. Later in the book we will return to a further discussion of boundaries. The concept of "boundaries" has many different connotations. I do not mean to imply that religion and science are completely distinct for everyone. Some scientists saw them very much as overlapping categories, different from the Nonoverlapping Magisteria (NOMA) that Stephen Jay Gould describes. See Gould, "Nonoverlapping Magisteria."

14. See Smith, *The Secular Revolution*; Schmalzbauer, *People of Faith*; and Schmalzbauer and Mahoney, *Religion*. Sociologist Christian Smith has called the secularization of the academy an intentional movement. And David Hollinger has argued there is an active movement to de-Christianize the academy, which he sees as a largely positive movement. See Hollinger, "Enough Already."

15. See, in particular, Bernstein, *Class, Codes and Control*. For more on lived religion, see Hall, *Lived Religion in America*. For more discussion of spirituality in American society, see Roof, *A Generation of Seekers* and *Spiritual Marketplace*. See also Wuthnow, *After Heaven*. These volumes are notable exceptions, taking seriously the importance of new forms of spirituality outside of religious institutions.

16. See the National Center for Education Statistics Report, June 2006, *U.S. Student and Adult Performance on International Assessments for Educational Achievement*.

17. See also Keeter, "What's Not Evolving is Public Opinion." Scott Keeter is the director of survey research at the Pew Research Center in Washington, D.C. He reports on research that shows roughly equal numbers of Americans believing that God created the universe in less than a week as those who believe that life on earth evolved over billions of years. See Editors, "Okay, We Give Up." In this tongue-in-cheek editorial, the editors of *Scientific American* argue that religiously based accounts of earth origins should not be taken as seriously as evolution. As evidence that there is public interest in volumes about religion by outspoken scientists, Richard Dawkins's *The God Delusion* was listed by *Publishers Weekly* as among the top five best-selling nonfiction hardcover books. It is also important to remember that "creationism" has different connotations among different groups of people. Often the term refers to the belief that God literally created the world in seven days. Among some, however, it indicates a view of a creator who is using evolution as the method of creation. This latter view is held by some religious scientists: see Collins, *The Language of God*.

18. Lakoff, "The Disconnect Between Scientists and the Public."

19. These figures come from the Science and Engineering Indicators of 2006, developed by the National Science Foundation's Division of Science Resources Statistics.

20. Ibid.

21. In making this choice for the sake of parsimony I recognize that many natural scientists, in particular, do not subscribe to the view that what they do is similar to sociology, economics, or psychology. Where there were sincere distinctions between natural and social scientists in terms of views on science or of religious perspectives I will be sure to point this out.

22. See Ross, *The Origins of American Social Science* in particular. It examines the evolution of the social sciences as disciplines. It is important to remember that these definitions of science are natural and social scientists' perceptions of *how their work relates* to science rather than the perceptions of the actual practice of science. There is an extensive literature in science-and-technology studies that examines conflicting definitions of science as well as the social construction of and social influences on science. See Hess, *Science Studies*. Where scientists departed from conventional definitions of science, I am careful to point out throughout the book.

23. These similarities may be indicative of a broader transition in the social sciences toward thinking about research in the way that natural scientists do, or they could be more a matter of working at an elite research university. For example, a sociologist in his late thirties (Soc. 20, conducted September 1, 2005) explained a view of reality and doing research that was perfectly in line with that of the natural scientists I interviewed. He said that there is an "idea of there being some kind of objective reality" and then that "the task of science is to try to understand that reality on the basis of evidence and logic and proof." This view of science closely aligns with the view held by many of the natural scientists in the sample. Throughout the book, I note the code with which I labeled each respondent so that the interested reader might see when quotes occur from

the same respondent. With these labels, I also include the date when the interview was conducted.

Chapter 2

1. Phys 23, conducted August 13, 2006.

2. Chem 38, conducted May 17, 2006.

3. The data for the general population comes from the 2006 General Social Survey, the most recent wave of the survey to contain a large number of questions on religion. Data for scientists was taken from the Religion among Academic Scientists survey (2005). Data from both of the populations has been weighted to allow meaningful analysis. The religious identification categories follow the scheme developed by Brian Steensland and coauthors in their article, "The Measure of American Religion." When we use statistical tests of significance to compare differences in proportion of adherents between scientists and the general population, the comparison is significant at the .05 level.

4. Test of significance comparing the percent of atheists and agnostics in the general public compared to their number among scientists is significant at the .01 level.

5. It is important to point out that I am referring to scientists' perceptions of how they became atheist, agnostic, or without religious belief rather than directly testing causality, which is not possible without following scientists over time.

6. See Budd, *Varieties of Unbelief*, for a further discussion of atheists and agnostics in English society from 1850 to 1960. Budd shows that there were a variety of reasons for rejecting faith, including reading books that impacted the shift to unbelief, such as Thomas Paine's *The Age of Reason*, which critiqued institutionalized religion and challenged the inerrancy of the Bible. Budd also mentions that, for those who already had doubts, the dubious moral actions of a minister were often a final push toward loss of faith. For an alternative view, see Larsen, *Crisis of Doubt*.

7. See Wright, *The Evolution of God*.

8. Merton, *The Sociology of Science* (281). See Merton as well as Zuckerman, "The Sociology of Science." There is a body of literature in science-and-technology studies that criticizes the normative structure of science. See, for example, Hess, *Science Studies*, and Knorr-Cetina, *Epistemic Cultures*. Those scientists I studied who thought that science necessarily disproves all forms of faith, however, were generally committed to a strict Mertonian definition of science. It is important to note that in the actual practice of their work, scientists do not always perfectly follow the normative structure of science. For this group of scientists, when they are comparing science to religion, science takes on a more pure, normative structure than it might really have.

9. PS 13, conducted August 30, 2005.

10. Psyc 38, conducted May 24, 2006.

11. For more on this topic, see Lakoff, *Moral Politics*, and Naugle, *Worldview*.

12. Intelligent design (ID) refers to the assertion that "certain features of the universe and of living things are best explained by an intelligent cause, not an undirected process

such as natural selection," according to Casey Luskin of the Intelligent Design and Evolution Awareness (IDEA) Center (see Luskin, "ID Uses Scientific Method," 2nd paragraph). Though many in the general public might find this explanation benign or even plausible, scientists across the board—including religious ones—consider ID, as it is applied today, to be detrimental to science. They've experienced it as a distraction at best and, at worst, a danger to the scientific enterprise. Their arguments against ID are not generally arguments against God or the idea that God created the universe. (Indeed most nonreligious scientists, as we've learned, don't take much time to consider the existence of God at all.) Rather they argue against the mixing of science and religion in such a way that God is considered a "proof" for something being considered scientifically. Even religious scientists (and learned nonscientists) have raised arguments against the ID movement, arguing that God (as a superior Creator) is completely outside of science and shouldn't be considered on the same level as a scientific experiment. Instead, religious scientists will often attest that the theory of evolution, the best theory they have for the origins of life on earth, in no way disparages a belief in an intelligent Creator. For works by Christian evolutionists, see Giberson, *Saving Darwin*; Collins, *The Language of God*; Miller, *Finding Darwin's God*; and Alexander, *Creation or Evolution? Do We Have to Choose?*

While none of the scientists I interviewed, religious or nonreligious, thought that ID theories had scientific merit, there was some disagreement over whether they should be addressed in science curricula. Most of the scientists in the study considered ID a part of religion, particularly evangelical Christianity, while ID theorists, such as Michael Behe, say that there is nothing religious about it, although they do employ supernatural explanations. For extensive discussion of arguments in favor of ID, see Michael Behe, *Darwin's Black Box*. Sociologists have examined ID as a case of how knowledge movements are structured and disseminated through a society, even when there are few members in the movement. See Binder, "Gathering Intelligence on Intelligent Design," and Fuller, "Intelligent Design Theory." Probably the most extensive volume ever written on the history of creationist movements is Numbers, *The Creationists*.

ID casts its shadow over my study in many ways, because a portion of the data was collected during 2005, when school boards in both Kansas and Pennsylvania were having heated discussions about teaching the theory of evolution and/or ID in public school classrooms.

13. Religious critics of embryonic stem cell research argue that it is unethical to destroy living human embryos for the sake of science, even if it advances research that might save other lives. For a more extensive discussion about how debates about human genetic engineering are constructed, see Evans, *Playing God?* See also Evans and Hudson, "Religion and Reproductive Genetics."

14. Soc 19, conducted August 30, 2005.

15. A roughly similar proportion of Jewish scientists were raised in a religious home (about 19 percent) as remained Jewish (about 16 percent), and this comparison is statistically significant at the .05 level. The comparisons for Protestants and Catholics are also significant at the .05 level. See also Leuba, *The Belief in God and Immortality* and

"Religious Beliefs of American Scientists," as well as Faia, "Secularization and Scholarship among American Professors."

16. Chem 32, conducted March 20, 2006.

17. Soc 22, conducted August 8, 2005.

18. See Durkheim, *The Elementary Forms of Religious Life*.

19. Chem 25, conducted March 1, 2006.

20. Chem 18, conducted September 15, 2005.

21. Although historians are not sure, it is thought that this phrase originated from an English judge in the late 1800s. See Foss, *Biographical Dictionary of the Judges of England*.

22. There is historical precedent for these views. Susan Budd, in *Varieties of Unbelief*, argues that many British during the Victorian period lost faith not because of science but because of the problem of evil, although they maintained a tenuous connection with Christianity that fit with their notion of an evil God. She writes, "most *de facto* atheists or agnostics were still nominal Christians not only because of the social consequences of an open atheism but because of fear of the possibility of hell" (118). And James R. Moore, in his chapter, "Of Love and Death: Why Darwin 'gave up Christianity,'" says, "Historians who have analyzed this so-called 'loss of faith' have reached the unsurprising conclusion that Victorians renounced Christianity as much or more for moral reasons as for intellectual ones" (195). For a totally contrasting view, see Larsen, *Crisis of Doubt*. Larsen argues that, when examining the true historical record, accounts of Victorian era loss of faith are vastly overblown. According to Larsen, "Future studies of nineteenth-century intellectual history should consider building in their framework a realization that faith was compelling to many Victorian thinkers. It is time to reintegrate faith positively into accounts of Victorian thought. Instead of discussions of faith merely serving as the set-up and foil for the imagined real story—one of the loss of faith— scholars would do well to learn to see that doubt has a subservient role in nineteenth-century Britain as the bugbear of a larger story, one of minds profoundly persuaded by the compelling nature of Christian thought" (253).

23. Chem 38, conducted May 17, 2006.

24. Chem 13, conducted September 21, 2005.

25. Bad Religion, "American Jesus," from their 1993 album *Recipe for Hate*, Epitaph Records. For an example of Graffin's academic work, see Graffin, *Evolution, Monism, Atheism and the Naturalist World-View*.

26. Phys 5, conducted July 12, 2005.

27. The "golden rule" is commonly understood to be "Do to others as you would have them do to you" (Matthew 7:12, NIV). For a further explanation of "golden rule Christianity," see Ammerman, "Golden Rule Christianity."

28. Edgell, Gerteis, and Hartmann, "Atheists as 'Other,'" 211. See this work for more information about how Americans view atheists. According to a Gallup Organization poll, 53 percent of Americans said they would not vote for an atheist. Compare this to those who would not vote for a woman (11 percent), a black American (5 percent), or a Mormon (24 percent).

29. Bio 2, conducted June 21, 2005.

30. Chem 26, conducted March 8, 2006.

31. See www.cyberhymnal.org/htm/f/a/faithoof.htm, accessed April 2, 2009, for words to the entire hymn and a further discussion of Faber's life.

32. When asked about the "importance of religion growing up," scientists had the option on the survey of choosing answers that ranged from "very important" to "not at all important." For a further statistical discussion of this data, see Ecklund and Scheitle, "Religion among Academic Scientists."

33. Test of significance for comparison between proportion of those in the general population raised Protestant when compared to proportion of elite scientists raised Protestant is significant at the .05 level. Similarly, the test of significance for comparison between those in the general population raised with no religion compared to percent of elite scientists raised with no religion is also significant at the .05 level. See Ecklund and Sheitle, "Religion among Academic Scientists," for more information about the survey data and an extensive discussion of how scientists' religion at age 16 might influence current religiosity.

34. PS 16, conducted August 21, 2005.

Chapter 3

1. For an example of popular books that convey the sentiment that science is against religion, see Dawkins, *The God Delusion*, and Winnick, *A Jealous God*.

2. Similar ideas about the responsibility of Christians to care for the world—especially as related to issues of environmentalism—can be found in the work of Calvin Dewitt, professor, Nelson Institute for Environmental Studies, University of Wisconsin. See in particular DeWitt, *The Environment and the Christian*.

3. See Ecklund and Scheitle, "Religion among Academic Scientists." This article contains fuller statistical analyses of the connection between the religion in which a scientist was raised and the likelihood of that scientist remaining religious. See also Ecklund, Park, and Veliz, "Secularization and Religious Change among Elite Scientists." According to the Religion Among Academic Scientists Survey 2005, 52 percent of scientists who were raised Protestant and 58 percent of scientists who were raised Catholic had switched to no tradition.

4. Econ 35, conducted June 8, 2006.

5. See Freese, "Risk Preferences and Gender Differences in Religiousness." See also Miller and Hoffman, "Risk and Religion," for theoretical explanations about why women tend to be more religious than men.

6. For a more detailed statistical explanation of this finding, see Ecklund and Scheitle, "Religion among Academic Scientists."

7. In the General Social Survey 2004, 49 percent of respondents 65 or older said they had a "strong religious preference," compared to only 29 percent of 18- to 30-year-olds, 39 percent of 31- to 44-year-olds, and 41 percent of 45- to 64-year-olds.

8. See the Carnegie Commission National Survey of Higher Education Faculty Study, 1969. The relationship between age and lack of religiosity is evident in the 1969

group of scientists. By 2005 a shift had occurred. Among those who responded to the 2005 survey, younger scientists are less likely than older scientists to have no religion.

9. Percentages for scientists in the table equal 101 percent because of rounding.

10. I draw the reader's attention to the complexity of the term "Jewish," which can connote both ethnic and religious categories. The survey data does not allow insight into the nuances individuals intended by this self-identification. For more in-depth analysis of the complexities that surround usage of the term, refer to Sarna, "American Jews in the New Millennium."

11. These statistics compare the General Social Survey 2006 to the Religion Among Academic Scientists 2005. Data are weighted.

12. When comparing the General Social Survey 2006 to elite scientists (2005), 1.1 percent of the scientists identify as Hindus, compared to 0.3 percent of the general public. The survey data is weighted to overcome differences in size of population, and results are statistically significant at the .05 level.

13. See Ecklund, Park, and Veliz, "Secularization and Religious Change among Elite Scientists." Here we discuss in further detail the impact the increasing proportion of scientists who are immigrants and non-U.S. citizens will have on the religious composition of the academy.

14. For example, see Giberson and Artigas, *Oracles of Science*; Miller, *Finding Darwin's God*; Collins, *The Language of God*; Giberson, *Saving Darwin*; and Falk, *Coming to Peace with Science*. For intelligent design literature (contrary to the above), see Behe, *Darwin's Black Box*, and Dembski, *Intelligent Design*.

15. Scientists were asked, "When compared to most Americans, where would you place your religious views on a seven-point scale, with 1 being 'Extremely liberal' and 7 being 'Extremely conservative'?"

16. When statistical tests compare the significance of differences in proportion of adherents between scientists and the general population, all values are significant at the .001 level. Comparison to the general public is taken from the General Social Survey 1998 because that is the most recent wave of the survey to ask this question. See Smith, Emerson, Gallagher, Kennedy, and Sikkink, *American Evangelicalism*, for a discussion of the core beliefs and practices of American evangelicals.

17. Respondents were asked, "Which one of the following statements comes closest to expressing what you believe about God?" For the purposes of this chapter, four respondent categories were collapsed into one category of belief in God: "I believe in a higher power, but it is not God," "I believe in God sometimes," "I have some doubts, but I believe in God," and "I have no doubts about God's existence."

18. See Berger, *The Sacred Canopy*, and Berger and Luckmann, *The Social Construction of Reality*. In both of these seminal works, Berger discusses the importance of the individual interacting in community with social structures—such as religious communities—as a way of figuring out his or her conception of reality.

19. While the term *plausibility structure* may be foreign to many religious people, they often embrace the concept but use different terminology. For instance, it is common among evangelicals to talk about God founding certain human social institutions

(such as marriage or the church) and those institutions in turn reinforcing certain ideas about God. Peter Berger's theories might even be understood in the context of biblical interpretation. Consider Acts 2:44, 46 (NIV), which describes the social benefits of religious plausibility structures: "All the believers were together and had everything in common. . . . Every day they continued to meet together in the temple courts. They broke bread in their homes and ate together with glad and sincere hearts." Also consider Hebrews 10:23–25 (NIV) as a description of how these structures uphold beliefs and practices: "Let us hold unswervingly to the hope we profess, for he who promised is faithful. And let us consider how we may spur one another on toward love and good deeds. Let us not give up meeting together, as some are in the habit of doing, but let us encourage one another—and all the more as you see the Day approaching."

20. See Merton, *The Sociology of Science*, and Zuckerman, "The Sociology of Science." Scientists' *perceptions* of how they conduct science (particularly concerning the point at which a groups reaches consensus) are often different from the reality of the scientific enterprise. Volumes have been written about these schisms in science (disharmony between perception and actual practice). See, for example, Gieryn, *Cultural Boundaries of Science*.

21. See Brooks, "A Man on a Gray Horse," for the influence of Reinhold Niebuhr on the life of David Brooks. See Niebuhr, *The Irony of American History*, as well as his magnum opus, *Nature and Destiny of Man*.

22. In particular see Lamont, *Money, Morals, and Manners*.

23. Bio 33, conducted April 12, 2006.

24. PS 4, conducted June 21, 2005.

25. PS 12, conducted August 9, 2005.

26. Bio 22, conducted February 14, 2006.

27. Bio 33, conducted April 12, 2006.

28. Psyc 9, conducted August 23, 2005.

29. A doubting Thomas is someone who needs physical evidence in order to be convinced of supernatural claims. The Bible tells the story of Thomas the Apostle, who after being told that the crucified Jesus had risen from the dead, said, "Unless I see the nail marks in his hands and put my finger where the nails were . . . I will not believe it" (John 20:25, NIV). According to the Bible, Jesus indulged his request (v. 27).

30. Bio 35, conducted April 24, 2006.

31. Bio 21, conducted February 9, 2006.

32. See Lindsay, *Faith in the Halls of Power*, 5–7, where Lindsay provides a concise and readable overview on the topic: "What's an Evangelical?" Lindsay and other scholars have argued that whether or not they find the label helpful, evangelicals share remarkable consensus about topics such as views of the Bible, Jesus, and Christian living. See also Smith et al., *American Evangelicalism*. For more information on the role of evangelicals in powerful sectors of society, see Lindsay, "Elite Power" and "Is the National Prayer Breakfast Surrounded by a 'Christian Mafia'?"

33. Econ 35, conducted June 8, 2006.

34. O'Reilly, Chatman, and Caldwell, "People and Organizational Culture."

35. Although scholars have argued that social scientists are generally much less religious than natural scientists (see, for example, Stark and Finke, *Acts of Faith*), in my research this strong culture was not disproportionately more prevalent in social science departments when compared to natural science departments.

36. Phys 29, conducted March 15, 2006.

37. See Thomas and Thomas, *The Child in America*, for a more in-depth discussion of perceptions and their role in directing behavior.

38. See Marsden, *Understanding Fundamentalism and Evangelicalism*, for a historical overview of the evolution of fundamentalism and evangelicalism as distinctively different religious types.

39. Soc 26, conducted October 27, 2005.

40. Chem 17, conducted November 1, 2005.

41. See Wuthnow and Evans, *The Quiet Hand of God*. I recommend this volume, which has a wonderful collection of essays about the various ways in which mainline Christians practice a quiet, publicly involved Christianity.

42. See, in particular, Allport, *The Nature of Prejudice*.

43. This is not to say that there was not some diversity in the ways that scientists viewed the process of science. Some scientists—both natural and social scientists—were critical of a definition of science that stressed strict falsifiability as a criterion (see Popper, *The Logic of Scientific Discovery*). In other ways, natural and social scientists disagreed about science, but this gap might be narrowing, particularly at elite universities. For more on how science changes over time, see Kuhn's influential *The Structure of Scientific Revolutions*. We are probably not witnessing the kind of violent intellectual revolution that Kuhn argues sometimes characterizes "paradigm shifts" in understandings of science. But perhaps we are, within elite research universities, witnessing something of an intellectual shift, characterized by blurring of the disciplines, where natural scientists are beginning to recognize some of the social influences on the construction of science, and social scientists are benefitting from the pursuit of empirical data in a way that has only previously characterized the natural sciences. For much more on the differences between social and natural sciences and the historical context(s) that have helped each establish legitimacy (as well as threaten legitimacy), see Gieryn, *Cultural Boundaries of Science*, especially Chapter 2. Some are critical of a natural science model having too much power over the social sciences. See, for example, Aronowitz and Ausch, "A Critique of Methodological Reason."

Chapter 4

1. Chem 18, conducted January 30, 2006.

2. See Schmidt, *Restless Souls*, and Kripal, *Esalen*, for a call for a more complicated understanding of American spirituality than that of Bellah et al., *Habits of the Heart*, and the particular stream of American sociology of religion that sees spirituality as uniquely individualistic. Data for the general population is weighted and taken from the General Social Survey 2006: very spiritual (28.44%, N=840) plus moderately spiritual (41.18%,

N=1217) equals total spiritual (69.63%). For a discussion of the overlap between religion and spirituality, see Underwood and Teresi, "The Daily Spiritual Experience and Scale." In addition to works of sociology, extensive literature has been published on the role of spirituality in medicine. For an overview, see Messikomer and Craemer, "The Spirituality of Academic Physicians"; Puchalski and Larson, "Developing Curricula in Spirituality and Medicine"; and Robinson et al., "Matters of Spirituality at the End of Life in the Pediatric Intensive Care Unit."

3. Wuthnow, *Loose Connections*, 22–23.

4. See Bellah et al., *Habits of the Heart*. But see also Wuthnow, *Loose Connections*, for a different view of the implications that the new spirituality has for American religious life.

5. See, for example, the activities of the Center for Contemplative Mind in Society at www.contemplativemind.org. See also Halpern, *Making Waves and Riding the Currents*.

6. See Bellah et al., *Habits of the Heart*. In addition, see Dillon, Wink et al., "Is Spirituality Detrimental to Generativity?," which argues that spirituality—in comparison to traditional religion—can lead to self-preoccupation. In contrast, see Lambert, "Religion in Modernity as a New Axial Age," for a discussion of how spirituality might actually be evidence of a renewed religious spirit in American society.

7. The comparisons with the general population are from General Social Survey 1998 and are significant at the .0001 level.

8. See Geertz, *The Interpretation of Cultures*.

9. Soc 28, conducted January 25, 2006.

10. Chem 15, conducted October 11, 2005.

11. Of the 275 qualitative interviews completed, about 23 percent at some point during the interview specifically described themselves as not spiritual or uninterested in spirituality; 22 percent did not mention spirituality; and 14 percent offered descriptions that could not be coded into a specific category.

12. See, for example, Barbour, *Issues in Science and Religion*. There is much debate over how different religion is from spirituality and about whether spirituality is a form of religion. See Bender, "Religion and Spirituality," for an excellent discussion of this topic. Bender argues that many of our definitions of religion and spirituality come from the way that surveys are conceptualized. Discussing studies of spirituality on college campuses, she says that in these studies "spirituality is private, emergent, emotional, and individual, and religion is corporate, public, and stable." The data analyzed in *this* book hopefully avoid this pitfall of conceptualization. They come both from in-depth interviews with respondents (where they defined religion and spirituality for themselves) and my survey of scientists, where they were asked whether they would describe themselves as a spiritual person and asked whether they participate in a variety of spiritual practices, such as meditation.

13. See www.washingtonpost.com/wp-dyn/content/article/2005/11/12/AR2005111 201080.html for a *Washington Post* article about the event.

14. Here, as in Chapter 2, we see a departure by scientists from the Mertonian model that science is ruled by the objectivity of the collective rather than the subjectivity of the

individual. It was actually scientists' self-image of being dedicated to individual inquiry that assured a central group of spiritual entrepreneurs that spirituality was more in line with science and scientific thinking than religion would be. Sociologists of science such as Bruno Latour and others would argue neither for individualism nor collective wisdom but would say that science only really changes when new power alliances and resources are formed that challenge existing structures, meaning that the views of individual dissenters are not readily incorporated. See Latour, *Science in Action*. In particular, consider Latour's second principle: "Scientists and engineers speak in the name of new allies that they have shaped and enrolled; representatives among other representatives, they add these unexpected resources to tip the balance of force in their favor" (259).

15. Marsden, *The Soul of the American University*, 6. See this and Smith, "Secularizing American Higher Education." And see Ross, *The Origins of American Social Science*, for more discussion of how American social science has developed.

16. Cherry, DeBerg, and Porterfield argue in *Religion on Campus* that the assertion that the academy is secularizing does not match the current reality of a resurgence of religion and spirituality among undergraduates.

17. Charles Taylor, winner of the 2007 Templeton Prize, reflects on the tensions between modernism and postmodernism in the push to secularization, arguing that the world's most difficult problems can only be solved through attention to both the secular and the spiritual. See Taylor, *A Secular Age*. See also Rosenau, *Post-Modernism and the Social Sciences*. It should also be noted that although postmodernism has taken hold in the social sciences more than in the natural sciences, the social scientists at these elite universities were often as much modernists as were the natural scientists I studied.

18. Bio 12, interview conducted August 19, 2005.

19. Sociologists of science, however, would strongly disagree with this view, pointing to the various ways in which science itself is based on systems of belief. See, in particular, Latour, *Science in Action*. See also Lynch and Bogen, "Sociology's Asociological 'Core.'" See also Zuckerman, "The Sociology of Science," and Gieryn, "Boundary-Work and the Demarcation of Science from Non-Science."

20. See Neff, "A New Multidimensional Measure of Spirituality-Religiosity for Use in Diverse Substance Abuse Treatment Populations."

21. These comparisons are significant at the .001 level.

22. Bio 9, conducted July 25, 2005.

23. See Weber, *Sociology of Religion*. In addition, see Durkheim, *The Elementary Forms of Religious Life*, where he discusses the early role of religion in society. Chaves, "Secularization as Declining Religious Authority," and Yamane, "Secularization on Trial," both discuss modern secularization as decline in religious authority, in the lives of individuals and in societal institutions.

24. Statistics comparing the general population are taken from the General Social Survey 1998. See Wuthnow and Cadge, "Buddhists and Buddhism in the United States." Based on data from a nationally representative survey conducted in 2003, Wuthnow and Cadge show that "one person in eight believes Buddhist teachings or practices have

had an important influence on his or her religion or spirituality" (363). For a general overview of Buddhism, see Seager, *Buddhism in America*.

25. Psyc 15, conducted October 19, 2005.

26. Conducted May 4, 2006. Less than 1 percent of the natural scientists and less than 3 percent of the social scientists self-described as black or African American. In order to protect his identity, it is important that I not mention his discipline.

27. See Wuthnow, *Creative Spirituality*.

28. Psyc 32, conducted April 26, 2006.

29. See Neff, "Exploring the Dimensionality of 'Religiosity' and 'Spirituality' in the Fetzer Multidimensional Measure," 453.

30. PS 28, conducted March 9, 2006.

31. Bio 9, conducted July 25, 2005.

32. Bio 12, conducted August 19, 2005.

33. Econ 21, conducted February 20, 2006.

34. For an overview of the place of nature in American spirituality, see Kripal, *Esalen*.

35. Bio 20, conducted January 24, 2006.

36. Phys 1, conducted June 17, 2005.

37. Bio 1, conducted June 17, 2005.

38. See Lamont and Molnar, "The Study of Boundaries Across the Social Sciences," for an extensive discussion of how the concept of "boundaries" is used in the social sciences. Boundaries are usually discussed as being between people, particularly in the way that some groups virtually or actually create a boundary between themselves and others.

39. Chem 15, conducted October 11, 2005.

40. Volunteer activities included church events, helping the homeless, political activism, distributing food to the needy, helping abused women or children, doing AIDS-related activities, doing environmental projects, building houses for the poor, school activities (such as PTA), other volunteer work, and donating money to a community-service organization. The table shows the results when all of the volunteer activities are combined (where 1=engaged in one or more volunteer activities and 0=not engaged in any volunteer activities). Comparisons are significant at the .001 level.

41. Tests were done for multicollinearity, a statistical condition where two or more variables are highly related, but none of the correlations resulted in a statistic greater than .29, revealing some correlation but not enough to make results of the model problematic.

42. Results come from ordinal logistic analysis of spiritual activities, religious attendance, and religious identity used as predictors of the likelihood of engaging in any volunteer activity. The complete table is included below:

43. PS 22, conducted October 6, 2005.

44. See Lamont, *Money, Morals, and Manners*, for a fuller discussion of the ways in which boundaries might have a moral component. For a further discussion of the importance of worldviews, see Naugle, *Worldview*.

TABLE 4.3. Logistic Regression Predicting Any Volunteer Activity

	Model 1	Model 2	Model 3
Any of Spiritual Activities[†]	1.858**	1.615**	1.691**
Frequency of Religious Service Attendance	-	1.319**	1.473**
Catholic (comparison group is Protestants)	-	-	.467*
Jew	-	-	2.315**
Other	-	-	1.242
None	-	-	1.513
Nagelkerke R^2	.102	.127	.147

*p<.05 **p<.01; [†]Data is weighted; exponentiated coefficient

45. Soc 15, conducted August 1, 2005.

46. Econ 21, conducted February 20, 2006.

47. See also Collins, *The Sociology of Philosophies*, and Lindsay, "Elite Power," "Is the National Prayer Breakfast Surrounded by a 'Christian Mafia'?" and *Faith in the Halls of Power*. See in particular Weber, *The Sociology of Religion*, 118–19, where he also helps us understand that religion can be shaped by particular aspects of the group characteristics of its practitioners. Scientists, then, are interesting because they could characterize the development and shape of spirituality. Insofar as scientists' spirituality truly is a coherent, engaged search for truth, it becomes less like the spirituality of the general public and more similar in character to what we see practiced by American evangelicals. Noted scholar of evangelicalism Christian Smith also describes evangelicalism as a distinctively engaged religion concerned with a search for an overarching truth. As Smith, "Secularizing American Higher Education," and Lindsay, *Faith in the Halls of Power*, show, this is especially true of elite evangelicals. This similarity between scientists and evangelicals is particularly fascinating, since many of them perceive themselves as very different from each other, providing a possible area for further research. See Emerson and Hartman, "The Rise of Religious Fundamentalism," for a discussion of another kind of religious sensibility that is on the other end of the spectrum. In terms of their ability to chart their own religious and spiritual destinies, Lindsay's elite evangelicals (see Lindsay, *Faith in the Halls of Power*) might be closer to my spiritual entrepreneurs on one end of a religion-spirituality spectrum than they are to fundamentalists on the other. Lindsay describes the elite leaders he studied as "cosmopolitan evangelicals." Similar to the spiritual entrepreneurs I describe among scientists, one facet of cosmopolitan evangelicalism is eschewing the groupthink of the broader evangelical public. As I mentioned within the text, spiritual entrepreneurs went out of their way to emphasize the norm of individual inquiry in order to distance themselves from groupthink. For more on the broad distinctions between evangelicalism and fundamentalism as religious movements, see Marsden, *Understanding Fundamentalism and Evangelicalism*.

Chapter 5

1. Phys 15, conducted August 30, 2005.

2. PS 13, conducted August 9, 2005.

3. Rawlings, "State of the University Address."

4. For a more in-depth explanation of the lawsuit brought by Christian high schools, see Fain, "Christian Schools Sue the University of California Over Credit for Courses." In August 2008, Judge Otero ruled against plaintiff ACSI, upholding the University of California's standards. The university had found that the books "didn't encourage critical thinking skills and failed to cover 'major topics, themes and components'" and were not appropriate preparation for college-level science courses.

5. The Higher Education Research Initiative (HERI) at University of California, Los Angeles, has surveyed university students about their religious beliefs and views about spirituality and found that students are overwhelmingly interested in spiritual matters. For more information about the study, see Bonderud and Fleischer, "College Students Show High Levels of Spiritual and Religious Engagement." For more evidence that spirituality and traditional forms of religion are increasing on university campuses, even elite university campuses, see Benne, *Quality Without Soul*. See Cherry et al., *Religion on Campus*, for a discussion of the four-university study that shows students are interested in traditional religion and even more interested in nontraditional forms of spirituality. See also Noden, "Keeping the Faith."

6. PS 21, conducted October 6, 2005.

7. For more information about language codes, see Bernstein, *Class, Codes, and Control*.

8. Chem 30, conducted March 15, 2006.

9. Bio 6, conducted July 8, 2005.

10. Chem 15, conducted October 11, 2005.

11. Separation of church and state as a concept can be traced to Thomas Jefferson's 1802 letter to the Danbury (Connecticut) Baptists, where he mentioned the first amendment of the U.S. Constitution as creating a wall that divides the church and the state. According to Jefferson, government should remain secular, and freedom of religious exercise should be protected. See Bergh, *The Writings of Thomas Jefferson*.

12. Econ 23, conducted February 28, 2006.

13. Based on quantitative analyses of the in-depth interviews, 20 of the 38 political scientists interviewed were asked directly if religion ever came up in teaching or personal interactions with students. Of these 20, all said that at some point religion had come into a classroom or informal teaching setting (such as meeting with students during office hours).

14. PS 8, conducted July 26, 2005.

15. For different views of how the public views evolution, see Hess, "Should Intelligent Design Be Taught in Social Studies Courses?" and Mazur, "Believers and Disbelievers in Evolution."

16. This point is in keeping with much of the science-and-technology studies literature. See, for example, chapter 5, "Hybridizing Credibilities," in Gieryn, *Cultural Boundaries of Science*.

17. Bio 9, conducted July 25, 2005.

18. Psyc 14, conducted September 9, 2005.

19. Sociologists of science commonly discuss the "demarcation problem," namely the ways different boundaries between science and nonscience are drawn. In particular, see Downey, "Reproducing Cultural Identity in Negotiating Nuclear Power"; Moore, "Organizing Integrity"; Gieryn, "Boundary-Work and the Demarcation of Science from Non-Science"; and Turner, "Public Science in Britain."

20. Econ 8, conducted September 3, 2005.

21. Chem 38, conducted May 17, 2006.

22. Soc 22, conducted August 8, 2005.

23. Bio 18, conducted September 15, 2005.

24. Chem 8, conducted August 22, 2005.

25. Phys 1, conducted June 17, 2005.

26. Econ 8, conducted September 3, 2005.

27. See Lamont and Molnar, "The Study of Boundaries across the Social Sciences," where they explain the need for more social-science work that examines the conditions under which boundaries are transgressed and changed. This book attempts to be such an example.

Chapter 6

1. See Roberts and Turner, *The Sacred and the Secular University*. Princeton University is not counted in the number of universities with active divinity schools, because Princeton Theological Seminary is not organically related to the university. The studied universities with active divinity schools on campus are University of Chicago, Duke, Yale, and Harvard. Some, however, might argue that the presence of divinity schools and/or departments of religious studies as separated from other disciplines and fields is evidence that secularization has occurred on university campuses. See, for example, Ammerman, "Christian Scholarship in Sociology: Twentieth Century Trends and Twenty-First Century Opportunities." See also Hart, "The Troubled Soul of the Academy: American Learning and the Problem of Religious Studies."

2. See, in particular, Reuben, *The Making of the Modern University*.

3. For more about changes in the Harvard seal from an evangelical Christian perspective see www.markdroberts.com/htmfiles/resources/harvardironies.htm.

4. See Bok, *Universities in the Marketplace*.

5. Historian James Gilbert argues, though, that nuclear proliferation after World War II resulted in a massive cultural shift, where the general public began to see science as morally culpable and even needing religion for moral grounding. See Gilbert, *Redeeming Culture*.

6. For more on Hollinger's ideas, see Hollinger, "Religious Ideas." For more from Reuben, see Reuben, *The Making of the Modern University*. Reuben describes these moral reforms as a series of stages, including the religious, occurring roughly from 1880 to 1910; the scientific, from 1900 to 1920; and the humanistic and extracurricular, from 1915 to 1930.

7. See Smith, "Secularizing American Higher Education." See also Schmalzbauer and Mahoney, "American Scholars Return to Studying Religion."

8. Quotations are from Schmalzbauer and Mahoney, "American Scholars Return to Studying Religion," 16, in which these scholars discuss the new social movement to revitalize religion on university campuses.

9. Full disclosure: Much of the research on which this book is based was funded by a generous grant from the John Templeton Foundation. I alone was responsible for the data collection, analysis, and conclusions drawn from the data.

10. See, for example, www2.asanet.org/section34, the web page for the Sociology of Religion section of the American Sociological Association. According to 2007 numbers for section membership, the Sociology of Religion Section was ranked 18th out of 44 sections in terms of overall membership. The section saw a 39 percent increase in membership between 2001 and 2007 and represented nearly 5 percent of the entire ASA membership of 14,000 sociologists. Statistics were provided by section chair Christian Smith in a personal communication to the section membership on July 21, 2008. Schmalzbauer and Mahoney write in "American Scholars Return to Studying Religion" that "with a 2007 membership of 640, the religion and politics section of the American Political Association has more members than the sections on political parties, race and ethnicity, public administration, urban politics, the presidency, and political communication" (19). For an overview of the Teagle Foundation's efforts, see www.teaglefoundation.org.

11. See Wuthnow, "Is There a Place for 'Scientific' Studies of Religion?"

12. See Astin and Astin, "Are Students on a Spiritual Quest?"

13. See Cherry et al., *Religion on Campus.*

14. See Wolfe, "A Welcome Revival of Religion in the Academy."

15. See Gross and Simmons, "The Religiosity of American College and University Professors."

16. Psyc 34, conducted May 4, 2006.

17. Scholars call this an organizational field, a group of organizations that influence one another in terms of ideologies, structure, and practices. See Powell and DiMaggio, *The New Institutionalism in Organizational Analysis.* See, in particular, Orru et al., "Organizational Isomorphism in East Asia," 361–389. Orru et al. discuss the role of "institutional isomorphism" in shaping how organizations look, arguing that organizations follow the ethos, structure, and practices of other organizations in their particular organizational field. As related to our particular topic, for example, Ivy League universities tend to look and function like other Ivy League universities. See also Dye, *Who's Running America?*

18. These percentages refer to the 275 qualitative interviews I did with scientists. Of these interviews, 191 individuals were asked how they would describe the place of religion in their university. The statistics are calculated from the proportion of those 191 individuals who provided an answer that could be coded as a "positive role," "negative role," or "mixed" role.

19. See National Science Foundation, "Science and Engineering Indicators 2008." In particular, see chapter 7, accessible at www.nsf.gov/statistics/seind08/c7/c7h.htm. See

Jacobson, "What Makes David Run," A8–12. See also Smallwood, "In a Clash of Academic-Freedom Titans, Civility Reigns," A16.

20. See Jacobson, "What Makes David Run."

21. In broader public dialogue outside the Religion among Academic Scientists study, see also Dawkins, *The Blind Watchmaker* and *The God Delusion*; Holden, "Subjecting Belief to the Scientific Method"; Kramnick and Moore, "The Godless University"; and Krauss, "When Sentiment and Fear Trump Reason and Reality."

22. See, in particular, Schuster and Finkelstein, *The American Faculty*, where they provide statistics on faculty life at different types of universities and colleges, according to discipline. On p. 463 they provide a table showing the average number of hours worked by faculty at research universities. The average hours per week for these faculty increased seven hours between 1972 and 1998.

23. See Wuthnow, *Communities of Discourse*, for an argument that the Enlightenment developed as a result of social and structural conditions in a particular historical period that made the cultural innovations of the Enlightenment possible.

24. See Evans and Evans, "Religion and Science." This *culture war* language comes from James Davison Hunter's work but has been applied in many different contexts. See Hunter, *Culture Wars*. See Gibson, "Culture Wars in State Education Policy," for application in a specifically scientific context.

25. Chem 24, conducted February 21, 2006.

26. See Schmalzbauer and Mahoney, "American Scholars Return to Studying Religion."

27. I am indebted to Rita Kasa for help with the task of ascertaining courses with a religion-and-science content at the particular universities studied. In order to obtain information about courses that deal with religion and science, or science and society, I accessed the home page of each respective university. In almost all cases, I had to further access home pages of schools and departments at the university in order to find listings of courses offered. In the majority of cases, undergraduate and graduate course lists were provided separately by schools and departments. When I started reviewing course listings, I looked at courses offered by every single department. After I had reviewed courses at five universities in this manner, I came to the conclusion that natural sciences departments do not offer these courses, or if they do, they cross-list them from humanities departments. From that point on, I continued reviewing courses offered only by social sciences and humanities departments, such as American studies, anthropology, history, philosophy, religious studies, and sociology. The decision to include courses in this list was based on the relevance of the course to the theme "science and society" or "science and religion" as presented in the course description or the title of the course. Except at Cornell, historians of science are rarely housed in natural sciences departments.

28. Econ 29, conducted April 20, 2006.

29. Econ 26, conducted March 14, 2006.

30. Chem 25, conducted March 1, 2006.

31. Bio 33, conducted April 12, 2006.

32. Soc 26, conducted October 27, 2005.

33. See Evans and Evans, "Religion and Science."

34. Phys 40, conducted May 16, 2006.

35. Soc 29, conducted January 31, 2006.

36. PS 35, conducted May 4, 2006.

37. Econ 33, conducted May 3, 2006.

38. See Collins, *The Language of God*. The Appendix specifically discusses this case.

39. See http://www.cornell.edu/about/mission/ retrieved April 30, 2009.

40. See Marsden, *The Soul of the American University*.

41. See Cadge and Ecklund, "Religious Service Attendance among Immigrants." The survey data is from the New Immigrant Survey-Pilot.

42. Soc 23, conducted September 20, 2005.

43. The quote is taken from the introduction to Marx, *Critique of Hegel's Philosophy of Right*.

44. Econ 21, conducted February 20, 2006.

45. Chem 9, conducted August 23, 2005.

46. This comparison is significant at the .001 level.

47. See, for example, Edgell et al., "Atheists As 'Other.'"

48. Psyc 23, conducted March 1, 2006.

49. See Gieryn, *Cultural Boundaries of Science*, particularly his category of "expulsion," where he says, "Expulsion often pits orthodox science against heterodox, mainstream against fringe." The intelligent design debates of 2005 were one example of such expulsion.

50. Phys 27, conducted March 14, 2006.

51. PS 38, conducted May 22, 2006.

52. See Douglas, *Purity and Danger*. See also Durkheim, *The Elementary Forms of Religious Life*.

53. Phys 23, conducted January 13, 2006.

Chapter 7

1. This quote is from Hutchinson, "Warfare and Wedlock," a transcript of a talk he has given several times on various university campuses.

2. For more information about the life of James Clerk Maxwell, see Domb, "James Clerk-Maxwell," in particular, 237: "The religious faith that had characterized his whole life became even more manifest . . . his mind remained clear to the end; in the words of Dr. Paget who attended him, 'No man has ever met death more consciously or more calmly.'" Hutchinson also gave the example of Francis Bacon, who said, "Let no one think or maintain that a person can search too far or be too well studied in either the book of God's word or the book of God's works." See Bacon (Kiernan, ed.), *The Advancement of Learning*, for further context about Bacon's ideas.

3. In Hutchinson, "Warfare and Wedlock," these same points are made.

4. For more on this topic, see Passmore, "Logical Positivism." Logical positivism is a close philosophical cousin to scientism.

5. Quotations from this lecture are taken from detailed personal notes recorded by research assistant Patrick Kelly during attendance at the lecture.

6. Physicist Sylvester Gates Jr. has done extensive work trying to promote science more broadly to the general public. To see a short clip of his views about religion as well as other issues relating to public science, see http://bigthink.com/sylvesterjamesgatesjr/scientific-literacy.

7. When a scientist like Hutchinson, who is well known and respected, talks about the connection between religion and science in a positive light, he is creating for his audience a larger retrievable story. See Schudson, "How Culture Works": "If a cultural object is to reach people, it must be 'available' to them" (161). See also Long, "Stories as Carriers of Theory."

See Collins, *The Sociology of Philosophies*, and Lindsay, *Faith in the Halls of Power*, for further discussion of how elites have the ability to change perceptions within the institutions they inhabit. Collins, in particular, sees the academy as one of the key institutions for knowledge dissemination and change in broader philosophical movements across the globe.

8. Of the 275 scientists I interviewed, 191 were specifically asked how they would answer the question, "What place should religion occupy in a university like yours?" And 42 percent of those asked mentioned a positive (productive and enriching) role.

9. Nationally, student-affairs professional organizations are rediscovering spirituality and teaching their members to draw on spiritual resources to help students. See www.naspa.org/kc/srhe/default.cfm. See also Schmalzbauer and Mahoney, *Religion: A Comeback on Campus*.

10. See Astin and Astin, *Meaning and Spirituality in the Lives of College Faculty*; Cherry et al., *Religion on Campus*; and Stamm, "Can We Bring Spirituality Back to Campus?"

11. Econ 37, conducted June 16, 2006, specifically mentioned faculty who teach at a university-affiliated medical school having the right to refuse to perform abortions if doing so would conflict with that physician's religious convictions.

12. Psyc 25, conducted March 16, 2006.

13. Phys 28, conducted March 14, 2006.

14. PS 37, conducted May 18, 2006.

15. Chem 27, conducted March 10, 2006.

16. Bio 38, conducted May 18, 2006.

17. See Hart, *The University Gets Religion* and "The Troubled Soul of the Academy," and Ammerman, "Christian Scholarship in Sociology."

18. Chem 26, conducted March 8, 2006.

19. PS 36, conducted May 10, 2006.

20. See Palca, "Possible Ethical Lapse Threatens Stem Cell Deals," accessible at www.npr.org/templates/story/story.php?storyId=5024028, for an example of how ethical scandals can derail scientific progress. See Evans, "Religion and Human Cloning," or for a lengthier discussion of how the public negotiates ethical issues related to human reproductive technologies, see Evans, *Playing God?*

21. Bio 13, conducted August 24, 2005.

22. Soc 30, conducted February 8, 2006.

23. See Weber, *The Methodology of the Social Sciences.*

24. PS 32, conducted April 19, 2006.

25. See Schmalzbauer and Mahoney, "American Scholars Return to Studying Religion." Organizations like the Templeton Foundation, the Pew Charitable Trust, the Lilly Endowment, and the Teagle Foundation, as well as visionary initiatives on the part of universities themselves, have played a role in establishing these cross-disciplinary centers. The center that the sociologist refers to in this paragraph, for example, is funded heavily by the Templeton Foundation. But it is the scientist leaders of these centers who apply for the funding and chart the vision.

26. Soc 31, conducted March 22, 2006.

27. See www.columbia.edu/cu/cssr for more information about the Center for the Study of Science and Religion, the Earth Institute at Columbia University.

28. Kanye West, "Jesus Walks," from his 2004 album, *The College Dropout*, Roc-A-Fella Records.

29. One notable exception is Cornel West, the famous African American studies professor, who has his own hip-hop CD. See www.cornelwest.com.

30. About 22 percent agreed with the statement, and 34 percent had no opinion on the issue.

31. Soc 34, conducted May 30, 2006.

32. Psyc 25, conducted March 16, 2006.

33. Psyc 17, conducted January 3, 2006.

34. See in particular Bernstein, *Class, Codes and Control*, for his discussion of language codes.

35. Soc 30, conducted February 8, 2006.

36. Schmalzbauer, *People of Faith*, 193.

37. Chem 31, conducted March 20, 2006.

38. Bio 21, conducted February 9, 2006.

39. Phys 34, conducted April 11, 2006.

40. Phys 29, conducted March 15, 2006.

41. Cadge and Ecklund, "Constructions of Religion and Spirituality in the Daily Boundary Work of Pediatric Physicians."

42. Econ 35, conducted June 8, 2006.

43. PS 21, conducted October 6, 2005.

44. See in particular Latour, *Science in Action.*

45. Phys 33, conducted April 10, 2006.

46. For the entire context of Singer's views, see Singer, "Taking Life." See also, Singer's more recent work, "America's Shame."

47. This discussion of "performance" for different audiences implicitly benefits from the work of Erving Goffman. See in particular Goffman, *Stigma.*

48. Humanities scholar Mark R. Schwehn discusses the role of professors further, particularly their role in students' character development, in Schwehn, *Exiles from Eden.*

Chapter 8

Epigraph: Chem 17, conducted November 1, 2005.

1. See Sagan, "Why We Need to Understand Science."

2. PS 24, conducted January 25, 2006.

3. Psyc 22, conducted February 22, 2006.

4. Psyc 40, conducted June 16, 2006.

5. Psyc 28, conducted March 28, 2006.

6. Such debates among secularists about how to respond to religious people are not new. See Budd, *Varieties of Unbelief*. Budd argues that among atheists and agnostics in late nineteenth-century English society, there was a strong disagreement between secularists about how to best advance the cause: militancy or respectability (with respectability being to soften the message against religion in the hopes of making it more widely accepted). Budd writes, "The strength of religion lay in its unexamined connections with every aspect of life, with its meaning as a *label* which marked off the church-goer . . . from those simply outside the understood pattern of life, excluded from the routine of Sunday school with buns and band, and funerals with ham. It was this aspect of religion which was so baffling to the secularist. Religious beliefs could be combated; but the relations between religious practice and life in the community were so intimate that religion could not be made into a separate target" (37). Similarly, the most secular of scientists I interviewed often lamented that religion was not problematic as long as it remained a personal, private belief system. It was when religion started influencing people in ways that motivated them to outward action—such as advocating changes in public policies that influence science—that it became most problematic.

7. Bio 12, conducted August 19, 2005.

8. Chem 8, conducted August 22, 2005.

9. Here, social constructivist approaches to science—which focus on the ways in which science is influenced by power structures, ideologies, and actors within and outside the scientific enterprise itself—are helpful in showing us that the way science responds to other institutions (such as religion) is based in a community of actors. These actors or individuals have their own histories and ideologies that shape their responses to religious people. Some of their conceptions of what religion is might need to be reframed in order for them to more effectively engage with religious people and communities for the cause of science. Hess, in *Science Studies*, talks about the aspects of science that are socially constructed. Gieryn, in *Cultural Boundaries of Science*, mentions specifically that science is constructed within bounds. Sociologists of science, then, should be concerned with uncovering the boundaries (and how they are constructed and how they change) around what is inside of science and what is outside of it.

10. Bio 17, conducted September 9, 2005.

11. Bio 27, conducted March 16, 2006.

12. Bio 1, conducted June 17, 2005.

13. Bio 20, conducted January 24, 2006.

14. For more on secularization theory, see Bruce, *God Is Dead*. For more on the opinions of those who argue for a revision to secularization theory, see Yamane, "Secularization on Trial." And for more on the view that secularization is not happening at all but that religion is simply restructuring and changing form, see Berger, *The Desecularization of the World*.

15. See Cadge and Ecklund, "Religion and Immigration," for an overview of recent research on the impact of religion on the lives of U.S. immigrants.

16. Soc 34, conducted May 30, 2006.

17. Psyc 17, conducted January 3, 2006.

18. Econ 23, conducted February 28, 2006.

19. Chem 17, conducted November 1, 2005.

20. PS 24, conducted January 25, 2006.

21. Phys 34, conducted April 11, 2006.

22. Phys 42, conducted May 25, 2006.

23. Brian,*Einstein*, 127. Einstein's God was not one, though, who "concerns Himself with the fate and the doings of mankind" (127).

24. Bio 20, conducted January 24, 2006.

25. Bio 23, conducted February 14, 2006.

26. See Peterson, "Demarcation and the Scientistic Fallacy."

27. PS 12, conducted August 9, 2005.

28. Various philosophers, both of science and of religion, have made similar arguments. For an argument directly related to how evolution actually defeats ideas related to naturalism, see Plantinga, *Warrant and Proper Function*.

29. Bio 7, conducted July 11, 2005.

30. See Gould, "Nonoverlapping Magisteria."

31. Bio 8, conducted July 22, 2005.

32. Bio 24, conducted February 15, 2006.

33. For a thorough discussion of boundary pioneers, see Chapter 3.

34. Bio 8, conducted July 22, 2005.

35. Ibid.

36. Soc 11, conducted July 14, 2005.

37. This sociologist's concern is particularly interesting in light of the fact that the American Sociological Association (ASA), the main association for U.S. academic sociologists, has made extensive efforts to advance a public sociology, including electing a president of the ASA who talked a great deal about the issue, developing a task force in 2004 to discuss how to make sociological research more relevant to a broader public, and publishing numerous articles in its newsletter about developing a public sociology. See www.asanet.org. Searching "public sociology" will bring up these and numerous other efforts on the part of the ASA to make sociological research more relevant to a broader American public.

38. PS 21, conducted October 6, 2005.

39. PS 38, conducted May 22, 2006.

40. Phys 16, conducted August 31, 2005.

41. See Numbers, *The Creationists*.

42. See Binder, "Gathering Intelligence on Intelligent Design."

43. Bio 14, conducted August 24, 2005.

44. Bio 25, conducted February 21, 2006.

45. Psyc 22, conducted February 22, 2006.

46. Bio 13, conducted August 24, 2005.

Chapter 9

1. Philosopher Maurice A. Finocchiaro persuasively argues that there is no real evidence that Galileo was tortured or jailed for his beliefs that the earth revolves around the sun (heliocentrism) rather than the other way around. See Finocchiaro, "That Galileo Was Imprisoned and Tortured for Advocating Copernicanism." See also Koestler, *The Sleepwalkers*. According to Koestler (p. 358), "The personality of Galileo, as it emerges from works of popular science, has even less relation to historic fact than Canon Koppernighk's. In [Galileo]'s particular case, however, this is caused . . . by more partisan motives . . . he appears . . . in rationalist mythography, as the Maid of Orleans of Science, the St George who slew the dragon of the Inquisition. It is, therefore, hardly surprising that the fame of this outstanding genius rests mostly on discoveries he never made, and on feats he never performed. Contrary to statements in even recent outlines of science, Galileo did not invent the telescope, nor the microscope; nor the thermometer; nor the pendulum clock. He did not discover the law of inertia; nor the parallelogram of forces or motions; nor the sun spots. He made no contribution to theoretical astronomy; he did not throw down weights from the leaning tower of Pisa, and did not prove the truth of the Copernican system. He was not tortured by the Inquisition, did not languish in its dungeons, did not say 'eppur si muove'; and he was not a martyr of science. What he did was to found the modern science of dynamics, which makes him rank among the men who shaped human destiny."

2. Phys 23, conducted August 13, 2006.

3. I should note that not all scholars agree with such an interpretation of the American spirituality movement. Schmidt, in *Restless Souls*, argues that liberal Protestantism was, at its root, a particular American form of individualized spirituality that sought to distance itself from conservative Protestantism and link to social justice and concern for the environment.

4. It should be strongly acknowledged here that this view of science as free from restrictive power structures is one that the entire field of science and technology studies, which emphasizes the social construction of science, has been set up to reject. See, for example, Evans and Evans, "Religion and Science"; Latour, *Science in Action*; and Knorr-Cetina, *The Manufacture of Knowledge*. These—among other experts—examine the ways that what is perceived as a scientific fact in science is actually influenced and/or even constructed by power structures within communities of scientists. Interestingly, among the natural scientists and even among the *social* scientists, I can count on one hand the number who held this view of science.

5. Chem 18, conducted January 30, 2006.

6. Institutional theorists argue that individuals more readily accept one cognitive schema (way of interpreting the world) when it is bundled with another cognitive schema that they find acceptable. See DiMaggio, "Culture and Cognition," who makes this point in greater detail. See also Long, "Stories as Carriers of Theory," who, in a 2007 address to the sociology of culture mini-conference held as part of the American Sociological Association, discussed the importance of stories as vehicles of central theoretical concepts related to the study of culture.

7. These figures come from the Science and Engineering Indicators of 2006, developed by the National Science Foundation's Division of Science Resources Statistics.

8. See Cadge and Ecklund, "Religion and Immigration."

9. See Wallis, *The Great Awakening*. See also www.sojo.net; search "science and religion."

10. Phys 15, conducted August 30, 2005.

11. Soc 22, conducted August 8, 2005.

12. Some scholars point out that this is not the case for certain religions—particularly Protestant fundamentalism. See Darnell and Sherkat, "The Impact of Protestant Fundamentalism on Educational Attainment," and Lehrer, "Religion as a Determinant of Educational Attainment." In particular, concerning views on evolution, see Ellison and Musick, "Conservative Protestantism and Public Opinion Toward Science." Sociologist Kraig Beyerlein points out in "Specifying the Impact of Conservative Protestantism on Educational Attainment" that under the label "conservative Protestant" evangelicals are as likely—if not more so—to be as highly educated as any other religious group, with the exception of Jews. (Because they often do not regard themselves as the same, evangelicals and fundamentalists are separated from one another in Beyerlein's analysis.) See also Smith, *American Evangelicalism*. For various views held by the American religious public on religion and science, see Brooke, *Science and Religion*. In particular, for various views on creation, see Brown, "Hindu and Christian Creationism." For the views of one evangelical Christian who is a noted scientist, see Collins, *The Language of God*.

13. See Smith, *American Evangelicalism*.

14. See, for example, Collins, *The Language of God*, and Miller, *Finding Darwin's God*.

Appendix A

1. After the RAAS study began, the "Top American Research Universities" project moved to Arizona State University. See http://mup.asu.edu/, accessed April 17, 2009.

2. These measures are similar to those used in other studies that examined elite universities. See, for example, Bowen and Bok, *The Shape of the River*, as well as Massey, Charles, Lundy, and Fischer, *The Source of the River*. The authors of these volumes used a similar strategy for designating a university as "elite" or "highly selective."

3. See, for example Rado, "Cultural Elites and the Institutionalization of Ideas," as well as Collins, *The Sociology of Philosophies* and Lindsay, "Elite Power" and *Faith in the Halls of Power*.

4. See, in particular, Gross and Simmons, "How Religious Are America's College and University Professors?" See also Gross and Simmons, "The Religiosity of American College and University Professors."

5. See, in particular, Larson and Witham, "Scientists Are Still Keeping the Faith" and "Leading Scientists Still Reject God."

6. Psyc 17, conducted January 3, 2006.

7. This individual did not participate in the survey.

8. For more on the preincentive, see Ecklund and Scheitle, "Religion among Academic Scientists" as well as Armstrong, "Monetary Incentives in Mail Surveys."

9. See Ladd and Lipset, "The Politics of Academic Natural Scientists and Engineers."

10. The 1998 GSS had 2,832 respondents, although only half of the sample was asked the expanded set of religion and spirituality questions. The 2004 GSS had 2,812 respondents. Where possible, I used data from the GSS 2006 for the comparisons of scientists with the general population. See Davis, Smith, and Marsden, General Social Surveys.

11. The Carnegie data set used the Gourman Report to indicate quality of universities. Since this study was specifically interested in faculty at elite universities the sample was restricted to faculty members at universities termed "high quality," using factors such as faculty publication records. Forty-three universities are indicated as "high quality" in the Carnegie dataset. Although the publicly available report about the data includes the names of these universities, the publically available data set does not indicate which particular institution faculty members are associated with, limiting the possibility to match specific institutions from the 1969 Carnegie data set with the 2005 RAAS data set. All of the 21 universities included in the 2005 survey, however, are also included on the list of 43 institutions that the Carnegie study defines as high quality research universities.

12. See Wuthnow, "Science and the Sacred," as well as Lehman and Shriver, "Academic Discipline as Predictive of Faculty Religiosity" and Lehman, "Academic Discipline and Faculty Religiosity in Secular and Church-Related Colleges." See also Stark and Finke, Acts of Faith. All of these authors write about the Carnegie Foundation (1969, 1984 surveys) research that compares the differences between natural and social scientists in their levels of religiosity.

13. See Strauss and Corbin, Basics of Qualitative Research.

BIBLIOGRAPHY

Alexander, Denis R. 2008. *Creation or Evolution? Do We Have to Choose?* Oxford, U.K.: Monarch Books.

Allport, Gordon W. 1979. *The Nature of Prejudice: 25th Anniversary.* New York: Perseus Books Group.

Ammerman, Nancy T. 1997. "Golden Rule Christianity: Lived Religion in the American Mainstream." In *Lived Religion in America*, edited by D. Hall, 196–216. Princeton, N.J.: Princeton University Press.

———. 2000. "Christian Scholarship in Sociology: Twentieth Century Trends and Twenty-First Century Opportunities." *Christian Scholars Review* 29:685–94.

Armstrong, Scott J. 1975. "Monetary Incentives in Mail Surveys." *Public Opinion Quarterly* 39:111–16.

Aronowitz, Stanley, and Robert Ausch. 2000. "A Critique of Methodological Reason." *Sociological Quarterly* 41:699–719.

Astin, Alexander W., and Helen S. Astin. 1999. *Meaning and Spirituality in the Lives of College Faculty: A Study of Values, Authenticity, and Stress.* Los Angeles: University of California, Los Angeles, Higher Education Research Institute. Retrieved April 15, 2009 (www.fetzer.org).

———. 2003. "Are Students on a Spiritual Quest?" *Dallas Morning News*, November 29.

Bacon, Francis. 2000. *The Advancement of Learning (The Oxford Francis Bacon)*, edited by Michael Kiernan. New York: Oxford University Press.

Barbour, Ian. 1971. *Issues in Science and Religion.* San Francisco: Harper & Row.

Behe, Michael J. 2006. *Darwin's Black Box: The Biochemical Challenge to Evolution.* New York: Free Press.

Bellah, Robert, Richard Madsen, William M. Sullivan, Ann Swidler, and Steven M. Tipton. 1985. *Habits of the Heart: Individualism and Commitment in American Life.* New York: Harper & Row.

Bender, Courtney. 2007. "Religion and Spirituality: History, Discourse and Measurement." Social Science Research Council Web Forum.

Benne, Robert. 2001. *Quality with Soul: How Six Premier Colleges and Universities Keep Their Religious Traditions.* Grand Rapids, Mich.: Wm. B. Eerdmans Publishing Co.

Berger, Peter L. 1967. *The Sacred Canopy: Elements of a Sociological Theory of Religion.* New York: Doubleday.

———. 1999. *The Desecularization of the World: Resurgent Religion and World Politics.* Washington, D.C., and Grand Rapids, Mich.: Ethics and Public Policy Center and Wm. B. Eerdmans Publishing Co.

Berger, Peter L., and Thomas Luckmann. 1966. *The Social Construction of Reality: A Treatise in the Sociology of Knowledge.* New York: Anchor Books.

Bergh, Albert E., editor. *The Writings of Thomas Jefferson.* 1905. Volume XV. Washington, D.C.: The Thomas Jefferson Memorial Association.

Bernstein, Basil. 1975. *Class, Codes and Control: Theoretical Studies Towards a Sociology of Language.* New York: Schocken Books.

Beyerlein, Kraig. 2004. "Specifying the Impact of Conservative Protestantism on Educational Attainment." *Journal for the Scientific Study of Religion* 43:505–18.

Biema, David Van. 2006. "God vs. Science: A Spirited Debate Between Atheist Biologist Richard Dawkins and Christian Geneticist Francis Collins." *Time,* 48–55. November 5.

Binder, Amy. 2007. "Gathering Intelligence on Intelligent Design: Where Did It Come From, Where Is It Going, and How Do (and Should) Progressives Manage It?" *Sociology of Education* 113:549–76.

Bok, Derek. 2003. *Universities in the Marketplace: Commercialization of Higher Education.* Princeton, N.J.: Princeton University Press.

Bonderud, Kevin, and Michael Fleischer. 2003. "Press Release: College Students Show High Levels of Spiritual and Religious Engagement, But New Study Finds Colleges Provide Little Support." Press release. Los Angeles: Higher Education Research Institute: Graduate School of Education and Information Studies, University of California, Los Angeles.

Bowen, William G., and Derek Bok. 1998. *The Shape of the River: Long-Term Consequences of Considering Race in College and University Admissions.* Princeton, N.J.: Princeton University Press.

Brian, Dennis. 1996. *Einstein: A Life.* See p. 127. New York: John Wiley & Sons.

Brooke, John Hedley. 1991. *Science and Religion: Some Historical Perspectives.* New York and Cambridge, U.K.: Cambridge University Press.

Brooks, David. 2002. "A Man On a Gray Horse." *The Atlantic,* September. Retrieved April 15, 2009 (www.theatlantic.com/doc/200209/brooks).

Brown, C. Mackenzie. 2002. "Hindu and Christian Creationism: 'Transposed Passages' in the Geological Book of Life." *Zygon: Journal of Religion & Science* 37:95–114.

———. 2003. "The Conflict between Religion and Science in Light of the Patterns of Religious Belief among Scientists." *Zygon: Journal of Religion and Science* 38: 603–32.

Bruce, Steve. 2002. *God Is Dead: Secularization in the West.* Malden, Mass., and Oxford, U.K.: Blackwell.

Budd, Susan. 1977. *Varieties of Unbelief: Atheists and Agnostics in English Society 1850–1960.* London: Heinemann Educational Books.

Cadge, Wendy, and Elaine Howard Ecklund. 2006. "Religious Service Attendance among Immigrants: Evidence from the New Immigrant Survey-Pilot." *American Behavioral Scientist* 49:1–22.

Cadge, Wendy, and Elaine Howard Ecklund. 2007. "Religion and Immigration." *Annual Review of Sociology* 33:17.1–17.21.

Cadge, Wendy, Elaine Howard Ecklund, and Nicholas Short. 2009. "Constructions of Religion and Spirituality in the Daily Boundary Work of Pediatric Physicians." *Social Problems* 56:702–21.

Chaves, Mark. 1994. "Secularization as Declining Religious Authority." *Social Forces* 72:749–74.

Cherry, Conrad, Betty DeBerg, and Amanda Porterfield. 2001. *Religion on Campus: What Religion Really Means to Today's Undergraduates.* Chapel Hill: University of North Carolina Press.

Collins, Francis. 2006. *The Language of God: A Scientist Presents Evidence for Belief.* New York: Free Press.

Collins, Randall. 1998. *The Sociology of Philosophies: A Global Theory of Intellectual Change.* Cambridge, Mass.: Belknap Press of Harvard University Press.

Darnell, Alfred, and Darren E. Sherkat. 1997. "The Impact of Protestant Fundamentalism on Educational Attainment." *American Sociological Review* 62:306–15.

Davis, James A., Tom W. Smith, and Peter V. Marsden. 1998, 2004. General Social Surveys 1998, 2004, 2006 [Computer files]. Chicago, Ill.: National Opinion Research Center.

Dawkins, Richard. 1996. *The Blind Watchmaker: Why the Evidence of Evolution Reveals a Universe Without Design.* New York: W. W. Norton.

———. 2006. *The God Delusion.* New York: Houghton Mifflin.

DeWitt, Calvin V. 1991. *The Environment and the Christian: What Can We Learn from the New Testament?* Grand Rapids, Mich.: Baker Books.

Dillon, Michele, and Paul Wink. 2007. *In the Course of a Lifetime: Tracing Religious Belief, Practice, and Change.* Berkeley: University of California Press.

Dillon, Michele, Paul Wink, and Kristen Fay. 2003. "Is Spirituality Detrimental to Generativity?" *Journal for the Scientific Study of Religion* 42:427–42.

DiMaggio, Paul J. 1997. "Culture and Cognition." *Annual Review of Sociology* 23: 263–87.

Domb, Cyril. 1979. "James Clerk Maxwell: 100 Years Later." *Nature* 282:235–39.

Downey, Gary L. 1988. "Reproducing Cultural Identity in Negotiating Nuclear Power: The Union of Concerned Scientists and Emergency Core Cooling." *Social Studies of Science* 18:231–64.

Douglas, Mary. 1966. *Purity and Danger: An Analysis of the Concepts of Pollution and Taboo.* New York: Routledge.

Draper, John William. 1874. *History of the Conflict Between Religion and Science.* New York: Appleton.

Durkheim, Emile. 1995 [1912]. *The Elementary Forms of Religious Life.* Translated by K. E. Fields. New York: Free Press.

Dye, Thomas. 2001. *Who's Running America? The Bush Restoration.* 7th edition. Englewood, N.J.: Prentice Hall.

Eckberg, Douglas Lee, and Alexander Nesterenko. 1985. "For and against Evolution: Religion, Social Class, and the Symbolic Universe." *The Social Science Journal* 22:1–18.

Ecklund, Elaine Howard, and Elizabeth Long. 2009. "The Coherent Spirituality of Scientists." Unpublished Manuscript.

Ecklund, Elaine Howard, Jerry Z. Park, and Phil Todd Veliz. 2008. "Secularization and Religious Change among Elite Scientists: A Cross-Cohort Comparison." *Social Forces* 86:1805–40.

Ecklund, Elaine Howard, and Christopher Scheitle. 2007. "Religion among Academic Scientists: Distinctions, Disciplines, and Demographics." *Social Problems* 54: 289–307.

Edgell, Penny, Joseph Gerteis, and Douglas Hartmann. 2006. "Atheists as 'Other': Moral Boundaries and Cultural Membership in American Society." *American Sociological Review* 71:211–34.

Editors, The. 2005. "Okay, We Give Up—We Feel So Ashamed." *Scientific American.* April 1.

Ellison, Christopher G., and Marc A. Musick. 1995. "Conservative Protestantism and Public Opinion toward Science." *Review of Religious Research* 36:245–62.

Emerson, Michael O., and David Hartman. 2006. "The Rise of Religious Fundamentalism." *Annual Review of Sociology* 32:127–44.

Evans, John H. 2002a. *Playing God? Human Genetic Engineering and the Rationalization of Public Bioethical Debate.* Chicago: University of Chicago Press.

———. 2002b. "Religion and Human Cloning: An Exploratory Analysis of the First Available Opinion Data." *Journal for the Scientific Study of Religion* 41:747–58.

———. 2009. "Religious Opposition to Science." Unpublished manuscript.

Evans, John H., and Michael S. Evans. 2008. "Religion and Science: Beyond the Epistemological Conflict Narrative." *Annual Review of Sociology* 34:87–105.

Evans, John H., and Kathy Hudson. 2007. "Religion and Reproductive Genetics: Beyond Views of Embryonic Life?" *Journal for the Scientific Study of Religion* 35:565–81.

Faia, Michael A. 1976. "Secularization and Scholarship among American Professors." *Sociological Analysis* 37:63–74.

Fain, Paul. 2005. "Christian Schools Sue the U. of California Over Credit for Courses." *Chronicle of Higher Education.* August 29.

Ferngren, Gary B., editor. 2002. *Science and Religion: A Historical Introduction.* See 105. Baltimore: Johns Hopkins University Press.

Finocchiaro, Maurice A. 2009. "That Galileo Was Imprisoned and Tortured for Advocating Copernicanism." In *Galileo Goes to Jail: And Other Myths About Science and Religion,* edited by Ronald Numbers. Cambridge, Mass.: Harvard University Press.

Fogg, Piper. 2005. "Study Finds Conservatives Are Less Likely to Advance in Academe." *Chronicle of Higher Education,* A12. April 8.

Foss, Edward. 1999. *Biographical Dictionary of the Judges of England*. Union, N.J.: The Lawbook Exchange.

Freese, Jeremy. 2004. "Risk Preferences and Gender Differences in Religiousness: Evidence from the World Values Survey." *Review of Religious Research* 46:88–91.

Fuller, Steve. 2006. "Intelligent Design Theory: A Site for Contemporary Sociology of Knowledge." *Canadian Journal of Sociology* 31(3):277–89.

Gallup, George Jr., and D. Michael Lindsay. 1999. *Surveying the Religious Landscape: Trends in U.S. Religious Beliefs*. Harrisburg, Pa.: Morehouse.

Geertz, Clifford. 1973. *The Interpretation of Cultures*. New York: Basic Books.

Giberson, Karl. 2008. *Saving Darwin: How to Be a Christian and Believe in Evolution*. HarperOne.

Giberson, Karl, and Mariano Artigas. 2007. *Oracles of Science: Celebrity Scientists Versus God and Religion*. New York: Oxford University Press.

Gieryn, Thomas F. 1983. "Boundary-Work and the Demarcation of Science from Non-Science: Strains and Interests in Professional Ideologies of Scientists." *American Sociological Review* 48:781–95.

———. 1999. *Cultural Boundaries of Science: Credibility on the Line*. Chicago: University of Chicago Press.

Gieryn, Thomas F., George M. Bevins, and Stephen C. Zehr. 1985. "Professionalization of American Scientists: Public Science in the Creation/Evolution Trials." *American Sociological Review* 50:392–409.

Gilbert, James. 1997. *Redeeming Culture: American Religion in an Age of Science*. Chicago: University of Chicago Press.

Gibson, Troy M. 2004. "Culture Wars in State Education Policy: A Look at the Relative Treatment of Evolutionary Theory in State Science Standards." *Social Science Quarterly* 85(5):1129–49.

Goffman, Erving. 1963. *Stigma: Notes on the Management of Spoiled Identity*. New York: Simon and Schuster.

Gould, Stephen Jay. 1997. "Nonoverlapping Magisteria." *Natural History* 106:16–22.

Graffin, Gregory W. 2004. *Evolution, Monism, Atheism and the Naturalist World-View*. Ithaca, N.Y.: Polypterus Press.

Gross, Neil, and Solon Simmons. 2007. "How Religious Are America's College and University Professors?" in *Social Science Research Council Web Forum*, edited by Social Science Research Council Web Forum. Cambridge, Mass.: Harvard University.

———. 2009. "The Religiosity of American College and University Professors." *Sociology of Religion* 70:101–29.

Hall, David, editor. 1997. *Lived Religion in America: Toward a History of Practice*. Princeton, N.J.: Princeton University Press.

Halpern, Charles. 2008. *Making Waves and Riding the Currents: Activism and the Practice of Wisdom*. San Francisco: Berrett-Koehler.

Hamer, Dean H. 2004. *The God Gene*. New York: Doubleday.

Harris, Sam. 2004. *The End of Faith: Religion, Terror, and the Future of Reason*. New York: W. W. Norton.

Hart, Darryl. 1992. "The Troubled Soul of the Academy: American Learning and the Problem of Religious Studies." *Religion and American Culture: A Journal of Interpretation* 2:49–77.

———. 1999. *The University Gets Religion: Religious Studies in American Higher Education.* Baltimore: Johns Hopkins University Press.

Hess, David J. 1997. *Science Studies: An Advanced Introduction.* New York: New York University Press.

Hess, Diana. 2006. "Should Intelligent Design Be Taught in Social Studies Courses?" *Social Education* 70:8–13.

Holden, Constance. 1999. "Subjecting Belief to the Scientific Method." *Science* 284:1257–59.

Hollinger, David. 2002. "Enough Already: Universities Do Not Need More Christianity." In *Religion, Scholarship and Higher Education*, edited by Andrea Sterk, 40–49. Notre Dame, Ind.: University of Notre Dame Press.

Hunter, James Davison. 1991. *Culture Wars: The Struggle to Define America: Making Sense of the Battles over the Family, Art, Education, Law, and Politics.* New York: Basic Books.

Hutchinson, Ian H. 2007. "Warfare and Wedlock: Redeeming the Faith-Science Relationship." *Perspectives on Science and Christian Faith* 59(2): 91–101.

Jacobson, Jennifer 2005. "What Makes David Run." *Chronicle of Higher Education*, A8–12. May 6.

———. 2006a. "Dangerous Minds." *Chronicle of Higher Education*, A6. Feb. 17.

———. 2006b. "Pennsylvania Hearing on Bias in Academe Draws Sharp Exchange Between Professor and Lawmaker." *Chronicle of Higher Education.* March 24.

Kaufman, Marc. 2005. "Dalai Lama Gives Talk on Science: Monk's D.C. Lecture Links Mind, Matter." *Washington Post.* November 13. Retrieved April 15, 2009 (www.washingtonpost.com/wp-dyn/content/article/2005/11/12/AR2005111201080.html).

Keeter, Scott. 2005. "What's Not Evolving Is Public Opinion." *Washington Post*, October 2. Retrieved November 12, 2009 (www.washingtonpost.com/wp-dyn/content/article/2005/09/30/AR2005093002083.html).

Knorr-Cetina, Karin. 1981. *The Manufacture of Knowledge: An Essay on the Constructivist and Contextual Nature of Science.* New York: Pergamon.

Knorr-Cetina, Karin. 1999. *Epistemic Cultures: How the Sciences Make Knowledge.* Cambridge, Mass.: Harvard University Press.

Koestler, Arthur. 1990. *The Sleepwalkers: A History of Man's Changing Vision of the Universe.* New York: Penguin Books.

Kramnick, Isaac, and R. Laurence Moore. 1996. "The Godless University." *Academe* 81:18–23.

Krauss, Lawrence M. 2005. "When Sentiment and Fear Trump Reason and Reality." *New York Times.* March 29.

Kripal, Jeffrey J. 2008. *Esalen: America and the Religion of No Religion.* Chicago: University of Chicago Press.

Krugman, Paul. 2005. "An Academic Question." *The New York Times.* April 5.

Kuhn, Thomas S. 1996 edition. *The Structure of Scientific Revolution*s. [First published 1962.] Chicago: University of Chicago Press.

Ladd, Everett Carll Jr., and Seymour Martin Lipset. 1972. "The Politics of Academic Natural Scientists and Engineers." *Science* 176:1091–1100.

Lakoff, George. 2002. *Moral Politics: How Liberals and Conservatives Think*. Chicago: University of Chicago Press.

Lambert, Yves. 1999. "Religion in Modernity as a New Axial Age: Secularization or New Religious Forms?" *Sociology of Religion* 60:303–34.

Lamont, Michèle. 1992. *Money, Morals, and Manners: The Culture of the French and the American Upper-Middle Class*. Chicago: University of Chicago Press.

———. 2000. *The Dignity of Working Men: Morality and the Boundaries of Race, Class, and Immigration*. New York and Cambridge, Mass.: Russell Sage Foundation at Harvard University Press.

Lamont, Michèle, and Marcel Fournier, editors. 1992. *Cultivating Differences: Symbolic Boundaries and the Making of Inequality*. Chicago: University of Chicago Press.

Lamont, Michèle, and Virag Molnar. 2002. "The Study of Boundaries Across the Social Sciences." *Annual Review of Sociology* 28:167–95.

Larson, Edward J., and Larry Witham. 1997. "Scientists Are Still Keeping the Faith." *Nature* 386:435–36.

———. 1998. "Leading Scientists Still Reject God." *Nature* 394:313.

Larsen, Timothy. 2006. *Crisis of Doubt: Honest Faith in Nineteenth-Century England*. New York: Oxford University Press.

Latour, Bruno. 1987. *Science in Action: How to Follow Scientists and Engineers through Society*. Cambridge, Mass.: Harvard University Press.

Long, Elizabeth. 2007. "Stories as Carriers of Theory." Paper Presented at American Sociological Society Culture Mini-Conference, New York.

Lehrer, Evelyn L. 1999. "Religion as a Determinant of Educational Attainment: An Economic Perspective." *Social Science Research* 28:358–79.

Lehman, Jr. Edward C., and Donald W. Shriver. 1968. "Academic Discipline as Predictive of Faculty Religiosity." *Social Forces* 47:171–82.

Lehman, Jr. Edward C., 1974. "Academic Discipline and Faculty Religiosity in Secular and Church-Related Colleges." *Journal for the Scientific Study of Religion* 13:205–20.

Leuba, James Henry. 1916. *The Belief in God and Immortality: A Psychological, Anthropological, and Statistical Study*. Boston: Sherman, French, and Company.

———. 1934. "Religious Beliefs of American Scientists." *Harper's* 169:291–300.

Lindholm, Jennifer, and Helen Astin. 2006. "Understanding the 'Interior' Life of Faculty: How Important Is Spirituality?" *Religion & Education* 33:64–90.

Lindsay, D. Michael. 2006. "Elite Power: Social Networks Within American Evangelicalism." *Sociology of Religion* 67:207–27.

———. 2006. "Is the National Prayer Breakfast Surrounded by a 'Christian Mafia'? Religious Publicity and Secrecy Within the Corridors of Power." *Journal of the American Academy of Religion* 74:390–419.

————. 2007. *Faith in the Halls of Power: How Evangelicals Joined the American Elite.* New York: Oxford University Press.

Luskin, Casey. 2008. "ID Uses Scientific Method; Infers Design by Testing Positive Predictions." (Answer to question, "Does Intelligent Design Have Merit?") *Opposing Views*. Retrieved April 15, 2009 (www.opposingviews.com/arguments/id-uses-scien-method-infers-design-by-testing-positive-predictions).

Lynch, Michael, and David Bogen. 1997. "Sociology's Asociological 'Core': An Examination of Textbook Sociology in Light of the Sociology of Scientific Knowledge." *American Sociological Review* 62:481–93.

Machamer, Peter, editor. 1998. *The Cambridge Companion to Galileo (Cambridge Companions to Philosophy)*. New York: Cambridge University Press.

Mahoney, Kathleen, John Schmalzbauer, and James Youniss. 2000. *Revitalizing Religion in the Academy: Summary of the Evaluation of Lilly Endowment's Initiative on Religion and Higher Education.* Chestnut Hill, Mass.: Lilly Endowment.

Marsden, George M. 1991. *Understanding Fundamentalism and Evangelicalism*. Grand Rapids, Mich.: Wm. B. Eerdmans Publishing Co.

————. 1994. *The Soul of the American University: From Protestant Establishment to Established Nonbelief.* New York: Oxford University Press.

Marx, Karl. 1978 edition. *Critique of Hegel's Philosophy of Right.* Translated by Annette Jolin and Joseph O'Malley. Cambridge: Cambridge University Press.

Massey, Douglas S., Camille Z. Charles, Garvey Lundy, and Mary J. Fischer. 2002. *The Source of the River: The Social Origins of Freshmen at America's Selective Colleges and Universities.* Princeton, N.J.: Princeton University Press.

Mazur, Allan. 2005. "Believers and Disbelievers in Evolution." *Politics and the Life Sciences* 23:55–61.

Merton, Robert K. 1973. *The Sociology of Science: Theoretical and Empirical Investigations.* Chicago: University of Chicago Press.

Messikomer, Carla M., and Willy De Craemer. 2002. "The Spirituality of Academic Physicians: An Ethnography of a Scripture-Based Group in an Academic Medical Center." *Academic Medicine* 77:562–73.

Miller, Alan S., and Rodney Stark. 2002. "Gender and Religiousness: Can Socialization Explanations Be Saved?" *American Journal of Sociology* 107:1399–1423.

Miller, Kenneth R. 2007. *Finding Darwin's God: A Scientist's Search for Common Ground Between God and Evolution.* New York: HarperPerennial.

Moore, James R. 1989. "Of Love and Death: Why Darwin 'Gave Up' Christianity." In *History, Humanity, and Evolution*, edited by James R. Moore, 195–229. Cambridge: Cambridge University Press.

Moore, Kelly. 1996. "Organizing Integrity: American Science and the Creation of Public Interest Organizations, 1955–1975." *American Journal of Sociology* 101:1592–1627.

Naugle, David K. 2002. *Worldview: The History of a Concept.* Grand Rapids, Mich.: Wm. B. Eerdmans Publishing Co.

Neff, James Alan. 2006. "Exploring the Dimensionality of 'Religiosity' and 'Spirituality' in the Fetzer Multidimensional Measure." *Journal for the Scientific Study of Religion* 45:449–59.

Newberg, Andrew, Eugene D'Aguili, and Vince Rause. 2002. *Why God Won't Go Away: Brain Science and the Biology of Belief*. New York: Ballantine Books.

Niebuhr, Reinhold, with an introduction by Andrew J. Bacevich. 2008 edition. *The Irony of American History*. Chicago: University of Chicago Press.

———. 1996 edition. *Nature and Destiny of Man: A Christian Interpretation*. Louisville, Ky.: Westminster John Knox Press.

Noll, Mark. 2009. "Science, Religion, and A. D. White: Seeking Peace in the 'Warfare Between Science and Theology'." Unpublished manuscript.

Numbers, Ronald L. 2006 edition. *The Creationists: From Scientific Creationism to Intelligent Design*. [First published 1992.] Cambridge, Mass.: Harvard University Press.

Numbers, Ronald L., editor. 2009. *Galileo Goes to Jail and Other Myths about Science and Religion*. Boston: Harvard University Press.

O'Reilly, C. A., J. Chatman, and D. F. Caldwell. 1991. "People and Organizational Culture: A Profile Comparison Approach to Assessing Person-Organization Fit." *Academy of Management Journal* 34:493.

Orru, Marco, Nicole Woolsey Biggart, and Gary G. Hamilton. 1991. "Organizational Isomorphism in East Asia." In *The New Institutionalism in Organizational Analysis*, edited by Walter W. Powell and Paul J. DiMaggio, 361–89. Chicago: University of Chicago Press.

Paine, Thomas. 1890. *The Age of Reason: Being an Investigation of True and Fabulous Theology*. Edited by Moncure D. Conway. New York: G. P. Putnam's Sons.

Passmore, John. 1967. "Logical Positivism." in *The Encyclopedia of Philosophy*. 1st edition. Edited by Paul Edwards. New York: Macmillan.

Peterson, Gregory R. 2003. "Demarcation and the Scientistic Fallacy." *Zygon: Journal of Religion and Science* 38:751–76.

Plantinga, Alvin. 1993. *Warrant and Proper Function*. New York: Oxford University Press.

Polkinghorne, John. 1998. *Belief in God in an Age of Science*. New Haven, Conn.: Yale University Press.

Popper, Karl. 1959. *The Logic of Scientific Discovery*. New York: Basic Books.

Powell, Walter W., and Paul J. DiMaggio, editors. 1991. *The New Institutionalism in Organizational Analysis*. Chicago: University of Chicago Press.

Pruett, Stephen B. 1999. "Silent Scientists." *Science* 286:901.

Puchalski, C. M., and D. B. Larson. 1998. "Developing Curricula in Spirituality and Medicine." *Academic Medicine* 73:970–74.

Rawlings, Hunter R., III. 2005. "State of the University Address." Ithaca, N.Y.: Cornell University, October 21.

Reuben, Julie. 1996. *The Making of the Modern University: Intellectual Transformation and the Marginalization of Morality*. Chicago: The University of Chicago Press.

Roberts, Jon H., and James Turner. 2000. *The Sacred and the Secular University*. Princeton, N.J.: Princeton University Press.

Roberts, David L., and Andrew R. Solow. 2003. "Flightless Birds: When Did the Dodo Become Extinct?" *Nature* 425:245.

Robinson, Mary R., Mary Martha Thiel, Meghan M. Backus, and Elaine C. Meyer. 2006. "Matters of Spirituality at the End of Life in the Pediatric Intensive Care Unit." *Pediatrics* 118:719–29.

Rogers, R. E. 1969. *Max Weber's Ideal Type Theory*. New York, Philosophical Library.

Roof, Wade Clark. 1993. *A Generation of Seekers: The Spiritual Journeys of the Baby Boom Generation*. San Francisco: HarperCollins.

———. 1999. *Spiritual Marketplace: Baby Boomers and the Remaking of American Religion*. Princeton, N.J.: Princeton University Press.

Rosenau, Pauline. 1991. *Post-Modernism and the Social Sciences*. Princeton, N.J.: Princeton University Press.

Ross, Dorothy. 1991. *The Origins of American Social Science*. New York, Cambridge, Mass.: Cambridge University Press.

Sagan, Carl. 1993. "Why We Need to Understand Science." *Mercury.* 22(2):52–55.

Sarna, Jonathan D. 2003. "American Jews in the New Millennium." In *Religion and Immigration: Christian, Jewish, and Muslim Experiences in the United States*, edited by Y. Y. Haddad, J. I. Smith, and J. L. Esposito, pp. 117–28. Walnut Creek, Calif.: Alta Mira Press.

Science and Engineering Indicators 2008. *National Science Foundation*, Arlington, Va. Retrieved April 15, 2009 (www.nsf.gov/statistics/seind08/c7/c7h.htm).

Schmalzbauer, John. 2003. *People of Faith: Religious Conviction in American Journalism and Higher Education*. Ithaca, N.Y.: Cornell University Press.

Schmalzbauer, John, and Kathleen A. Mahoney. 2008. "American Scholars Return to Studying Religion." *Contexts: Understanding People in Their Social Worlds.* Winter: 16–21.

———. *Religion: A Comeback on Campus*. Unpublished manuscript.

Schmidt, Leigh Eric. 2005. *Restless Souls: The Making of American Spirituality*. New York: HarperCollins.

Schudson, Michael. 1989. "How Culture Works: Perspectives from Media Studies on the Efficacy of Symbols." *Theory and Society* 18:153–89.

Schuster, Jack H., Martin J. Finkelstein. 2006. *The American Faculty: The Restructuring of Academic Work and Careers*. Baltimore: Johns Hopkins University Press.

Schwehn, Mark R. 1993. *Exiles from Eden: Religion and the Academic Vocation in America*. New York: Oxford University Press.

Seager, Richard Hughes. 2000. *Buddhism in America*. New York: Columbia University Press.

Singer, Peter. 1993. "Taking Life: Humans." In *Practical Ethics*, 2nd edition, 175–217. Cambridge: Cambridge University Press.

Singer, Peter. 2009. "America's Shame: When Are We Going to Do Something about Global Poverty?" *Chronicle of Higher Education*, B6–B10. March 13.

Smallwood, Scott. 2006. "In a Clash of Academic-Freedom Titans, Civility Reigns." *Chronicle of Higher Education*, A16. April 7.

Smith, Christian. 2003. "Secularizing American Higher Education." In *The Secular Revolution: Power, Interests, and Conflict in the Secularization of American Public Life*, edited by Christian Smith, 97–159. Berkeley: University of California Press.

Smith, Christian, Michael Emerson, Sally Gallagher, Paul Kennedy, and David Sikkink. 1998. *American Evangelicalism: Embattled and Thriving*. Chicago: University of Chicago Press.

Stamm, Liesa. 2004. "Can We Bring Spirituality Back to Campus? Higher Education's Re-Engagement with Values and Spirituality." *Journal of College and Character*. Retrieved April 15, 2009 (www.collegevalues.org/articles.cfm?a=1&id=1075).

Stark, Rodney. 1963. "On the Incompatibility of Religion and Science." *Journal for the Scientific Study of Religion* 3:3–20.

———. 2003. *For the Glory of God: How Monotheism Led to Reformations, Science, Witch-Hunts, and the End of Slavery*. Princeton, N.J.: Princeton University Press.

Stark, Rodney, and Roger Finke. 2000. *Acts of Faith: Explaining the Human Side of Religion*. Berkeley: University of California Press.

Steensland, Brian, Jerry Z. Park, Mark D. Regnerus, Lynn D. Robinson, W. Bradford Wilcox, and Robert D. Woodberry. 2000. "The Measure of American Religion: Toward Improving the State of the Art." *Social Forces* 79:291–318.

Strauss, Anselm, and Juliet Corbin. 1990. *Basics of Qualitative Research: Grounded Theory Procedures and Techniques*. Newbury Park, Calif.: Sage Publications.

Taylor, Charles. 2007. *A Secular Age*. Cambridge, Mass.: Harvard University's Belknap Press.

Thomas, William I., and Dorothy Thomas. 1929. *The Child in America: Behavior Problems and Programs*. 2nd edition. New York: Alfred A. Knopf.

Thurs, Daniel Patrick. 2008. *Science Talk: Changing Notions of Science in American Culture*. Rutgers, N.J.: Rutgers University Press.

Turner, Frank M. 1980. "Public Science in Britain, 1880–1919." *Isis* 71:589–608.

Underwood, Lynn G., and Jeanne A. Teresi. 2002. "The Daily Spiritual Experience and Scale: Development, Theoretical Description, Reliability, Exploratory Factor Analysis, and Preliminary Construct Validity Using Health-Related Data." *Annals of Behavioral Medicine* 24:22–33.

Wallis, Jim. 2008. *The Great Awakening: Reviving Faith and Politics in a Post–Religious Right America*. New York: HarperCollins.

Weber, Max. 1963 [1922]. *The Sociology of Religion*. Boston: Beacon Press.

Weber, Max, Edward A. Shils [trans.], and Henry A. Finch [trans.]. 1949. *The Methodology of the Social Sciences*. New York: Free Press.

White, Andrew Dickinson. 1955. *A History of the Warfare of Science with Theology in Christendom*. London: Arco.

Winnick, Pamela. 2005. *A Jealous God: Science's Crusade Against Religion*. Nashville, Tenn.: Thomas Nelson.

Wolfe, Alan. 1997. "A Welcome Revival of Religion in the Academy." *Chronicle of Higher Education*, B4. September 19.

———. 2005. "Reality in Political Science." *Chronicle of Higher Education*, B19. November 4.

Wright, Robert. 2009. *The Evolution of God*. Boston: Little, Brown.

Wuthnow, Robert. 1985. "Science and the Sacred." In *The Sacred in a Secular Age*, edited by Phillip E. Hammond, 187–203. Berkeley: University of California Press.

Wuthnow, Robert. 1989. *Communities of Discourse: Ideology and Social Structure in the Reformation, the Enlightenment, and European Socialism.* Cambridge, Mass.: Harvard University Press.

———. 1994. *Sharing the Journey: Support Groups and America's New Quest for Community.* New York: Free Press.

———. 1998. *Loose Connections: Joining Together in America's Fragmented Communities.* Cambridge, Mass.: Harvard University.

———. 1998. *After Heaven: Spirituality in America Since the 1950s.* Berkeley: University of California Press.

———. 2001. *Creative Spirituality: The Way of the Artist.* Berkeley: University of California Press.

———. 2003. "Is There a Place for 'Scientific' Studies of Religion?" *Chronicle of Higher Education*, B10–11. January 24.

Wuthnow, Robert, and John H. Evans, editors. 2002. *The Quiet Hand of God: Faith-Based Activism and the Public Role of Mainline Protestantism.* Berkeley: University of California Press.

Wuthnow, Robert, and Wendy Cadge. 2004. "Buddhists and Buddhism in the United States: The Scope of Influence." *Journal for the Scientific Study of Religion* 43:363–80.

Yamane, David. 1997. "Secularization on Trial: In Defense of a Neosecularization Paradigm." *Journal for the Scientific Study of Religion* 36:109–22.

Zuckerman, Harriet. 1988. "The Sociology of Science." In *Handbook of Sociology*, edited by N. J. Smelser, 511–74. Newbury Park, Calif.: Sage Publications.

INDEX

adolescent struggles, of scientists, 30

African American, Irving as, 60

After Heaven: Spirituality in America Since the 1950's (Wuthnow), 51

age, religion relating to, 32

agnosticism, of Tobin, 30

agnostic scientists, 15, 30, 36

Allport, Gordon, 49

American evangelicals, 49

Americans: as Protestants, majority of, 15*t*, 32, 33, 49, 191n33; resistance of, to science, 129; science and, 9–10; scientists v., 34

Anthony: classroom discussions of, 83; as lapsed Catholic, 14; as scientist, 14–15, 18

anticonversion, 20, 26

Arik: definition of religion, 13, 19; Judaism and, 13, 19; as scientist, 13–14, 18, 19–20

atheism, science as closer to religion than to, 108

atheists: dislike of, 24; myths about, 150; spiritual, 6, 7, 58–60; stereotypes of, 151; village, 10

atheist scientists, 15, 16, 58

bad religion, in society, 22–23

beliefs: of Christians, 38–39, 45; core, 34; in God, 16*t*, 21, 35–36, 39, 58*t*, 117, 192n17; in God, public v. scientists, 16*t*, 35; of Irving, 90; scientific, of Raymond, 72, 154; of Tobin, 30, 40

Bellah, Robert N., 52, 53, 55, 195n6

Berger, Peter, 36

Bernstein, Basil, 26–27, 76

best practices, implementation of, 146–47

bias, personal, in religion, 17, 120

Binder, Amy, 143–44

biologists, 42, 111, 113

biology, religion and, 40–41, 139–41

Bok, Derek, 88

born-again Christian, 130

boundary ideology, 38

boundary pioneers, 6, 7, 45–47, 140, 186n13

Budd, Susan, 16, 188n6

Buddhism, scientists and, 34, 59, 60, 153, 196n24

campus: faith on, making room for, 107–25; religion's resurgence on, 90, 92; student ministries on, 98; support of religion on, 110, 122

carriers, scientists as, 6–7

Catholic Church, 19

Catholic scientists, 49

Catholics, 14, 20, 33, 34, 42, 117, 130, 144, 152, 189n15

chaplaincy service and public chapel, at universities, 98

Christian doctrines: equality and respect for humanity, 38; human pride and sinfulness, awareness of, 38

Christian fundamentalist family, Evelyn from, 21

Christianity, 23, 34, 46, 99, 119, 192n14; golden rule, 23, 190n27; liberal, progressive tradition of, 39; philosophers influenced by, 73; questioning core tenets of, 41

Christians, 153; beliefs of, 38–39, 45; born-again, 130; evangelical, 29, 74, 100, 155; mainline, 49; moral commitment of, 39

Chronicle of Higher Education (Wuthnow), 89

church: Catholic, 19; Lutheran, Raymond relating to, 71; Roman Catholic, 137; and state, separation of, 78–79, 98, 104, 105, 199n11